LOUIS SPOHR'S

GRAND

Violin School.

From the Original German.

DEDICATED TO

Professors of the Violin,

By the Translator

C. RUDOLPHUS.

THIS WORK IS COPYRIGHT.

Ent. Sta. Hall.

Vienna, T. Haslinger.   Paris, S. Richault.

and

London,

EDWIN ASHDOWN.

(Limited)

BOSTON.   TORONTO.
218, TREMONT STREET.   144, VICTORIA STREET.

19, HANOVER SQUARE.

Printed in England

INDEX.

PREFACE. Addressed to PARENTS and MASTERS 1

PART I.

Page.

Introduction 3

CHAPTER 1 On the Structure and the separate Parts of the Violin 3

2 On the Arrangement of the Violin 4

3 On Stringing the Violin 6

4 On the Difference in the Quality and Value of Violins 8

5 How the Violin should be kept 8

6 On the Violin Bow 9

7 Of Rosin 10

PART II.

8 Of Notes, Staves and Clefs 10

9 Of Holding the Violin and Bow 11

10 On the motion of the right arm 12

11 On the motion of the fingers of the left hand 15

12 On the Shape of the Notes and their duration, and on Rests 23

13 On the Bar and Measure of time and its signature 25

14 On Triplets, Sextoles, dotted notes, Rests, Slurs, and Syncopation 34

15 On Scales or Keys, Accidentals, and Signatures 40

16 On Intervals, Major and Minor Keys, Diatonic, and Chromatic Scales 56

17 On Shifts, the extension of fingers, and Harmonics 74

18 On the management of the bow and the different bowings 110

19 On Double Stops, broken-Chords and Arpeggios 124

20 On Graces, Ornaments, or Embellishments 140

PART III.

21 On Delivery or Style in General 179

22 On Delivery or Style of Playing Concertos 180

23 On the Method of Studying New Concerto Compositions 229

24 On Delivery or Style of Quartett Playing 230

25 On Orchestra Playing and on Accompaniment 231

Conclusion 233

PLATE A. to SPOHR'S VIOLIN SCHOOL.

Fig. I.

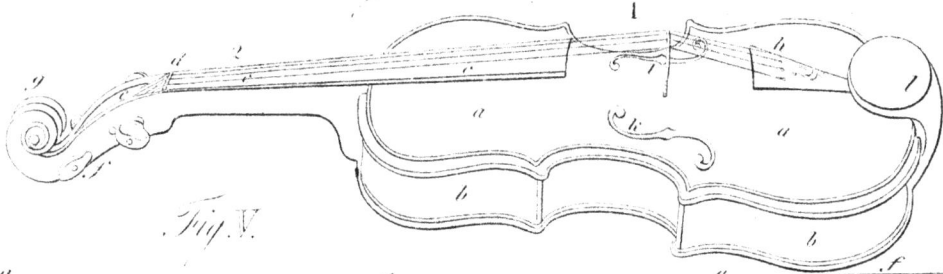

Fig. V.

Fig. II.

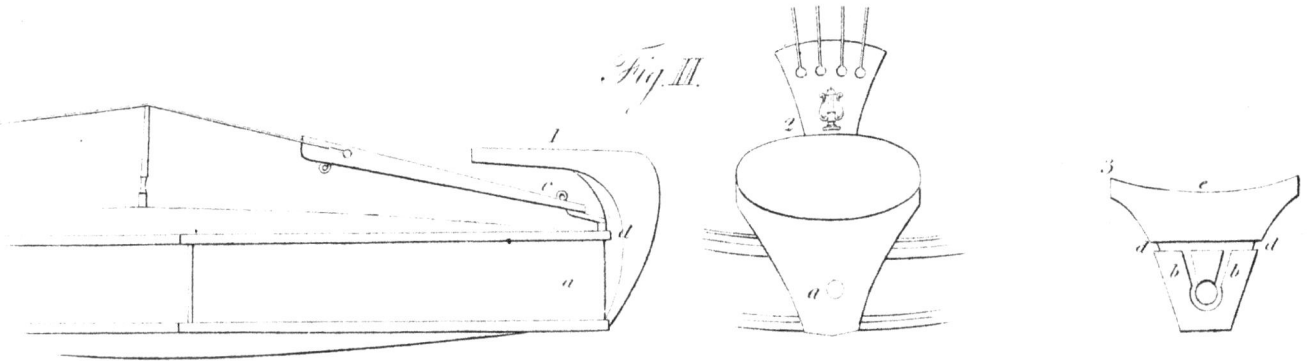

Fig. IV.

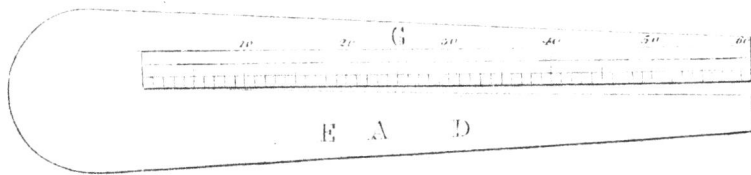

Fig. III.

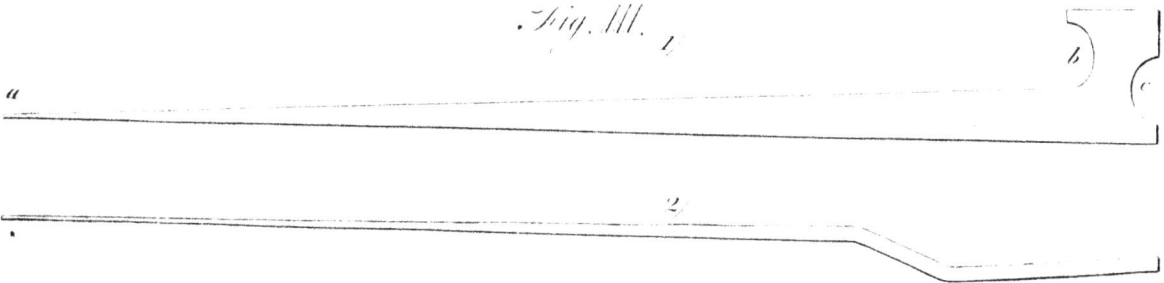

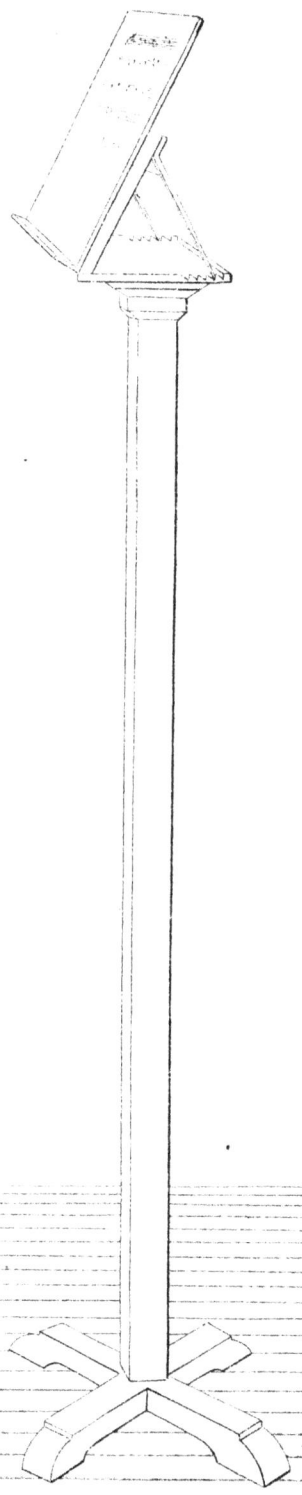

PLATE C. to SPOHR'S   VIOLIN SCHOOL.

Fig. 1.

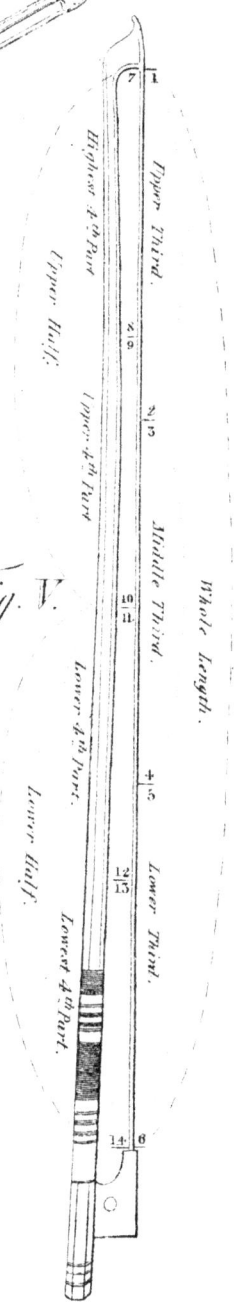

Fig. V.

Whole Length.

Upper Third.

Highest 4th Part.

Upper Half.

Upper 4th Part.

Middle Third.

Lower 4th Part.

Lower Half.

Lower Third.

Lower 4th Part.

Fig. II.

Fig. III.

Fig. IV.

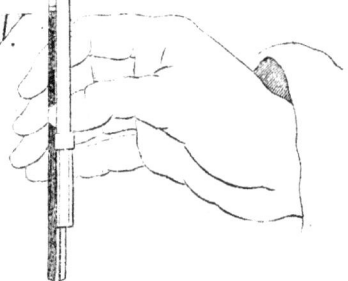

Preface addressed to Parents and Masters,

The Violin School which I herewith present to the Musical World, is less calculated for self Tuition than as a Guide for teachers; It begins with the first rudiments of music, and gradually proceeds to the most finished style of performance, so far as that can be taught in a book.

It has been my aim to make the first elementary lessons more agreable to the Scholar, by at once uniting them with the practical part of Violin playing, and which is not to be found in other works; consequently according to my Method, the Violin may be given into the pupil's hands at the first lesson.

To a parent, desirous of having his Son instructed according to my plan, I beg to address the following observations.

The Violin is a most difficult instrument, and is really only calculated for those who have great inclination for music, and who from advantageous circumstances are enabled to study the art thoroughly. To the Amateur, (if he likewise possess the requisite talent) it is only recommendable if he can set apart for practice at least two hours every day. _ With such application, if he do not attain to the greatest proficiency, he may nevertheless, make such progress as to afford himself and others great enjoyment of music, in quartett playing, in accompanying the Pianoforte, or in the Orchestra.

Whether a youth be intended for the Profession or not, it must be the Parents' first care to choose for him a qualified and conscientious master. This is of more importance as regards the Violin than any other instrument. Faults and bad habits are too easily acquired, which time and great labour can alone remove. It is for this reason, I would at once have an experienced master for the pupil, in order to avoid all these evil consequences of first neglect; and such teacher should be bound to adhere closely, to the rules contained in this Instruction-book.

As it is difficult, nay almost impossible, before the commencement of instruction, to ascertain whether a boy have talent for music, or not; the parent will do well to wait till he shews a decided inclination for music in general, and for the Violin in particular. After a few weeks the master will be enabled to determine with certainty whether the boy have the requisite talent for Violin playing, and judgment sufficient to enable him to acquire a pure intonation, without which, it would be better to discontinue the Violin, and to choose some other Instrument, on which the intonation does not depend on the player, namely, the Pianoforte.

At what age the instruction on the Violin should be commenced, must mainly depend on physical structure. If strong, and healthy in the chest, 7 or 8 years of age is a proper time. At all events it must be in the age of boyhood, as the muscles then are most tractable; the fingers and arms being more easily managed then, than at a more advanced period of life.

Unless the boy be very young, a Violin of the ordinary size may be given to him; a smaller one only, if he find that inconveniently large. A good and old Instrument will materially assist him in producing a good tone, and neat fingering.

One hours instruction every day, if time and circumstances permit, is requisite for the first months, and as the pupils first eagerness very soon abates, and a daily practise between the hours of lessons being nevertheless very necessary, he should be encouraged as much as possible, and the occupations of the day be properly regulated, to prevent either mental or bodily fatigue from too long continued practice.

Parents also may beneficially influence the improvement of their Son, by shewing them selves interested in his progress; they should sometimes attend his lessons, and as an encou_ragement and reward for farther diligence, take him to Concerts and other places, where he may have the opportunity of hearing good music If the parents themselves be musical, it will prove a great inducement to the Son to let him join (according to his abilities) in their mu_sical parties.

In the application of this Violin School, by which I hope materially to facilitate the Master's laborious occupation, the following observations should be attended to.

If the Scholar be quite ignorant of Music, the Master must then strictly adhere to the order of instruction, as here laid down. From Part 1st he will however at first only choose what may ap_pear necessary to him, to give the Scholar an idea of the Instrument, its mechanical parts, the bow &c. The rest to be deferred. As early as possible the Scholar must himself learn to string his Instrument, as well as to keep it in order, in the manner indicated in Chapter 5th

Every Chapter should be perfectly understood before another is attempted; a repeated questioning of that just learnt will best satisfy the Master on this point.

Great patience must be bestowed on the 11th Chapter in which the foundation for a per fect intonation is laid down. It will save the Master for the future a vast deal of trouble if he rigorously insist from the first on a perfect intonation. I recommend the same attention to the 12th Chapter in regard to time and measure.

Several Exercises for every division of instruction are given in this School, either elementary or practical; the master therefore need not have recourse to any others. Should the pupil however grow fatigued with the sameness of the subject and the Master feel inclined to use other compo_sitions. these ought to be in accordance with the Exercises of this School, written and calculated for the intended purpose: the bowing and fingering of which must be marked with great care.

Among the Exercises in this book, there is often one more difficult than the rest; this the pupil may at first pass over, and afterwards take up when the exercises are repeated and he has ac_quired more facility of execution.

When the Scholar has come to the end of the 2^{d} part, it will be found necessary, besides the re petition of the Exercises, to introduce also other compositions, to guard him against any particular style. For this purpose I recommend as most useful, Duets for two Violins; the bowing, fingering &c. of which the Master must mark according to my Method.

A Master undertaking to teach a pupil who, has already been instructed in Music and Violin playing. should ascertain by an attentive examination, whether his attainments correspond in regard to the holding of the Violin &c &c with the rules laid down in this work; which rules, if the pupil wishes to be instructed according to this Method, he must strictly attend to and acquire, previous to farther progress.

Every thing else the Master will find in the School itself, partly in the text, partly in the notes.

Finally, the Author requests that experienced Masters, after having used this School for some time, will be pleased to afford him their instructive hints as to the practicability of his Method of Instruc tion in all cases, which in the event of a 2^{d} Edition he might with advantage apply in the improvement of his work.

CASSEL, March 1833.   LOUIS SPOHR.

FIRST PART.

INTRODUCTION.

Among all the now existing Musical Instruments, the Violin holds the first rank; not only on account of the beauty and equality of its tones, its variety of expression of light and shade the purity of its intonation, which cannot be so perfectly attained by any Wind instrument but principally, on account of its fitness to express the deepest and most tender emotions;where in indeed of all instruments, it most nearly approaches to the human voice.

The Violin does not possess the extent and completeness (Vollgriffigkeit) of the Piano-forte, nor the fulness and power of the Clarionet; however, these deficiencies are more than compensated for, by the soul and richness of its tones, the power of sustaining and binding them, and the great er equality in even the most distant notes.

With such advantages, it is not to be wondered at that the Violin for centuries has continued to be the leading instrument in all complete Orchestra music. For 300 years no change has ta.. ken place in its form; it remains in its original simplicity, and altho' all the other then known, or since invented instruments, have undergone innumerable improvements, the Violin continues to be acknowledged the most perfect instrument for Solo performance

It is, however, this very simplicity in the structure of the Violin, which demands such extraordi_ nary accurate mechanism of playing, and which must consequently of all other instruments, make it the most difficult to attain. For this reason, the Amateur who on another instrument, for example, the Pianoforte or Flute is able to perform in a passable, nay, even pleasing manner, would be intolerable on the Violin. It is only by a perfect command over the instrument that its advantages can be shewn to the fullest extent.

FIRST DIVISION.

CHAPTER 1.

ON THE STRUCTURE, AND THE SEPARATE PARTS OF THE VIOLIN.

The Violin is an instrument of wood, constructed of the following parts. (see Plate A figure 1) 1. the belly, comprising the arched roof, (a) and the likewise arched back, both ornamentally inlaid; and (b) the ribs serving to connect them together at the edges; and 2. the neck, to which is fastened the fingerboard (c), and the nut (d). At the upper part of the neck is the head, (e) with its cheeks to carry the pegs (f) round which the strings are fastened. The neck ter minates in an elegant winding called the scroll (g). At the lower part of the ribs is the tail pin, to which the tail-piece (h) is fastened by a cat-gut string, receiving the lower ends of the four strings, these again rest on the bridge (i). Close to this are two openings (k) intended for the emission of sound, called (from their shape) f holes, or sound holes

In the interior of the Violin, for the support of the bridge and under its right foot is a small cylinder of wood, called the sound post; and under the left foot is a beam, called the bar, a piece of wood glued on lengthways to the roof. The projecting corners of the Violin are filled up and glued on with small blocks of wood, to give the instrument more durability The neck is

---

The Tenor and Violoncello partake of the advantages of the Violin over Wind Instruments.

likewise attached to a block of somewhat larger dimensions.

The back, ribs, and bridge are of maplewood, the belly, inside bar and sound post of fir, the finger_ board, nut, tail piece and pegs, consist generally of ebony. In order to guard the instrument against damp and dust the exterior is varnished.

On the lower part of the Instrument (Fig:1.) near the tail piece is the representation of a contri_ vance of my own invention, called the fiddleholder (*l*) which after more than 10 years experience, has convinced me, my numerous Scholars and many other Violinists, of its great utility, and about which I may therefore be permitted to say a few words here.

The modern style of playing which so frequently obliges the left hand to change its position, makes it absolutely necessary to hold the Violin with the chin. To do this unfettered and without bending down the head, is difficult; no matter whether the chin rest on the left or on the right side, or even on the tail piece itself. It may also, in the quick sliding down from the upper positions, easily draw the Violin from under the chin, or at least, by moving the instrument, disturb the tranquility of bowing. These evils the fiddleholder perfectly removes, and in addition to a firm and free position of the Vio. lin the advantage is gained of not hindering the full vibration of the instrument, and thereby injuring the sound and force of the tone, which the pressure of the chin on the belly or the tail piece must cause. The Violin being held with the fiddleholder, exactly in the middle over the tail piece and more away from the face, allows of greater freedom and regularity in bowing

The following description will be useful to any one desirous of trying the experiment on his own instrument.

The fiddleholder is made of ebony of the form represented on plate A, Figure II. 1.2 3. seen here from different side and fastened with a peg (*a*) in the opening, which previously was occupied by the tail pin. The cat gut to which the tail pin is fastened runs in a farlow (*b*) which is made for it.

The Knot (*c*) is tied over the tail piece, but so as not to touch the fiddleholder. For the little nut on which the strings rest, as well as for the edges of the Violin a farlow, is also made, to enable the fiddle_ holder to be closely attached to the sides. The surface is hollowed out in the middle. (*e*) which gives the chin a firmer and more comfortable hold. The peg (*a*) must fit the opening very exactly, that the force of the draft of the string may not push it out.

CHAPTER II.

ON THE ARRANGEMENT OF THE VIOLIN.

Under arrangement of the Violin is meant, 1. the situation of the neck and fingerboard, the height of the bridge and strings over the fingerboard, in reference to the ease of playing; 2. also, the pla cing of the sound post and the bridge, their strength, as well as making choice of proper wood, in re_ ference to the tone of the instrument.

The former is certainly the business of the manufacturer, but the Violinist should be able to su perintend and direct the same. The following remarks may therefore be in their proper place.

The neck of the Violin must be placed so far back as, to make the fingerboard rise in the di_ rection of the bridge, as much as the height of the latter requires, without the necessity of hav_ ing a block of wood put between the neck and fingerboard; in which case, the neck loses the due proportion of its strength, and inconveniences the player when changing the position of the hand

The bridge is shaped as follows, the right side sloping considerably more than the left.

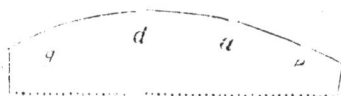

The broad end of the fingerboard is shaped somewhat flatter

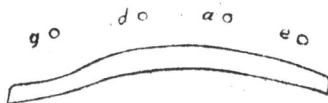

Under the G string on the fingerboard of my Violin I have the here to be observed excavation, which gradually lessens in width towards the nut. The advantage it affords to this string is, a great er room for its vibrations, and it also obviates the unpleasant jarring so often heard under a forced pressure, whilst the D string, with less vibration, lies so near the fingerboard, that it can be easily pressed down, and in any position is sensible to the most delicate touch.* The above sketch, shows the distance of the strings at the broad end of the fingerboard; so arranged as never to jar.

Our attention must now be directed to the bridge and sound post, to give the instrument the best possible tone. The Violinist can only attain the requisite knowledge by his own experiments; he should not leave it to the instrument maker, who, in general does not possess the necessary facility in playing the Violin, nor a good ear for judging of the right tone.

Ascertain first the breadth and height of the bridge. The Rule for the breadth is; that with e qual distance from the sound holes, the middle of the left foot of the bridge must exactly stand o ver the bar. The height is regulated by the arch of the belly. A high arch requires generally a higher bridge; this also is best decided by experiments.

Knowing the right size of the bridge, have a number of bridges made of the oldest and driest wood, some stronger, some weaker, some of soft, others of hard wood. Try them one after another, to as certain which gives the best tone.

The feet of the bridge must exactly adhere to the arch of the belly, the back edge coming in straight line with the inner cross cuts (or notch) of the sound holes.

The changes in trying the different bridges, should be performed as expeditiously as possible, other wise the ear cannot nicely distinguish the difference in sounds. To save time, it is therefore not ne_ cessary to loosen the strings every time of change; but place another equally high bridge half an inch before the other, which lessens the pressure on the one to be removed.

The bridge must be lifted up with force to prevent the sharp edges of the feet from damaging the varnish.

Before however any experiment with the bridges can be made, it is requisite first, to fix the sound post, and previous to that to take down the strings, bridge, and fiddleholder.

For placing the sound post, an iron instrument is made use of (see plate A, figure 1 & 2) The point (a) of the iron stick is driven into the sound post, half an inch from the end intended to be the upper part; thrust it through the right sound hole into the Violin and place it upright, first pressing the lower end of the sound post firmly on the back, and next, the upper part towards the belly, by drawing back the iron stick.

The iron stick is now turned, and with the hook (b) draw, or with the hollow (c) push at both ends of the sound post, till it is in the right place. This is in general close behind the right foot of the bridge, its foremost edge appearing parallel with the back edge of the bridge.

The sound post must stand perfectly upright, and must exactly fit to the upper and lower arch This latter is very difficult, and can only be overcome by looking thro' the aperture of the tail pin into the interior of the Violin: with a thin file move then the sound post, till it everywhere closely adheres. It is well first to blunt the upper edge of the sound post, to prevent, when moved, its pressing into the soft wood of the belly.

To ascertain whether the upper end of the sound post, in the direction from the sound hole to the

* This excavation is the invention of B. Romberg. who originally had it made for the C string of his Violoncello. I adopt ed his plan 25 years ago on the Violin. since which time it has proved of great utility.

wooden bar stands in the right place, take a thin wire, bent at one end in the form of a hook, and measure its distance from the edge of the sound hole; after that, hold the measure over the belly, and compare whether the distances correspond. If they do, the lower end of the sound post must then be moved and brought in the perfect upright position. By alternately viewing it thro' the sound hole, and the aperture of the tail-pin, the correctness is soon ascertained.

The sound post must neither be so long as to raise the belly, nor so short as to shift or perhaps to fall down, through breaking of a string or any other motion. Without strings, it should only slightly adhere, and be easily moved backward and forward.

The sound post should be so placed, that the grain of the wood may be crossed by the grain of the wood forming the belly. It will prevent injury to the latter.

Whether the sound post should be large or small, of wide or close grain, can only be decided by repeated trials; in general, a Violin with a thick belly of wood, will bear a thick sound post better than one of less wood.

If in following these directions the Violin should nevertheless not sound free enough, or is uneven in tone, then the sound post must be moved backward and forward, till the place be found which will give all the four strings the most powerful, clear, and equal tones, of which the instrument is capable.

I may observe, if the tone, altho' even, is yet rough and hard, move the sound post from the foot of the bridge a little backward. Should the fine strings be piercing, and the lower ones on the contrary weak, then move the sound post towards the bar; On the other hand, if the lower notes are harsh, and the upper ones feeble, then, the sound post should be drawn towards the sound hole.

The original place in making these experiments in the direction towards the sound holes, must not be lost sight of, as the inequality of the belly, causes the sound post either to be too short, or too long.

Should a point different from the first place of the sound post, happen to be particularly favorable to the tone, examine, after again taking down the strings, thro' the opening of the tail-pin, whether the sound post on the new spot be of proper length, and adheres closely both above and below; if not, it must of necessity be altered, or else a new one made.

In moving the sound post, care is to be taken to prevent its turning, and to keep its front side (distinguished by the perforated hole) always in the original position.

All experiments must be made with the greatest care, and the sharp edges of the iron be rounded off, to guard the sound holes against injury.

These experiments ought never to last long, as the ear soon becomes fatigued, and insensible to the nicety required in distinguishing the tones.

CHAPTER III.
ON STRINGING THE VIOLIN.

The Violin is strung with cat-gut, the lowest string having silver-wire spun round it.

The goodness of a silver string depends: 1, on being even, knotless, and clear toned; 2, on having been previously sufficiently expanded; and 3, on the exactness and equality of the spinning. If spun too tight, it sounds with difficulty, and is rough, even after some use; if spun slack, the wire, when the gut dries, soon loosens, and occasions a jarring sound.

The worst cat-gut strings are too often made use of by the spinner, it is therefore best to pick the cat-gut strings from your own stock, and to cause them to be spun under your own direction. Before the spinning they should be expanded on an unused Violin, tuned in C and should remain thus for several days.

In order to obtain a full and powerful tone, the largest strings the instrument can bear are generally preferred, such as will easily and quickly produce all tones without at all damping the sounds of the instrument. But if a Violin loses nothing in the quality of its tone by using smaller strings, those of middling size are to be preferred; for besides their full and effective tone, the player has more command over his instrument, and can add elegance and taste to his performance

The relative proportion of the power of the strings, must be such, as to give every one an equal share of richness and volume of tone; experiment is the only guide in this matter. An unevenness in the tone of a string which could not be remedied by the sound post and bridge, may sometimes be equalised, by the more or less tone of another string.

When the size of the strings is once fixed, let it not be changed. A frequent alteration from small to large is detrimental both to the player and to the instrument; the strings which are purchased ought therefore always to be the most suitable to the instrument: in choosing them, a gage (see plate A, fig 4.) is the surest guide. This instrument is a metal plate of silver or brass divided into graduated slits, by sliding the string into these slits, the place where it stops will show its size; if these places are marked with letters (as on plate A.) all mistakes will be obviated.

Attention to the quality of the strings is equally necessary. There are manufactories of them in every country; but those of Italy, (altho' differing considerably) have always proved the best. In general, the Neapolitan are preferable to the Roman, and the Roman again, to those of Padua and Milan. A good string should be white, transparent and glossy; if the gloss has been produced by furbishing with pumice stone, they will always be false and squeak. Some fifths (E strings) have three and four threads, that is, such as are spun from 3 or 4 cat guts. The latter are dearer and generally in higher estimation by Violinists; but experience has shown that perfect 4 thread fifths are very scarce; they also sooner become fibrous and worthless.

As the cat gut strings spoil, when long laid by (and the thinner sort are soonest affected,) it is best to purchase only as many of them as may be wanted in 5 or 6 months. Old and damaged strings are easily known by their dull yellow colour and want of elasticity.

On drawing up a string it ought to be observed, that the length (from the bridge to the nut put in vibration by the bow) should be: 1. perfect in itself; and 2, should agree in fifths with the other strings. A string is perfect when its vibrations are regular; these are so, when the string is found to be of equal power and compactness in every position or shift. As so much depends on a good choice, cut out of a whole string that part only, which is most even. Having found one which is of the proper size, smooth and uniform to the eye and touch, then try, before drawing it up, whether its vibrations are regular; by taking the ends between the thumb and first finger of both hands and expanding the string with moderate force, let it vibrate with the fourth finger of the right hand. It is perfect if the vibrations are like the following figure

and may then be used. It will be false and useless, if the vibrations cause it to form a third line, as

Two adjoining strings are called perfect, if, when pressed down, they give in all positions, perfect fifths A string may however be in itself and with others, correct, yet be false in fifths. This is easily explained: almost all strings (consequently nearly every single length) are thinner at one end than at the other; if this thinning is equalised thro' the whole length, it will nevertheless give regular vibrations and sound perfect; but in this case the octave is not exactly in the centre, and the intervals lie, comparatively, nearer the stronger than the weaker end. Two of these strings, drawn up with their thin ends opposite, will, though in themselves perfect, always sound false in the fifths If, therefore, for all four strings, no lengths can be found of equal size at

the ends, all the thin ends should be carried to the bridge under the bowing place, as they res-
pond so much easier to the touch.

CHAPTER IV.

ON THE DIFFERENCE IN THE QUALITY AND VALUE OF VIOLINS.

Every new Violin at first, even of the oldest wood, has always a rough unpleasant tone, which only wears off, after a number of years of constant use.

For Solo playing those instruments only are best adapted, which have been made free and
mellow toned by age and much use.

Among these, those of the three Cremona makers, ANTONIO STRADIVARIO, GIUSEPPE GUAR-
NERIO, and NICOLO AMATI, who flourished in the second half of the 17th and at the beginning of
the 18th century, have the greatest reputation. The Violins of these makers unite in themselves,
if well preserved, all the advantages of a good instrument, viz: a strong, full and mellow tone,
equality on all the strings and in all keys, and an easy and free touch in every position. They
differ however in form, and in the characteristics of their tones.

These excellent Instruments are scattered over all Europe; but being mostly in the hands of
rich amateurs, they are scarce and dear; every year enhances their value, and a young beginner will but seldom find an opportunity of becoming possessed of one. He must therefore con-
tent himself with an instrument by a less famous maker. Among these are: a second, but elder
ANTONIO STRADIVARIO, ANDREA and PIETRO GUARNERIO, FRANCESCO RUGGERIO, GUADAGNINI,
(Italians), JACOBUS STAINER (Tyrolian), BUCHSTETTER, MAUSIELL, KLOTZ, WITHALM, SCHEINLEIN,
(Germans) and of later times: two Frenchmen. LUPOT and PIC. All these makers, and particularly the five first, have made excellent instruments, though not equal to those of the three
first named.

Should an opportunity offer to purchase a good instrument, it would be a pity to let it slip,
for want of information. Endeavour therefore, as much as possible, to become acquainted with the
characteristics of the instruments of these celebrated makers, notice their peculiarities of structure,
shape, height of the body, the bending of the sides, the arches of the belly and back, the cut of
the sound holes and scroll, the ornamental workmanship, the colour of the varnish &c: and im-
press on your ear the quality of their tones.

With perseverance and attention, it will gradually give a knowledge of the Violin and secure you
against imposition, particularly as there are many close imitations of the old makers. In really
old instruments, it will easily be discovered from the tone, whether they are still perfect or
have been partly renovated. Some 40 or 50 years ago, many of the old instruments were
much injured, from an idea of improving their tone, by scraping the wood from off the interior
of the belly. These scraped Violins give, particularly on the lower strings and when the greatest force is used, a hollow dull sound, which is only heard at a short distance. Consequently, if
a Violin be really manufactured by an old maker, and still preserves a good exterior, it must nevertheless lose all real value if it has suffered from the above stated defect. In later times
trials have been made to remedy these scraped instruments, by glueing on wood, but without
success. They only become dry in the touch and duller in tone.

CHAPTER V.

HOW THE VIOLIN SHOULD BE KEPT.

The Violin is a brittle instrument easily liable to be damaged, and therefore requires the utmost care from the beginning.

Always place the case in which it is kept, in a dry spot, but not exposed to heat. Let it be locked up in a well lined case, and further guard the Violin against the effects of air, by a wadded silken covering. After use, never let the Violin lay outside the case, nor be sent home without being well packed and locked up.

Accustom yourself to wipe the Violin often, and always after it has been used, with a dry cloth, to prevent the accumulation of dust, of rosin, and other filth, particularly on the belly, as it not only disfigures but obstructs vibration and attracts humidity.

In all cases of repairs, address yourself only to a person of known experience and integri_ty. If convenient, see to the repairs yourself as often as possible.

I have already recommended, the greatest care in the experiments with the sound post and bridge. This attention must be increased with old instruments, as frequently from the many years pressure, the places under the bridge have already considerably suffered.

CHAPTER VI.

ON THE VIOLIN BOW.

The Violin Bow (see plate A, fig:5) consists of the stick, (a) the nut, (b) and the ferrel, (c) with which the hair (d) is screwed in.

The hair is fastened at the upper end of the face, which is part of the head (e), and at the lower end in the nut.

The bow at the lower part of the stick has a lapping of silk, for holding it more firmly. The stick is made of Pernambuco wood, the nut of ebony or ivory, the ferrel and nut are inlaid with mother_of_pearl.

Since the old makers, the art of making Violins has rather declined than otherwise, which may perhaps be principally attributed to the cheapness of the new ones; but the bow has been so much altered for the better, that it seems no longer capable of further improvement.

The best and most approved are those of Tourte in Paris; he has gained them an European celebrity. Their superiority consists of: 1, the trifling weight, with sufficient elasticity of the stick; 2, in a beautiful, uniform bending, by which the nearest approach to the hair is exactly in the middle between the head and the nut, (see the representation of the bow plate C, fig. III) and 3, in the very exact and neat workmanship.

Most of the bows of other makers, though often corresponding in appearance with those of Tourte, do not possess the before mentioned advantages, simply because the manufacturers do not understand the principles of making them. Therefore in purchasing, endeavour to get one as nearly resembling Tourte's as possible.

The tail hair of white horses is always used by bow makers, being stronger and whiter, and not so oily as that of mares. All fine and split hairs must be thrown out. The ordinary quan_tity in a good bow, is from 100 to 120 hairs, fastened in straight lines and in a width of near_ly half an inch.

All new hair at first gives a rough thrilling tone; the bow must therefore be used 3 or 4 weeks before it is fit for good playing.

For Solo playing, the bow must not be screwed too much, but only so tight that, the stick in the middle of the line, with a moderate pressure can still be bent to the hair. If the stick possess the necessary elasticity, it will appear as on plate C, fig: III. For Orchestra playing the bow must be drawn tighter.

After playing unscrew the hair, it will preserve the elasticity of the bow. It should also be fastened in its place in the case; if left laying about it will soon become bent.

CHAPTER VII.
OF ROSIN.

Good rosin is generally of a light brown colour and transparent; but there is a good quality (Russian which is yellow and not transparent. When purified, it is sold in small boxes at every instrument seller's. In applying it, take it in the left hand, the bow in the right hand, and draw the hair the whole length 8 or 9 times across.

A new haired bow, requires at first to be rubbed in with finely pulverised rosin. The dust, which hangs to the stick, must frequently be wiped off with a soft cloth.

END OF THE FIRST PART.

SECOND PART.

CHAPTER VIII.
OF NOTES, STAVES AND CLEFS.

Before the Violin is given into the Scholar's hands he must learn the notes. These are signs, by which the situation and duration of tones are represented. They have the names of seven letters of the Alphabet, C, D, E, F, G, A, B, which in their continuation, are repeated as often as the extent of notes makes it necessary. Their names are determined by the place in which they appear on the staves. The staff consists of five parallel lines and their four spaces, counted upwards thus:

five lines.   four spaces

In order to be enabled to represent on the staves the whole extent of all the notes, different clefs have been invented, every one of which gives to the staves other names: however the young Violinist has at present only to learn the Violin clef,

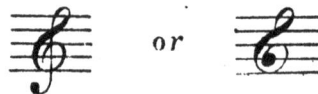

or

It is placed, with the termination of the ring or point on the 2d. line, and gives the note of this line the name of G, wherefore it is also called the G clef. From this clef being placed at the beginning the notes of the five lines are denominated:

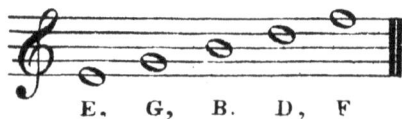

E, G, B, D, F

those of the four open spaces.

F, A, C, E,

and the lines and open spaces combined in succession are:

E, F, G, A, B, C, D, E, F,

. But the Violin has a much greater extent of notes; to write these in continuation or exten_ sion of the notation, short lines are used called ledger lines,

on, above, or below which, the remaining notes are placed. They are:

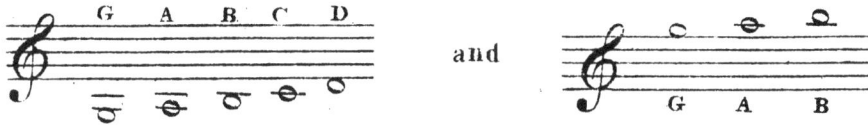

G A B C D

and

G A B

The extent of all the notes the Scholar is for the present required to know, therefore, is:

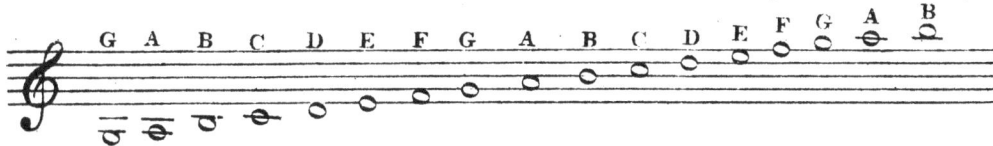

G A B C D E F G A B C D E F G A B

The Scholar must be able to answer and point out the notes, as the Master should indiscri _ minately question him, before he permits him to proceed to the following chapter.

CHAPTER IX.

OF HOLDING THE VIOLIN AND BOW.

The Violin rests with the lower edge of the back on the left collar _ bone, and is held fast by pressing the chin on the fiddleholder.*) The left shoulder for the support of the lower part of the Violin, is moved a little forward, giving it thereby an inclination towards the right side (in an angle of 25 to 30 degrees), (see plate C, fig: 1.) The neck of the Violin rests be_ tween the thumb and the forefinger of the left hand, held gently over the first joint of the thumb, and at the third joint of the forefinger, so, that it cannot sink down to the depth of the division between finger and thumb. (see the left hand Fig: II, plate C.) That part of the hand, where the little finger is, is brought near the fingerboard as much as possible, in order that this shorter finger, like the others with bent joints, may also fall perpendicularly on the strings.

The ball and palm of the hand must however, remain further from the lower part of the neck. The elbow of the left arm is drawn inwards under the middle of the Violin; but let it not touch the body, as then, it would sink the Violin too much towards the neck. (see plate C, Fig: II.)

The bow is held with all five fingers of the right hand, (see plate C, fig: III and IV and the right hand of fig: II.) The thumb is bent with the point against the stick (or rod) of the bow, close to the nut, and opposite the middle finger. With the fore and middle finger clasp the stick, so as to rest it in the hollow of the first joint.

The third and fourth fingers are placed loosely on the stick, and the points of the four fin gers are joined without leaving any vacant space. The hand ought to have an elegant, curved

* If the Scholar will not use the fiddleholder, he must place his chin partly on the belly on the left side of the tail piece and partly on the tail piece itself.

form, and to avoid shewing the knuckles. (see plate C, fig: II and IV.)

Next, place the upper part of the bow with the hair on the strings at the distance of an inch from the bridge, and incline the stick a little towards the fingerboard. The wrist must be held high the elbow, however, low, and as close to the body as possible. The position should be noble and free, facing the desk, the eye looking over the bridge, the left hand being opposite to the music page. (see plate B.)

CHAPTER X.

ON THE MOTION OF THE RIGHT ARM.

When the Scholar has learned to hold the Violin and Bow, as represented by the figures on the plates, as taught in the last chapter, he may now begin to draw the length of one third part at the upper end of the bow, to the point, slowly backward and forward. The first requisite to a regular bowing is; to hold the bow always parallel with the bridge, and at a right angle with the strings. To keep the bow in the hand in this position, it is requisite that it move backward and forward between the thumb and forefinger. With a down-bow the stick gradually approaches the middle joint of the forefinger, whilst the little finger is by degrees drawn back towards the stick; but with an up-bow the stick at the forefinger is drawn back in the hollow of the first joint, and the point of the little finger is moved a little beyond the stick.

The following Exercise on the open strings is intended for teaching the short bowing. Before the Scholar begins, he must know the four strings of the Violin. The lowest silver string is called G, the next D, the third A, the fourth and thinnest E. Their places on the staf are:

From the commencement, the Scholar should study to produce a clear and full tone. As already stated, the first requisite is straight bowing. But it is here also necessary to ascertain, how gentle or strong, the pressure of the bow on each of the four strings ought to be, in proportion to the rapidity of the bowing, in order to produce a light and clear touch, and how near the bridge the hair may be permitted to approach on the different strings. In regard to the former, the rapidity of bowing must increase in the same proportion as the pressure of the bow on the strings becomes greater; and, as a thick string is more difficult to be put in vibration by bowing than a thin one, so, the bow on the lower strings must not approach the bridge so nearly as on the higher ones. The Scholar will be better guided by his ear, when he feels the want of a fine tone, in using the proper bowing necessary to produce it, than by any theory.

The bow is either drawn downwards (down-bow, ____ tiré) or pushed upwards (up-bow, ____ poussé.) *

The first note of the following Exercise is played with a down-bow in the others the bow is throughout pushed up, and drawn down alternately.

The strokes must be all of equal length, and the tones of equal duration.

---

* The Master should let the Scholar place himself at his left, to have his bowing better under his observation The Master will also be attentive that the holding of the Violin and Bow, as well as the position of the body are in accordance with the foregoing rules. The second lines are for the Master who by accompanying in strict time will

As the above Exercise is to be played on the two highest notes, the elbow may remain un_moved in its position; but in the following Exercise which, includes also the two lower notes, this is no longer possible. The elbow then, at the second note D, is a little raised, somewhat more at the third note G, and gradually falls to the A and E. But the elbow must neither move forward nor backward, as the bowing would not remain straight; it also must only be raised so much as, is actually necessary to reach the lower strings. On no account must the Violin change its position, whether you play on the lower or higher strings.

In double notes, where two strings are played upon at once, the pressure of the bow must be equal on both, and not one of the notes stronger than the other.

enable the Scholar to sustain the notes in equal proportion, and thus imbibe a proper rhythmetical feeling

The following Exercise shews a new difficulty, that of leaping from a lower, to a higher string, without touching the intermediate one or two.

This is done at the moment of changing the bowing, by rapidly dropping the elbow without the bow being taken off the strings. The leaping from a high to a low note, is done in the same manner, by quick-ly raising the elbow.

When the Scholar has learned to make the short bowings with the upper third part of the bow, evenly, and with a stiff back-arm, he may commence whole bowings. This cannot be done without also moving the back-arm. Begin with an up-bow. The first third part of the bow (1 - 2) being bowed up with a stiff back-arm, the remainder of the bow must now follow, the elbow continuing to be moved forward, but the hand is moved as previously directed, towards the strings. When the nut, with a constant parallel position of the bow and the bridge, has reached the strings, the same thing in a contrary way is to be observed with the down-bow.

What has been said before about the motion of the bow, between the thumb and middle-finger in short bowing, is still more applicable in long bowing.

The nut of the bow then approaching the strings, let the little finger stretch its point more and more over the stick; but if the bow is drawn down to the point, then the little finger is gradually drawn back to the stick.**

For exercising these bowings with a whole bow, the Scholar may now repeat the three first lessons, untill he is also enabled to produce a good tone with these long bowings.

What before has been said of the duration of notes and pauses is also to be regarded in these repetitions, only, that these exercises are now played slower than before.

The Scholar must not advance to the following Chapter till he has obtained so much command over the bow, as not to interfere with his attention to the fingers of his left hand.

CHAPTER XI.

ON THE MOTION OF THE FINGERS OF THE LEFT HAND.

It has already been stated that the part of the hand, where the little finger is, should be as near as possible to the fingerboard, the ball and the joint of the hand however must be kept apart from the neck of the Violin. The forefinger is drawn a little back, and the three first fingers placed one after another with bended joints and with the fleshy part of the point firmly on the E string, after first bowing this open string. Thereby the following tones are produced.

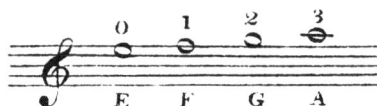

*) It has been suggested to the Translator, that in the application of the different bowings which the Author in all parts of the School makes use of, a more intelligible mode of expressing his meaning, without in the least deviating therefrom, might be introduced
The Translator with the approbation of several Professors of eminence, has therefore taken the liberty to introduce a plan (see Fig V. Plate C.) showing at a glance all the divisions of the bow, which the Author requires?
The evident advantage in this sketch is, that by thus marking the divisions on the bow, the Author's meaning will be more precisely understood when he speaks of a third, a fourth, &c:&c: part of the bow.
Whenever therefore a note in the Exercises has for instance the number 1-2 or II-1 UNDER IT, the meaning is, that that part of the bow is to be used which is between these figures, and so on for the rest.
* It will be necessary that the master in the first difficult experiments of the whole length bowing, guide the arm of the Scholar, and see that these bowings are made straight, and that the elbow is not moved too far from the body

16

To find the proper places for the three last notes on the fingerboard, the scholar must before hand be told, that the spaces between the seven notes already known to him, viz: C, D, E, F, G, A, B, are not all of equal distance, and that there are two intervals of only half the distance of the others, namely those spaces between E_F and B_C.

Of the four first notes to be played on the E string ♦ the E and F lie close together, the following two however lie at double that distance. The F is therefore taken close to the nut, the G from the F doubly as far off, and the A in the same proportion. When the scholar shall with the assistance of his master and his own ear, find out the places for the three fingers requisite for true intonation, he must play the following exercise accompanied by the master. Here are applied whole length bowings, but those notes with a ⌢ are slurred together in one bow. An equal division of the bow is here to be observed, each of the two notes obtaining half of the bow. The notes marked with 5-6 are to be played with a short bow, namely both the E's with the lower third part, (because the bow in the preceding note has been pushed up to the nut); both the G's, however must be played with the upper third part of the bow, (1-2) because at the F, it has again been drawn down to the point.

On the A string the short interval is between B and C. The first fin_ger is placed therefore at a distance from the nut, the second must however be quite close to the first, and the third more distant from the second. When the scholar has learned to intonate these notes, he should play the following Exercise. The four first notes are slurred in one long bow; for the next take only a third part of the bow and so on, i.e. for four notes, whole bows, for two or single notes, short bows, the latter with a stiff back‑arm.

No. 5.

18

In the following Exercise on both strings, the scholar has principally to attend to the different positions of the first finger, which as already stated, is placed on the E string, close to the nut, but on the A string at a distance. At the marks * * these different positions follow each other successively.

On the D string the short interval E_F is likewise between the first and second finger, consequently the positions being the same as on the A string, do not therefore require a separate practice.

On the G string the short interval B_C is between the second and third finger: the first finger is therefore placed at a distance from the nut, the second at a distance from the first, but the third is placed close to the second.

The following Exercise on the two lowest strings, begins with a whole bow, but from the place where each note requires a separate bowing, use the short bow with a stiff back-arm.

The signs (:‖ and :‖ in the middle or at the end of the following Exercise are called Repeats, and signify that the notes included within them are to be played twice. If the sign has only dots on one side, :‖ or ‖: then the notes on that side are repeated: if the dots are on both sides the preceding, as well as the following notes, are repeated.

No. 7.

No. 8.

The next Exercise on all four strings, is played throughout, (except the accented notes) with whole length bows.

Hitherto the little finger has not been employed, to prevent the accumulation of too many difficulties at once. It is now time that the scholar begin to place and move it. The little finger must like the others, be bent in its joints, and fall perpendicularly on the strings; it should never lay flat, not even on the G string.

At first learn to take the E of the A string, to produce the same sound as the open E [music] and in the same manner the A on the D string, [music] the D on the A string, [music] and lastly the B on the E string, [music]

To obtain firmness in stopping with these fingers, play the following Exercise with short bowings.

Like the above, the scholar will find the following three Exercises, marked for all four fingers and strings, whether the note be taken on the open string, or with the fourth finger, or on the lower string. The four notes marked with 1º are played the first time, and the repetition those of 2º omitting the 1º.

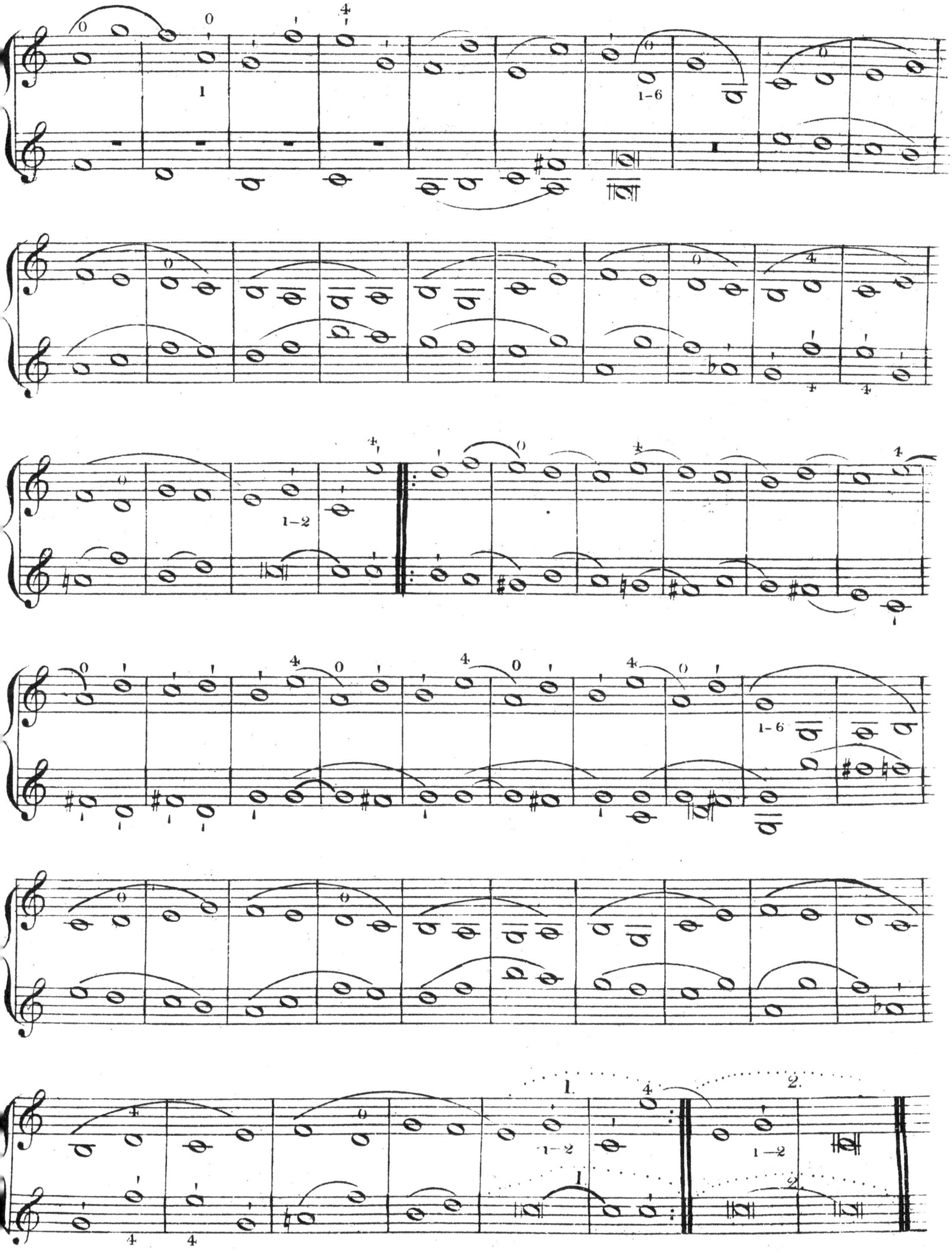

No 11.

No 12.

Segue.

CHAPTER XII.

ON THE SHAPE OF THE NOTES AND THEIR DURATION, AND ON RESTS.

The Scholar hitherto knew the notes only, in regard to the places on which they appeared on the staves, and which determined their names; he will now have to acquaint himself with their various **forms**, by which their value, time, or duration is determined.

The note ![semibreve] in the fourth Exercise is a whole note, or semibreve. A tail at its side ![minim] makes it half a note, or minim; the head filled up ![crotchet] makes it a $\frac{1}{4}$ note, or crotchet; a hook to this ![quaver] makes it $\frac{1}{8}$ note, or quaver; two hooks ![semiquaver] make it $\frac{1}{16}$ note, or semiquaver; three hooks ![demisemiquaver] makes it $\frac{1}{32}$ note, or demisemiquaver; and four hooks ![semidemisemiquaver] make it $\frac{1}{64}$ note, or semi‑demisemiquaver.

---

*)
Before the Master proceeds to the 12th Chapter, he should let the Scholar play the preceding exercises (particularly the three last) untill he be enabled, for every one of its notes, to find instantly the proper stopping, as well as the requisite place for a true intonation. In proportion as the Scholar advances in execution with his left hand, as well as in activity of bowing, the exercises may gradually be taken quicker, yet not more at each practice, than he can play without interruption to strict time.

The master has to observe that the scholar does not for a moment swerve from the manner of holding the Violin the bow and body, or addict himself to bad habits: such as: lowering of the Violin, shrugging of the shoulders, making grimaces, loud breathing, &c:

The following table shows the relative value and duration of notes to each other.

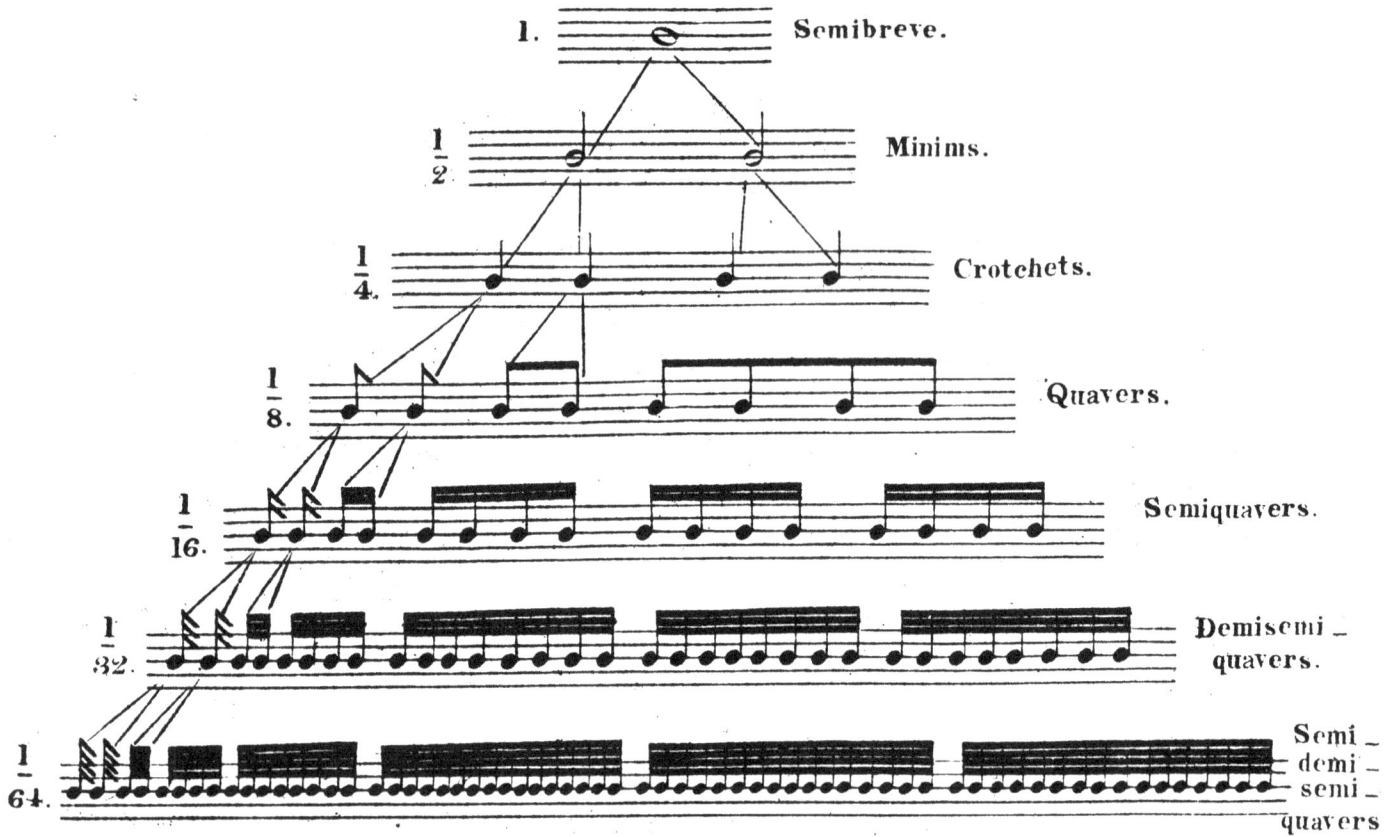

| 1. | | Semibreve. |

$\frac{1}{2}$ Minims.

$\frac{1}{4}$ Crotchets.

$\frac{1}{8}$ Quavers.

$\frac{1}{16}$ Semiquavers.

$\frac{1}{32}$ Demisemi‑quavers.

$\frac{1}{64}$ Semi‑demi‑semi‑quavers

From this may be seen that, during the time of one semibreve, two minims must be played; in the time of one minim, two crotchets; &c: &c: The 64 notes in the last line, are consequently performed in the same time as, the semibreve in the first line.

In ancient music, notes of different forms and value were used, but of which only the breve representing two of our modern notes or semibreves, is occasionally employed.

When pauses occur in playing, marks called rests are used, to show the duration of the time not employed, i.e.

Whole Bar Rest. | Minim Rest. | Crotchet Rest * | Quaver Rest. | Semiquaver Rest. | Demisemiquaver Rest. | Semidemi‑semiquaver Rest.

* In Germany the mark is generally used for a crotchet rest.

CHAPTER XIII

ON THE BAR AND ON THE MEASURE OF TIME AND ITS SIGNATURES.

All Musical Compositions are subdivided into bars, in order to facilitate the reading of the variously shaped notes and rests. A Bar, is formed by those groups of notes with or without rests, which, are contained within the space of two lines, drawn perpendicularly across the staff.

The Time (Italian "Tempo") of the bar between these lines, is determined, by placing at the commencement of each musical piece the signature, which, influences every bar of the piece, or, until a new time begins. The time from the first line of the bar to the next remains unchanged, no matter whether many or few notes or rests are introduced.

There are three kinds of time, common, triple, and compound. Common time, is that which contains an equal number of parts. Triple and Compound times, are those, which, are divisible into three equal parts.

Common simple four crotchet time is represented by

the two four crotchet time by $\frac{2}{4}$ and the Allabreve or two minims or $\frac{2}{2}$

Simple Triple time is represented by:

The three minim - time $\frac{3}{2}$

The three crotchet - time $\frac{3}{4}$

and the three quaver - time $\frac{3}{8}$

Compound Time is represented by:

The six quaver - time $\frac{6}{8}$

The six crotchet - time $\frac{6}{4}$

The twelve quaver - time $\frac{12}{8}$

and the nine quaver time by $\frac{9}{8}$

To perform bars of music so as to allot to each its requisite length, is called playing in time, which the Scholar has next to learn

26

The acquisition of keeping time may be greatly facilitated, and a clear view of the division of the various times obtained, if the master beforehand, teach the scholar how to mark or beat the time. This consists in a visible, yet inaudible marking of the bars, by moving the right hand quickly through the air, and then resting till the next bar

If four beats are to be marked, the first beat is made perpendicularly, the second towards the left side, the third to the right side and the fourth upwards, according to this figure.

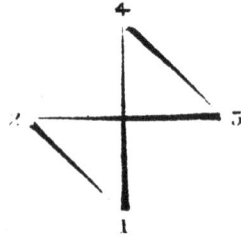

For three beats it is:

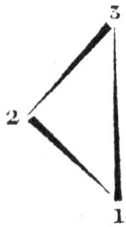

For two beats the first is downwards, the second upwards.

For common time (C), and twelve quaver time $\left(\frac{12}{8}\right)$, beat four times; for three minim time $\left(\frac{3}{2}\right)$, three crotchet time $\left(\frac{3}{4}\right)$, three quaver time $\left(\frac{3}{8}\right)$, and the nine quaver time $\left(\frac{9}{8}\right)$, beat three times; for the two four crotchet time $\left(\frac{2}{4}\right)$, the allabreve or two minims $(\mathcal{C})$, $\left(\frac{2}{2}\right)$, the six crotchet time $\left(\frac{6}{4}\right)$, and the six quaver time $\left(\frac{6}{8}\right)$, beat twice.

In case a musical piece in any one of the latter mentioned times is to be played very slowly, it becomes requisite to beat the six parts of a bar separately, therefore, the two first beats are made downwards, the third to the left, the fourth and fifth to the right, and the last upwards.

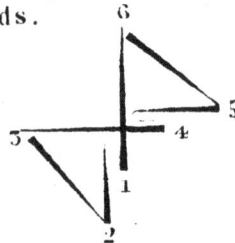

If a musical piece in common $\left(\frac{3}{4}\right)$ or $\left(\frac{3}{8}\right)$ time, is to be played very quick, then only two beats are given in common time, in lieu of four, and only one beat at the commencement of every bar in the others.

The accentuation falls on the first note of the bar, and on the one with which the second half of the bar begins; the first is therefore called the strong, the other the weak portion of the bar. Consequently in common time, the first crotchet receives a greater accent than the third, in three crotchet time the first note only is accented, in six quaver time, the first and fourth notes of the bar are accented.

For regulating the quicker or slower movement of time of a musical piece, certain Italian terms are used, of which one is always placed at the commencement of every piece. The Scholar for the present need only to be acquainted with ADAGIO, slow; ANDANTE, moderately slow; ALLEGRETTO, rather lively; ALLEGRO, cheerful and lively; and PRESTO, very quick.

Yet all these indications of movements were formerly left in uncertainty, and rather to be guessed at from the character of the musical piece. Frequently it was only found out after repeated playing, and often wholly mistaken.

This evil is now remedied by the invention of Metronomes, by which the time can be strictly determined. Maelzel's Metronome has met with the greatest approbation, for the last ten or fifteen years, we therefore find it generally annexed to the Italian terms of time. For instance; Andante is fixed by ♩ 66, Maelzel's Metronome (abbreviated M.M.) thus four crotchets in the bar of the Andante movement, require four of such beats of Maelzel's Metronome.

The indication of Time according to Maelzel, is used throughout this School. The following exercise, the Scholar should however at first practise a little slower, until he is enabled to play it strictly in the required time, and with perfect intonation.

In order to awaken in the Scholar a feeling for rhythm, and accustom him to a proper division of bars, it will be useful, if the master play the Exercises Nos 13 to 18, and let the scholar beat time, in the manner above indicated, and count the bars aloud.* When the Scholar can do this perfectly, as well as accentuate the notes correctly, he may be allowed to proceed.**

* If necessary the Metronome may also be used.
** The Master from the beginning must insist upon a strict division of the measure, and by no means yield to the Scholar. The following four notes in the Exercise must be marked in the manner stated, to produce the desired effect. In the other measure the same is to be observed, but not longer than until the Scholar begins without assistance to play in time

28

Andante ♩ 66 „ Maelzel's Metronome.

N.º 13.

All the foregoing Exercises were intended to be played with a third part of the bow, and whole bow; but in the following we shall require the use of all the parts of the bow; for besides the whole bowings, (or the length between 1 – 6 on fig: V plate C.) and the short or third part bowings, half bowings are introduced, marked under the notes; if with the upper half of the bow by 7 – 10, if with the lower half of the bow by 11 – 14, and if with the middle of the bow by 3 – 4, (see fig: V, plate C.)

The rules for the motion of the right arm, and the right hand in these half bowings, have already been given in those for whole bowings, it needs therefore only to be remembered that in bowings with the upper third part of the bow (1-2) the elbow remains stationary, and that all short half and whole bowings must always be parallel with the bridge.

Andante, ♩ 88.

N.º 14.

* The whole length bow is marked by 1 – 6.

Before the Master proceeds to teach a new measure, the Scholar should first learn to beat the time of it.

The next exercise has two notes before the first bar, called introductory notes, and not for_ming a full bar. These introductory notes whether one or more, are generally unaccented, or at least, conclude with an unaccented note, which is generally taken with an up_bow, in or_der to employ for the first or accented note of the next bar, the down_bow. The down_bow has on account of the nearness of the hand to the strings, and the thereby occasioned pressure of the bow on the same, more weight than the up_bow, and it is the ancient rule that every bar should commence with the down_bow, and finish with the up_bow.

Modern playing has however caused frequent deviations from this rule, as the Scholar will observe in the notation of the bowings in the following exercise, the necessity of which I shall explain hereafter.

The two introductory notes, of the following exercise are not to be slurred, but played in two bowings, and must, to conform to the old rule, be begun with the down_bow. Thereby the first note of the full bar obtains the down_bow, as also the first note of each succeeding bar.

No. 16.

Allegretto. ♩=92
tiré. Segue

With the upper third part of the bow. (1,2)
Segue

No. 17.

Andante. ♩=100.
tiré.

tiré.

The introductory Note in the next exercise is made with a short up_bow near the nut, in order
to employ the whole bow to the six notes of the succeeding bar. In the 5th and 13th bar, at the quaver
pauses, the bow is lifted up and moved on through the air, so that its whole length finishes at the same
time with the end of the bar.

Adagio, ♪ 96

Nº 18

Regarding the pauses, it is necessary to repeat here, that the whole pause ▭ not only denotes silence for the duration of a whole bar in common time, but also in all other measures, as for example the first bar in $\frac{6}{8}$ in the accompaniment of the above exercise.

Two or more pauses are written

Above that number the simple cut is often substituted.

The following exercise is to be played throughout with a stiff back-arm, and between 1-2 of the bow. For the motion of the bow on two strings, the Scholar should use only the hand-joint, and raise and lower the elbow only a little, when he has to pass over three or four strings.

The bowings in every succeeding exercise become more varied, their correct execution according to the marking, is therefore the more necessary; as, even if only one were missed, the bowing would immediately be thrown wrong through the whole piece.

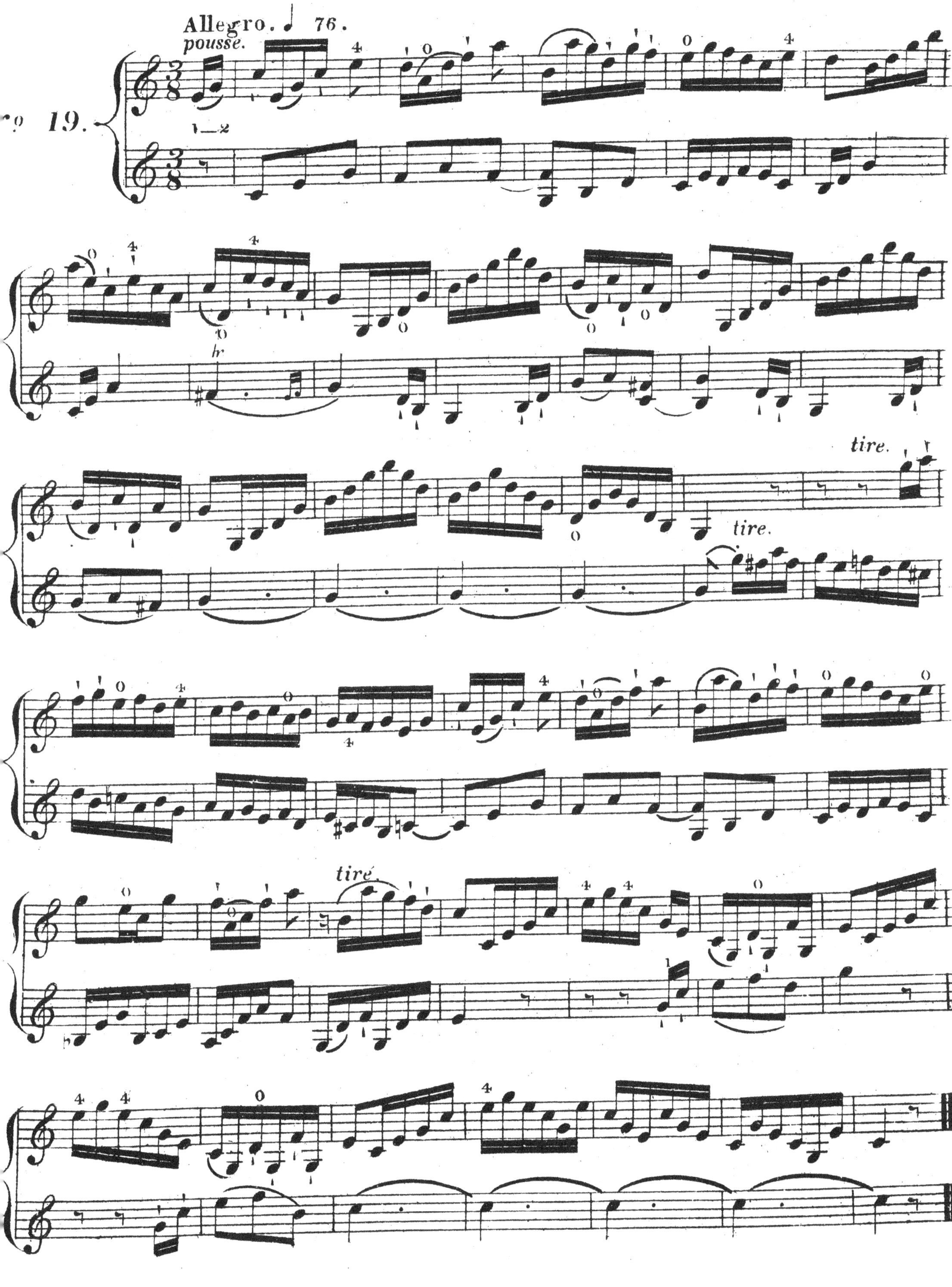
N° 19.
Allegro. ♩ 76.
pousse.
tire.
tire.
tire.

CHAPTER XIV

ON TRIPLETS, SEXTOLES. DOTTED-NOTES. RESTS. TIES, & SYNCOPATION.

In changing the movement of the quavers of the $\frac{12}{8}$ or $\frac{6}{8}$ time into common, or crotchet $\frac{2}{4}$ time, a system of notes is created called Triplets.

Every note divided into three, instead of two parts, makes a triplet.

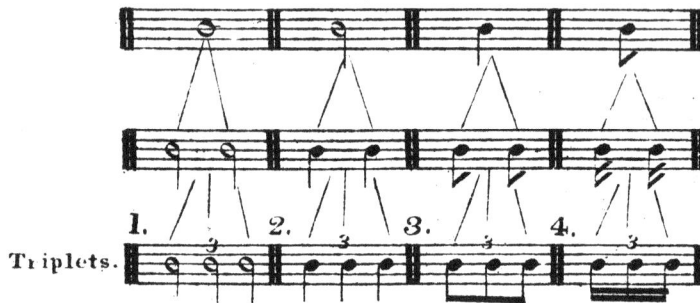

Triplets.

The first is called Minim _ triplet, the second crotchet _ triplet, the third quaver_triplet, and the fourth semiquaver _ triplet. The figure 3 distinguishes triplets from notes of simi_lar appearance. Over quaver or semiquaver triplets, the figure is however not always used, or is only placed over the first triplet, as they can be distinguished by their being tied in three's.

Frequently, instead of a note there is a rest.

Sometimes two quavers are compressed into one crotchet.

The Triplet having been doubled forms the Sextole.

Triplets.

Sextoles.

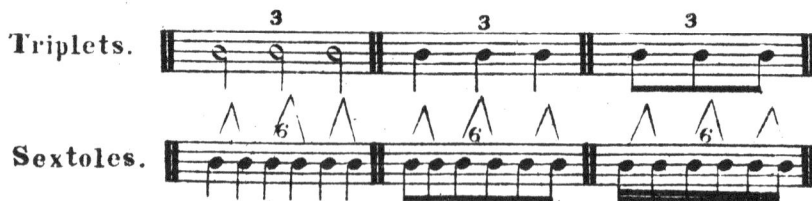

Two triplets are often tied together in this manner, and marked by a 6 (although incorrectly) as a Sextole They differ from the first, by having the accent on the first, and fourth note. Sextoles have the accent on the first, third, and fifth notes.

Triplets.   Sextoles.

The following exercise has for its object, to teach the Scholar the division of Triplets and Sextoles; they are therefore mixed up with the other species of notes. In the 10th 21st and 22nd bar are several triplets successively, commencing with a rest; but con_ sisting only of unaccented notes, they must in accordance with the old rule be all play_ ed with an up–bow. For the rest the bow is raised from the string, drawn back in the air, and at every triplet again placed at the point.

The dot prolongs the duration of the note behind which it is placed, one half in addition to its original value.

The minim with the dot, has therefore the duration of three crotchets; a crotchet with the dot, the duration of three quavers. If two dots are placed behind a note, the second dot gives an additional quarter to the length of the original note.

It is the same with the dots after the rests.

The first dot has half the length of the rest, the second the half of the first dot.

Where a note could not be prolonged by a dot, either because the prolongation consists of less than half of the note, or because it was divided on account of the bar, the prolongation is made by a note with a tie over it.

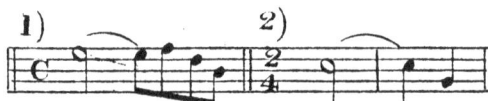

Such tied notes are likewise played as one. In lieu of the tie across the bar, the dot at 2 is also frequently used:

The following exercise contains simple and double dots, at notes, and rests, as well as slurs.

It is a frequent fault with beginners, to hurry the notes with dots too much, and thereby overstep the time. The Master should therefore require a strict holding of the time in each division.

In the 15th bar occurs a new bowing. Two notes should be played in one bow, but each be separately heard, as if it had a separate bowing. Before the second note is played, the bow must therefore remain momentarily fixed. The pause thereby occasioned, should be very short, at the utmost only a demisemiquaver.

Nº 21.

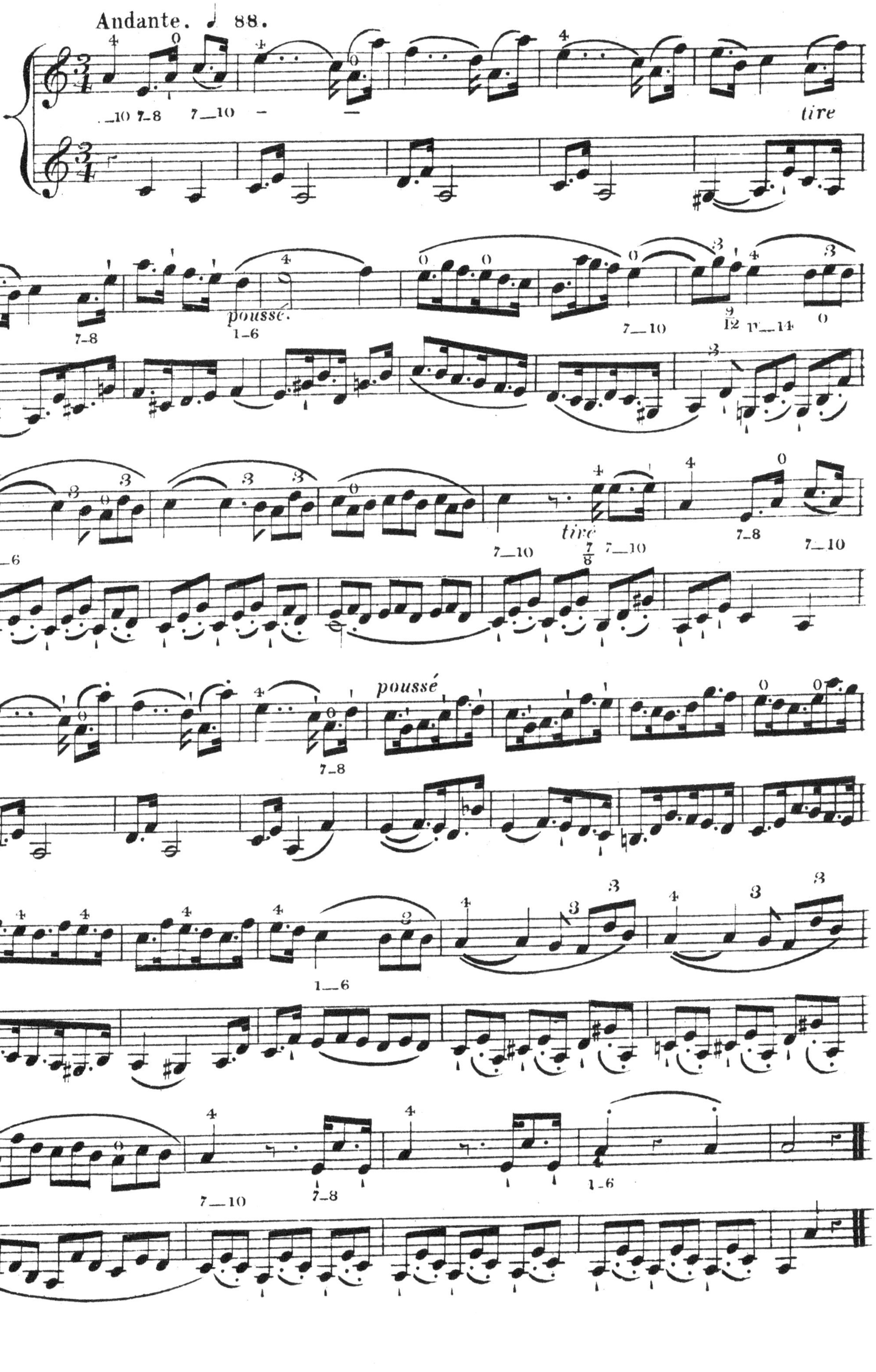

If two notes are at sundry times, successively tied, of which each time, the first is unaccented and the second accented, they are called Syncopes.

With notes of a shorter duration, the two tied notes are tied across the bar.

It is the characteristic of Syncopes, that the accented note forms always the beginning of a bar, and therefore receives more naturally the accent or pressure. The manner often used by Violinists to accent each note of the second half of the bar by a parti_cular pressure of the bow,

is therefore incorrect, because to a certain extent it destroys the peculiarities of Synco_pation.

The next exercise gives the Scholar an opportunity of practising the division and manner of playing syncopes, as well as the other kind of notes named above.

The last 10 Exercises are to be repeated till the Scholar is enabled to play them, not only in perfect intonation, and according to the stated bowings, but more particularly in correct time. His success in the latter, the master may try by letting him here and there play, to the beats of the metronome, but not too long, as otherwise the playing soon becomes stiff and awkward. If the Scholars execution does not come up to the required Tempo, the Master may place the Metronome a few degrees slower.

CHAPTER XV

ON SCALES OR KEYS, ACCIDENTALS, AND SIGNATURES

The natural and gradual succession of tones, C, D, E, F, G, A, B. and again to C. is called the Scale. The Scholar has already been told that the distance from one tone to another is not always the same, and that between E, F, and between B and C is only half the distance of the other tones. Consequently this scale consists of five whole and two half tones.

whole tone · whole tone · half tone · whole tone · whole tone · whole tone · half tone

As the succession of the above tones begins at C, it is called the Scale or Key of C.

But the want of modulating from the above tones to others, and thereby to create new scales is soon felt. In order to obtain the necessary succession of two whole tones a half, then three whole tones, and again a half tone for a scale, it is requisite to lower or raise one or more of the above tones, either half a tone lower or higher.

The raising of a tone is determined by a sharp ♯ prefixed to the note, a C with a ♯ is called C sharp, and F with a ♯ is called F sharp, &c.

The new Scales created by putting one or more sharps before tones, are firstly G, because it requires only one sharp.

whole tone · whole tone · half tone · whole tone · whole tone · whole tone · half tone

G   A   B   C   D   E   F♯   G.

The next is the scale of D requiring two sharps.

whole tone · whole tone · half tone · whole tone · whole tone · whole tone · half tone

F♯   C♯

The Scale of A, three sharps.

half tone   half tone

C♯   F♯   G♯

The Scale of E, four sharps.

half tone   half tone

F♯   G♯   C♯   D♯

and the Scale of B, five sharps.

C♯ D♯   F♯ G♯ A♯

Among these scales the Scholar will miss that of F. But this can only be round by lowering the tone of B half a note, whereby the first half tone following the two whole tones is obtained.

The lowering of a tone is determined by a flat ♭ prefixed to a note, a C with a ♭ is called C flat; a D with a ♭ D flat; &c: F the first of the new scales is created by lowering the tone B.

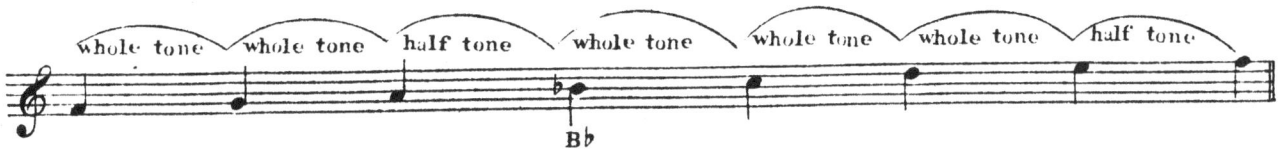

whole tone   whole tone   half tone   whole tone   whole tone   whole tone   half tone

B♭

A new scale can now be created from the lowered tone B, by lowering the fourth note which is the E.

Scale of B♭, with two flats.

half tone   half tone

B♭   E♭   B♭

Commencing from the second lowered note E♭, and lowering the fourth note A, we form the scale of E♭, with three flats.

half tone   half tone

E♭   A♭ B♭   E♭

In the same manner, commencing from the third lowered note A♭, we form the Scale of A♭ with four flats.

half tone   half tone

A♭ B♭   D♭ E♭   A♭

and commencing from the fourth lowered note D♭, we form the scale of D♭, with five flats.

half tone   half tone

D♭ E♭   G♭ A♭ B♭   D♭

But new Scales can also be created from those tones raised by sharps, we must therefore add here the scale of F♯, with six sharps.

half tone

F♯   G♯   A♯   C♯   D♯   E♯   F♯

With this, the twelfth Scale, all major Scales are exhausted. For in forming a new scale from the next raised tone C♯. it will be just the same as the scale in D flat, as C♯ and D♭ although differently called, are one and the same tone. In raising namely the C by a ♯, or lowering the D by a ♭ they amalgamate on the same note, consequently the difference exists only in name, not in sound.* In like manner, a scale from the fifth lowered note the G♭ amalgamating with the F♯, forms only one and the same scale.

One of these scales will appear to predominate in every composition, for Ex: in the Exercises Nº 13, 14, 15, 16, 17, 19, 20 & 22. as the scale of C predominates they are said to be in the key of C. There are as many keys as scales, namely, twelve.

The sharps and flats requisite for the formation of scales are not always repeated through the whole composition, but are only given once at the beginning, immediately after the clef, thus influencing its whole duration. From the signature therefore will immediately be seen the predominant scale and key in which the piece is composed.

Next follow all the twelve keys, with their signatures, with which the Scholar must be well acquainted.

Key of **C.** — without signature.

Key of **G.** — with one sharp.

Key of **D.** — with two sharps.

Key of **A.** — with three sharps.

Key of **E.** — with four sharps.

Key of **B.** — with five sharps.

Key of **F♯.** — with six sharps.

Key of **F.** — with one flat.

Key of **B♭.** — with two flats.

Key of **E♭.** — with three flats.

Key of **A♭.** — with four flats.

Key of **D♭.** — with five flats.

If one of these sharps or flats is to be contradicted, to restore the note to its original pitch, the sign ♮, called a Natural, is placed before it.

F♯ F♮   B♭ B

___

*These notes similar in sound, though different in name, are called Enharmonic, and by substituting the one for the other, i.e. the C♯ for D♭, or F♯ for G♭, and the reverse, is called the Enharmonic change or movement.

This sign consequently lowers the tone when it contradicts a sharp, and raises it if it be a flat.

These three signs ♯, ♭, and ♮, are called accidentals, as exemplified below. In the following Exercise, one ♯ only is before F, consequently the scholar has to take the F half a note higher through the whole piece.

On the E string the first finger then, is not to be placed any longer close to the nut, but close to the second finger, and on the D string, the second finger which hitherto was kept close to the first, is now to be placed at a distance from it, quite close to the third finger.

The fourth bar of the exercise modulates into the key of D therefore in this and the following bars, the scale of D with two sharps predominates. The scholar, besides the F, has also to take the C half a note higher, and to place on the A string, the second finger at a distance from the first, close behind the third finger. In the four last bars, the scale of G is again predominant, therefore the C must be taken on its original place.

The following Exercise has likewise a sharp put after the clef, and therefore the scale of G is predominant. But if the 5th 6th and following bars, by modulation into other keys, the scales of C E A, and D, are introduced. Attention to the signature is therefore requisite, and at each sharp to move the finger half a note upwards, and at each ♮ to return to the original place. From the 8th bar the modulation is in D, and the scale of D predominates to the 17th bar.

Allegro. ♩ 100.

Nº 24.

tire.

poussé.

tiré.

The following Exercise has two ♯, the key is therefore D, all F's and C's are to be taken half a note higher.

The sharps and flats placed after the clef are called essential signatures, those which appear in the course of the piece, accidentals. These latter only influence one bar at a time, and must be placed again in the next bar before the note, if the same is to be raised or lowered, unless it be connected with another note of the following bar by a tie or in which case also the note of the new bar is raised or lowered.

But in the space of a bar, every note of the same kind, even if it stands in different Octaves is changed by *one* accidental. In the 13th bar of the next exercise the ♯ before the A, not only influences the 1st but likewise the fifth note, and in the 28th bar the ♮ lowers the G sharp to G, as well as the 7th and 9th note.

The essential sharps of the following Exercise are F, C, and G, sharp, consequently the key is A.

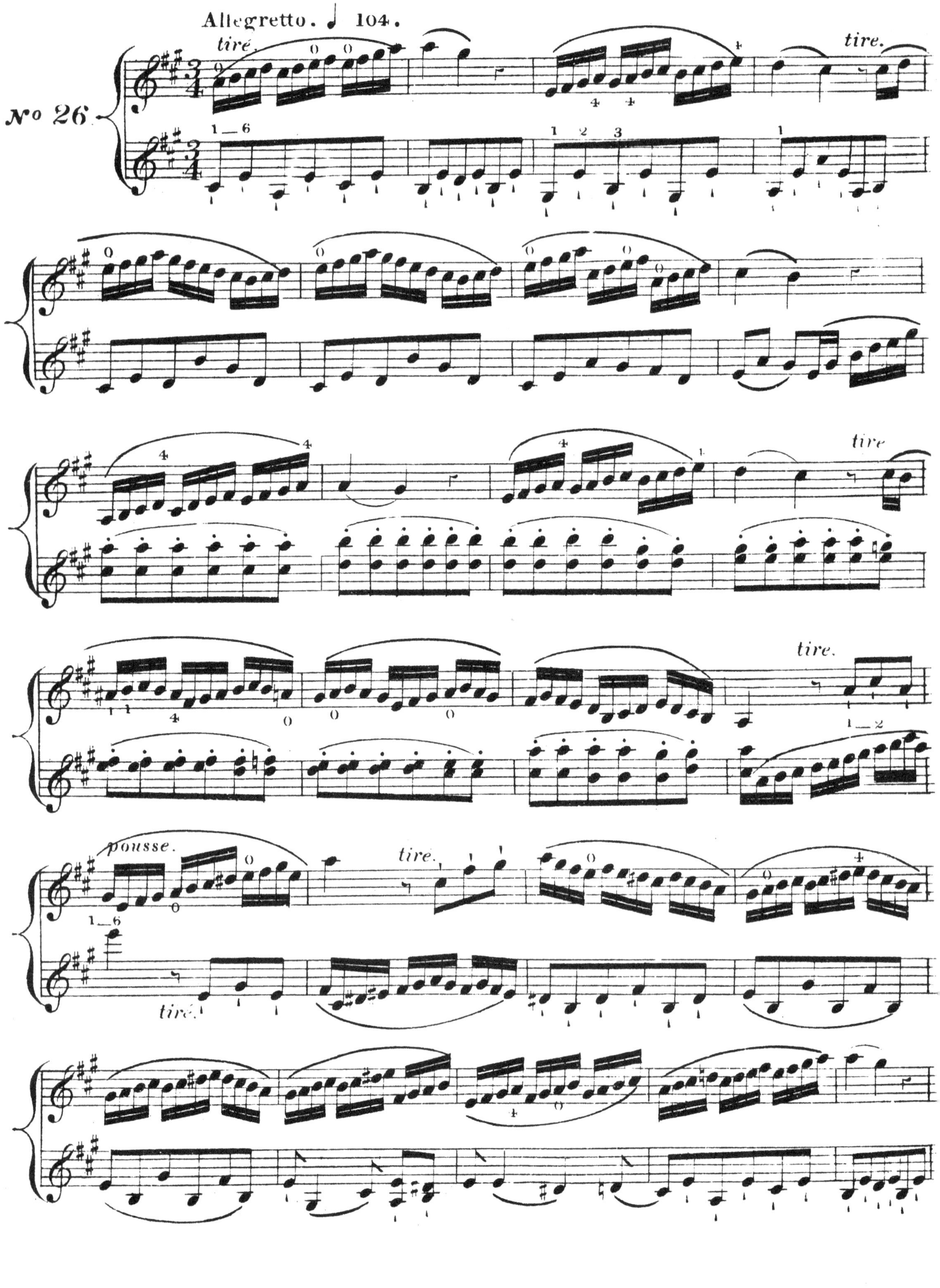
Allegretto. ♩ 104.
Nº 26.
tiré.
tire.
tire
tire.
pousse.
tiré.
tiré.

The Scholar hitherto has played with an equal strength of tone. The Violin however admits of various degrees of strength of tone, and it is now time that the scholar should try to produce them. In the following Exercise they are marked down in the usual manner below the staf, i.e. with the Italian mode of Expression. For the present it will suffice to know: *piano*, (abbreviated *p*) soft; *pianissimo* (*pp*) very soft; *forte* (*f*) loud; *fortissimo* (*ff*) very loud; *crescendo* (cres:) gradually increasing in strength, and *decrescendo* (decres:) gradually decreasing in power. Each of these words continue to influence the music, till some new modification is expressed.

At the forte the bow is pressed more firmly on the string with the first finger, more quickly moved and brought nearer the bridge; at the piano however the bow is lifted a lit_ tle by the pressure of the little finger, moved slower and further from the bridge. At the cres: and decres: a gradual swelling and diminishing of tone from one to the other takes place. The Scholar should take pains at the *p* and *f* to draw always a fine tone from the instrument. A regular bowing and a firm placing of the finger of the left hand on the finger- board, are here the first requisites

50

The following Exercise has a ♭, after the clef all B's, are therefore taken half a note lower. Besides this essential signature, various accidentals are introduced, which must be well noticed by the Scholar

Andante. ♩ 100.

Nᵒ 27.

*) The P and f. of the upper line applies also to the second part.

decres.
pp
7_10
1_6
cres.
f
decres.
p
cres.
f
p
cres.
decres.
cres.
decres.
p
pp

The following Exercise has two Flats, therefore all B's and E's are to be taken half a note lower.

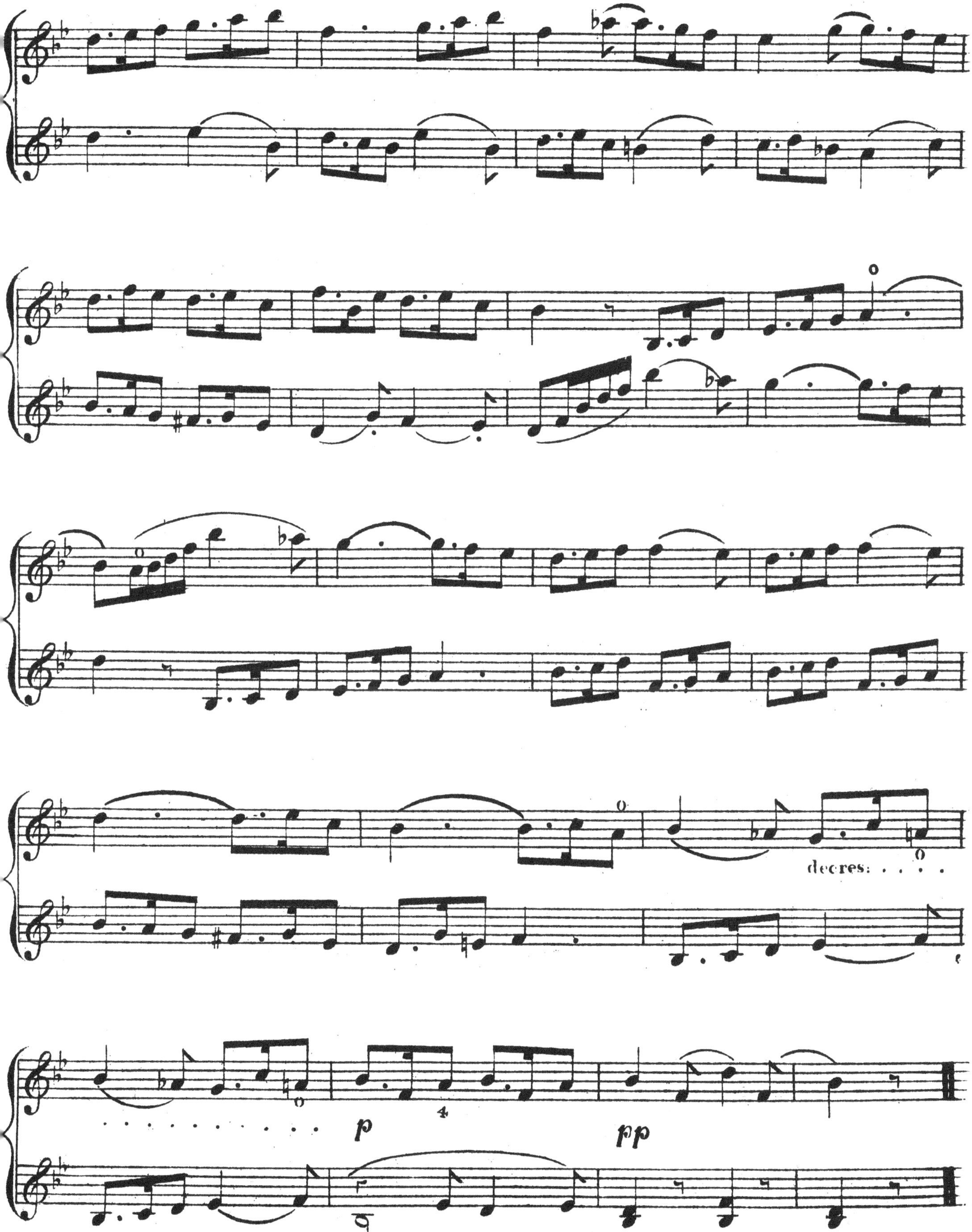
decres: . . . .
p
pp

The following Exercise has three Flats. therefore all B's, E's, and A's are to be taken half a note lower.

Allegretto ♩=108.

№ 29.

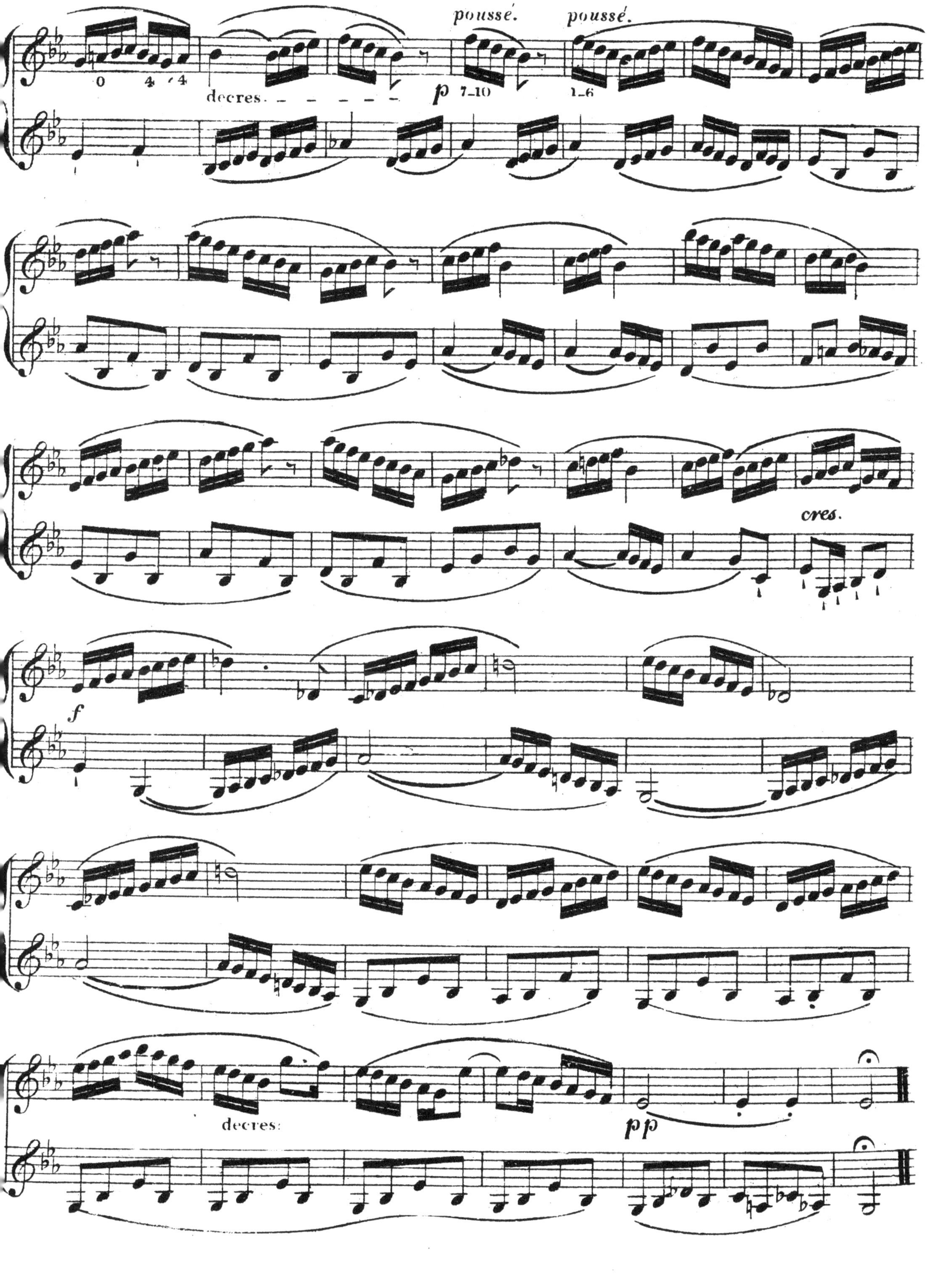
poussé.
poussé.
0 4 4
decres.
p 7-10
1-6
cres.
f
decres:
pp

CHAPTER XVI.

ON INTERVALS, MAJOR, and MINOR KEYS, DIATONIC, AND CHROMATIC SCALES.

The distance from one tone to another is called an Interval. The number of degrees or notes which it includes determines its name, for Ex: a second; from a third: from a fourth; and so on

But as these notes can be raised or lowered, they cause a variety of intervals, distinguished by the terms major, minor, sharp, and diminished.

The following intervals are most commonly used.

When the interval extends above the tenth, it then is counted from the Octave of the fundamental note, and again called fourth, fifth, &c:

All other intervals the scholar will learn in studying Harmony. It may as well be observd that, to become a clever musician, this study cannot be dispensed with.

The scale which the scholar has hitherto studied in twelve different positions, has in ascending and descending, both the third and the sixth major.

There is still another scale, differing from this principally on account of the third and sixth being minor, the first in ascending, the latter however only in descending:

Besides the sixth, it will be observed the seventh in descending has also a flat (mi_nor *)

This scale consists like the others, of five whole and two half tones, but in different succession.

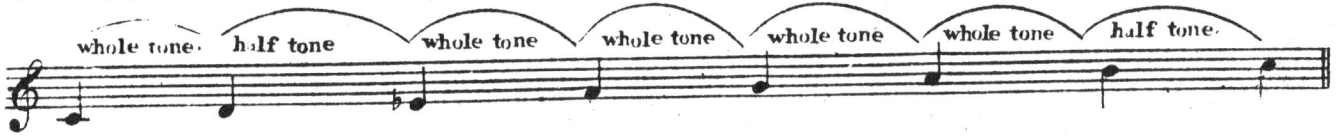

In ascending, after the first whole tone, immediately follows half a tone, then four whole tones, and lastly the second half tone.

In descending we find at first two whole tones, then half a tone, then again two whole tones, next a half tone, and lastly a whole tone.

The scale with major third, and major sixth is denominated the *Major* scale; the scale with minor third ascending, and minor seventh, minor sixth and minor third descending, is called the *Minor* scale.

The minor scale like the major scale, can be transposed eleven times. Consequently there are 12 major, and 12 minor scales. The former the scholar knows already, the latter follow here with their signatures; at first the one of A, because on this key, no essential signature is necessary, yet it requires two accidentals for raising the sixth and eventh in ascending.

---

* Mr Gottfried Weber in his Theory of Music objects to this hitherto used Minor scale and advocates another having both ascending, and descending the minor sixth and major seventh.

In his view "the scale is the number of tones of which the peculiar harmonies of a key is composed" he is certainly right to object to the major sixth in ascending, and the minor seventh in descending, as being foreign to the minor scale. But as the minor scale is mostly employed as a melody to the principal harmony of the minor scale, namely to the triad of the fundamental note, yet (as he states) it still ought to be ascending and descending as hitherto customary

and as his scale but seldom occurs in ascending & only in descending when in the harmony of the 7th of the dominant.

consequently the hitherto customary scale is in practice more frequently heard than his scale. I have therefore thought it better for my purpose to adhere to the old style, and to accustom the scholar's ear to the scales which he would have most often to play.

SCALE of A, without signature

1.

of E, with one sharp.

2.

of B, with two sharps.

3.

of F♯, with three sharps

4.

of C♯, with four sharps.

5.

In order to raise the seventh in the next minor scale of **G** sharp (with five sharps) it requires an accidental, with which the Scholar is not yet acquainted. This is the double-sharp ×, which raises the note (already raised half a note by a sharp) another half note, or altogether a whole tone. The simply raised note receives for the second raising the denomination of double, as F double sharp, E double sharp, &c.

The natural ♮ annuls the double sharp, but a ♯ is added if the note is to remain simply raised.

MINOR.

SCALE of G♯, with five sharps:

6.

of D♯, with six sharps.

7.

of D, with one flat.

8.

of G, with two flats.

9.

of C, with three flats.

10.

of F, with four flats.

11.

of Bb, with five flats.

12.

The Scholar will have observed, that each of these minor scales has the same clef and signatures as the major scales have, both in ascending and descending, they are there - fore called *relative*.

The relative minor mode or key to a major mode lies a minor third lower, the relative key of C major consequently is A minor, of G major, E minor &c: The following are all the major and minor keys or modes with their different signatures.

C major.		G major.		D. major.		A major.	
A minor.		E minor.		B minor.		F♯ minor.	
E major.		B major.		F♯ major.		F major.	
C♯ minor.		G♯ minor.		D♯ minor.		D minor.	
B♭ major.		E♭ major.		A♭ major.		D♯ major.	
G minor.		C minor.		F minor.		B♭ minor.	

To a beginner on the Violin not possessing any knowledge of Harmony, it will generally be difficult to know in what key (whether major or minor) a composition is written, observe therefore that:

In the beginning of most compositions the triad, i.e. the chord of the key in which they are written, consists of the fundamental note, third, fifth, and octave. Without sharps or flats after the clef, it is therefore the chord of C major, or A minor, In comparing these two chords it will be seen that two tones, C and E, belong to both, but that the G belongs to the major, the A to the minor chord. If a musical piece therefore, without sharps or flats after the clef begins with a G, this first tone decides it to begin the major key, if with an A, it is in the minor key, if it com_ mence with C or E, then the continuation of the melody must determine the key If after C and E, or after both tones immediately follows the G or A, one or the other of these tones decides the key. If the melody proceeds by diatonic degrees, the F and G is to be observed in ascending, for if both are raised, as for instance:

or only the G, it is in the minor key; if without sharps, as:

or then it is in the major key. If the melody descends *gradually*, it must be pursued to where it turns or closes, where the A or G generally decides the key. This will be exemplified by the following examples, N⁰ 13. to 19

In N⁰ 13 the second note G, shews the key to be major. In N⁰ 14 the key remains in the 1st bar undecided, as the same notes might also appertain to A minor, the first note of the second bar G however shews it to be C major. In N⁰ 15 the first note immediately announces the minor key In N⁰ 16 the 3d note indicates the major key. In N⁰ 17 the third note likewise shows the major key. In N⁰ 18 it remains undecided till the beginning of the second bar, the A of which shews it to be minor In N⁰ 19 the second note indicates at once the major key.

The Scholar may now try from the foregoing examples, how to find out the key of compositions with sharps or flats. If after this he is still in doubt as to the key, he may, to be certain, look to the last note, as every regular composition ends in the same key in which it begins, even if it modulates in the middle into other keys * Generally the first Violin ends like the Bass, with the principal and fundamental note of the key. The above examples N⁰ 13 to 19 may likewise serve as illustrations, for they all end in G or A, according as they are major or minor.

The following Exercises are intended for practising the minor scales, ascending and descending, the latter sometimes with the minor, sometimes with the major seventh. The numerous accidentals must be carefully attended to.

*A composition in a Minor key, not unfrequently ends in the Major of the same tone, Ex: A—minor in A—major.

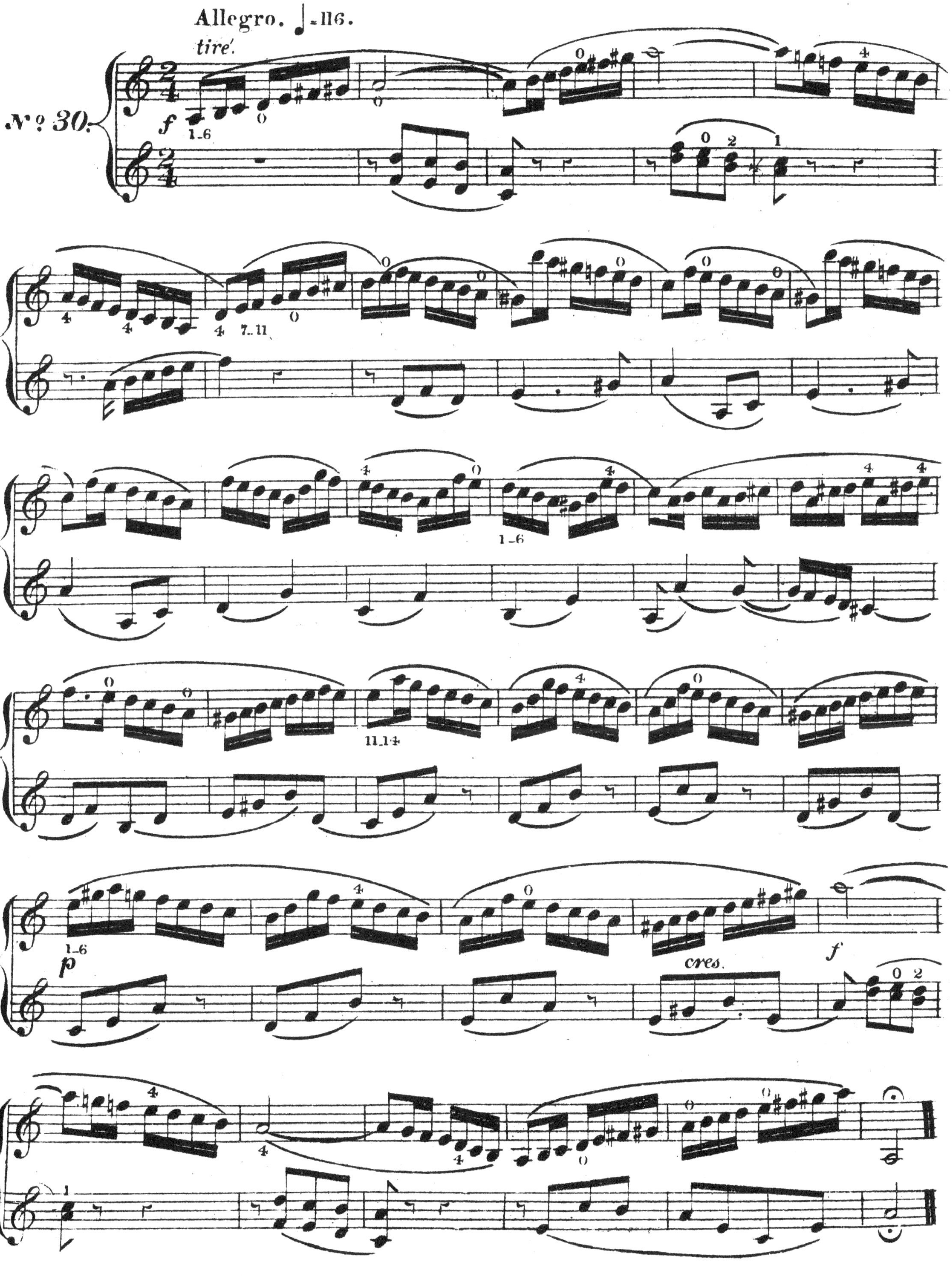
Allegro. ♩=116.
tiré
№ 30.
f
p
cres.
f

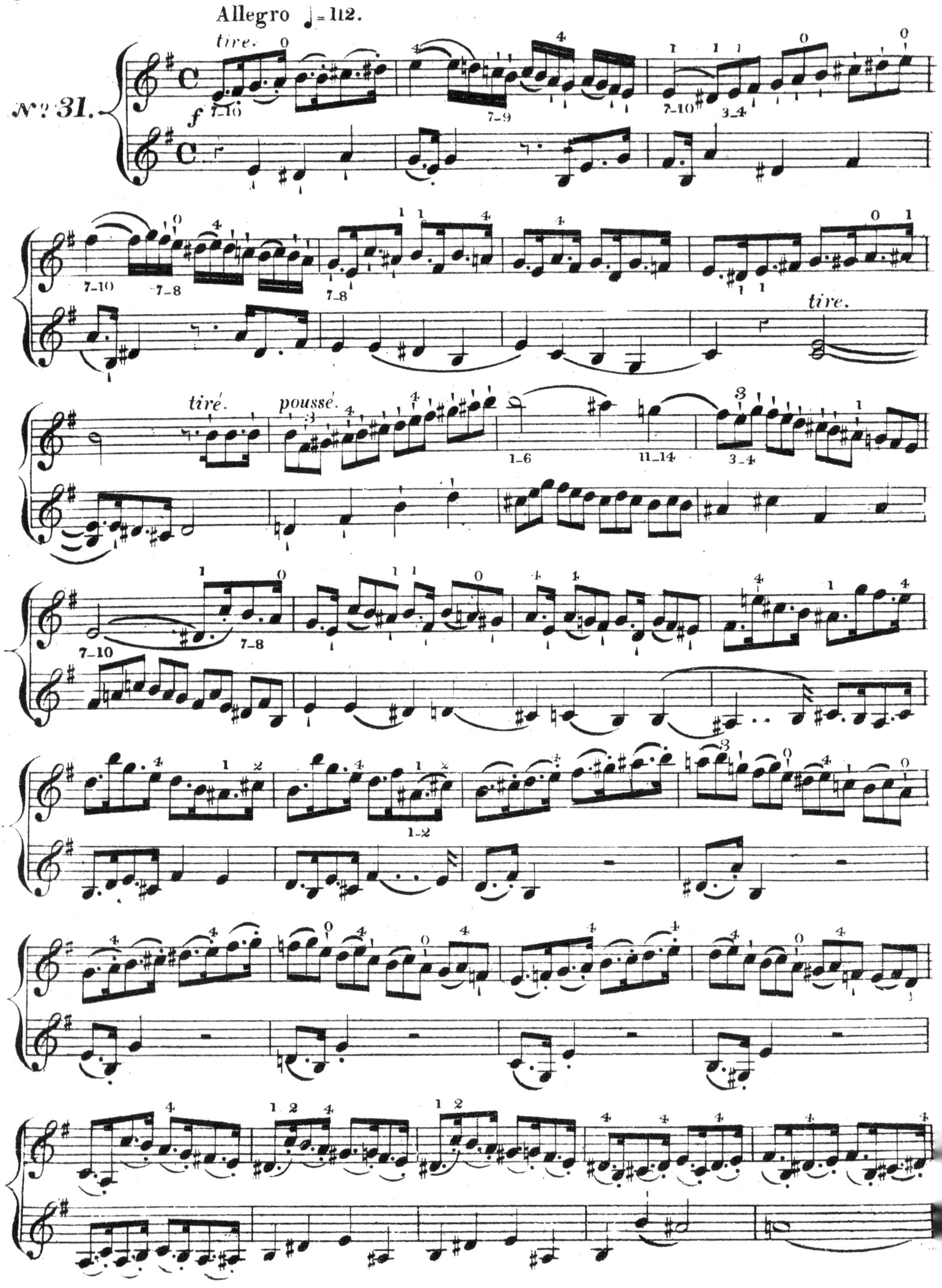
Allegro ♩=112.
Nº 31.
tire.
f
tire.
tiré.
poussé.

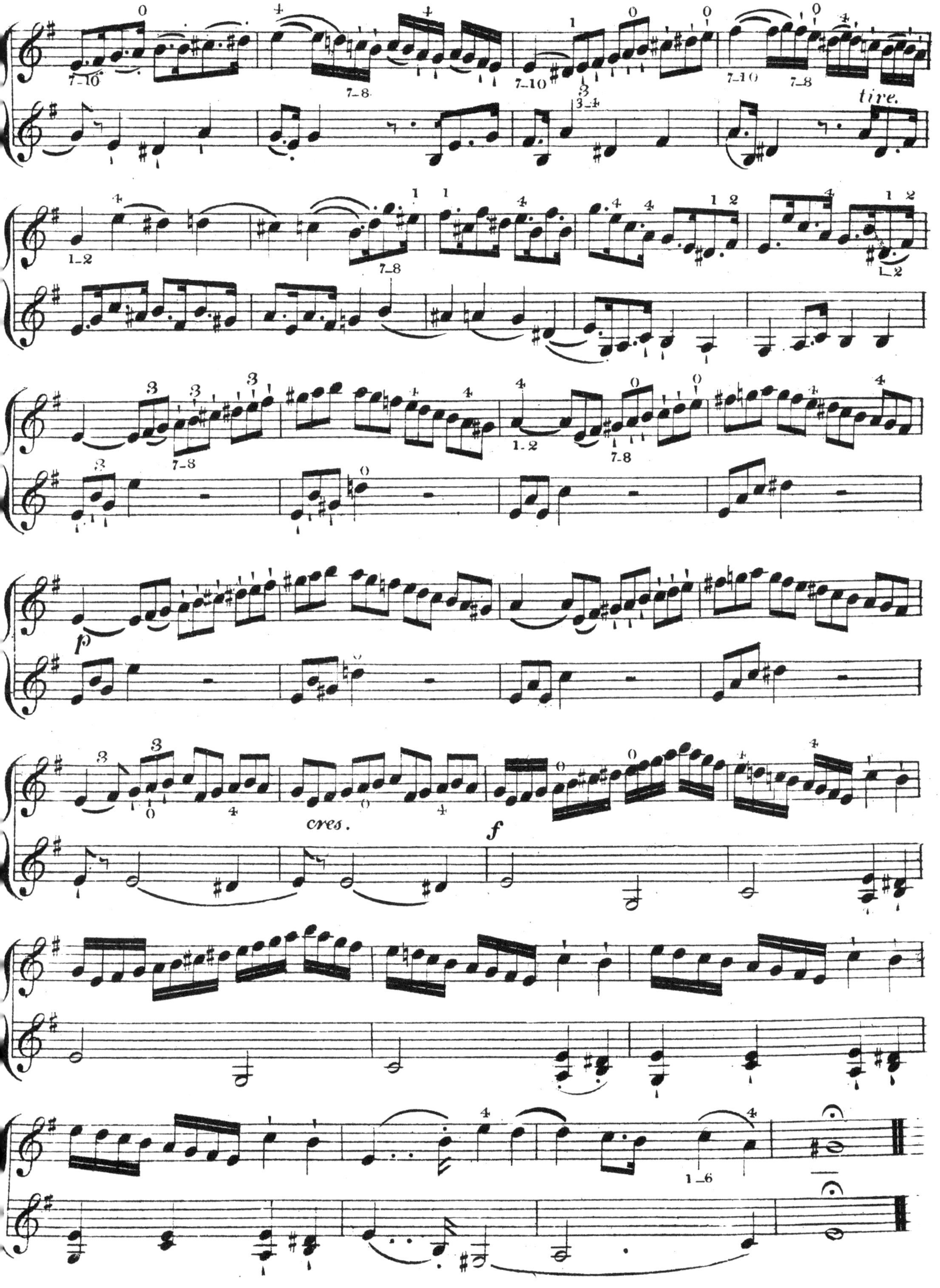
tire.
p
cres.
f

№ 32.

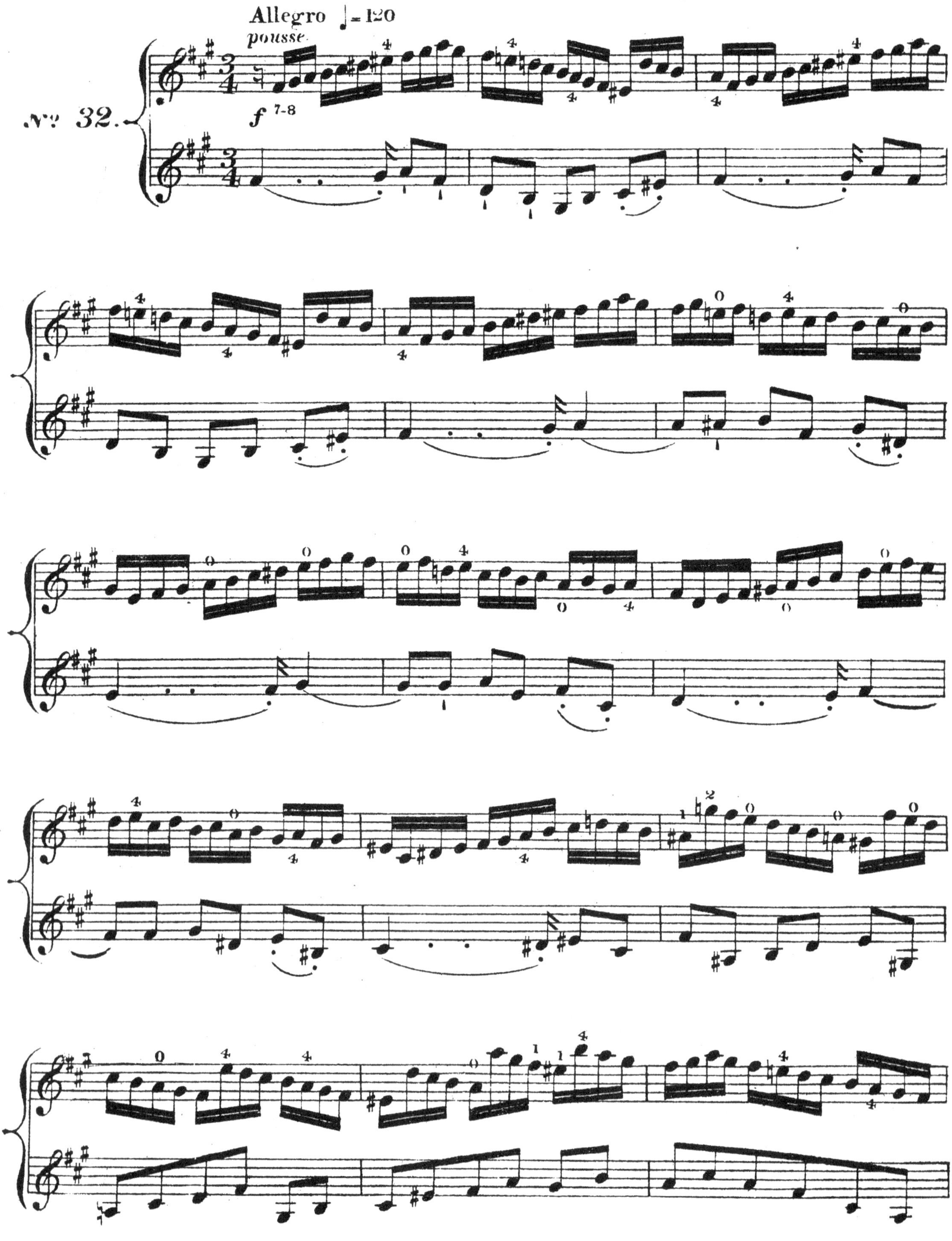

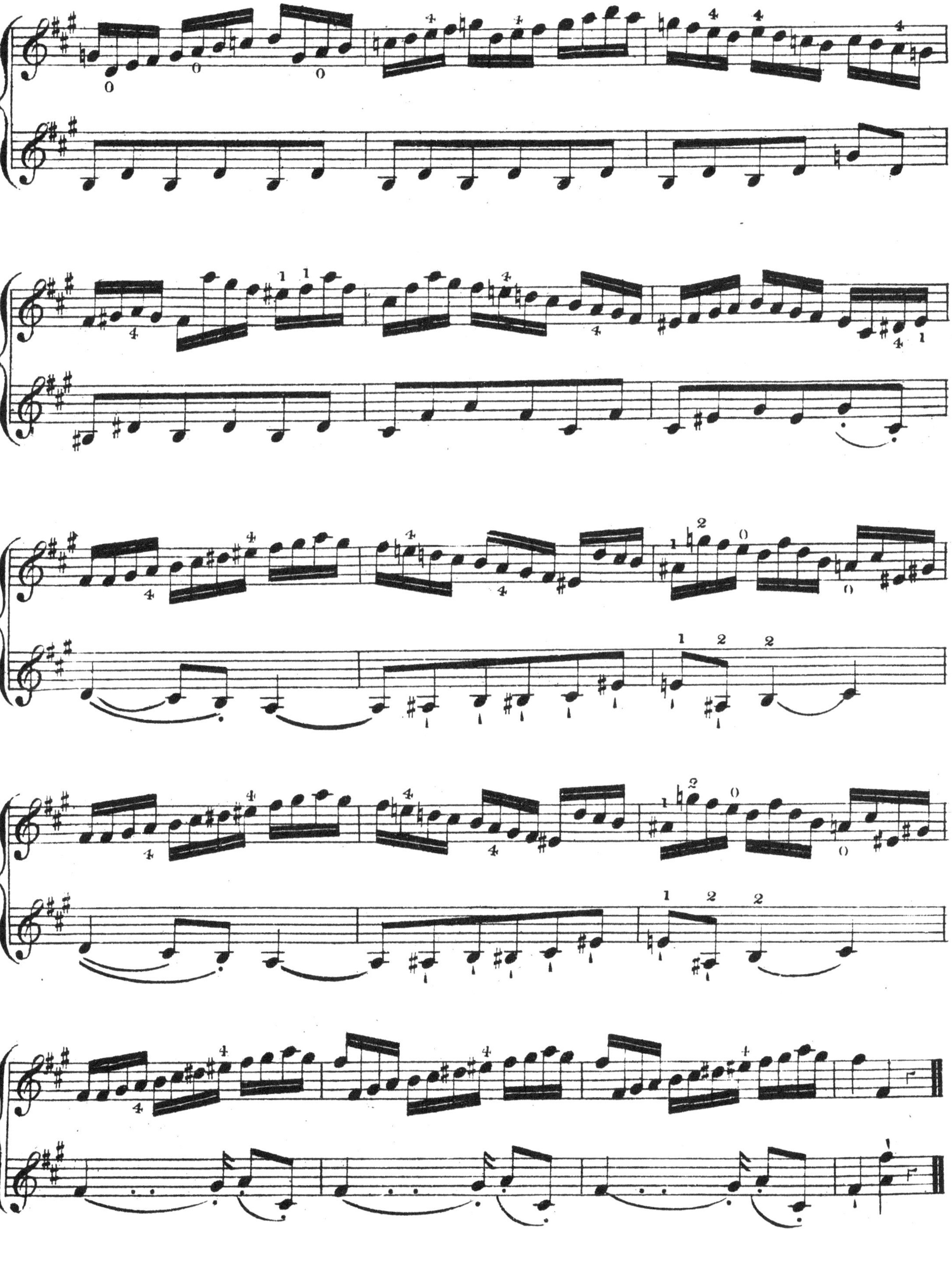

66

In the following Exercise, the rule that the Accidentals in a bar influence the higher or lower Octaves must also be remembered.

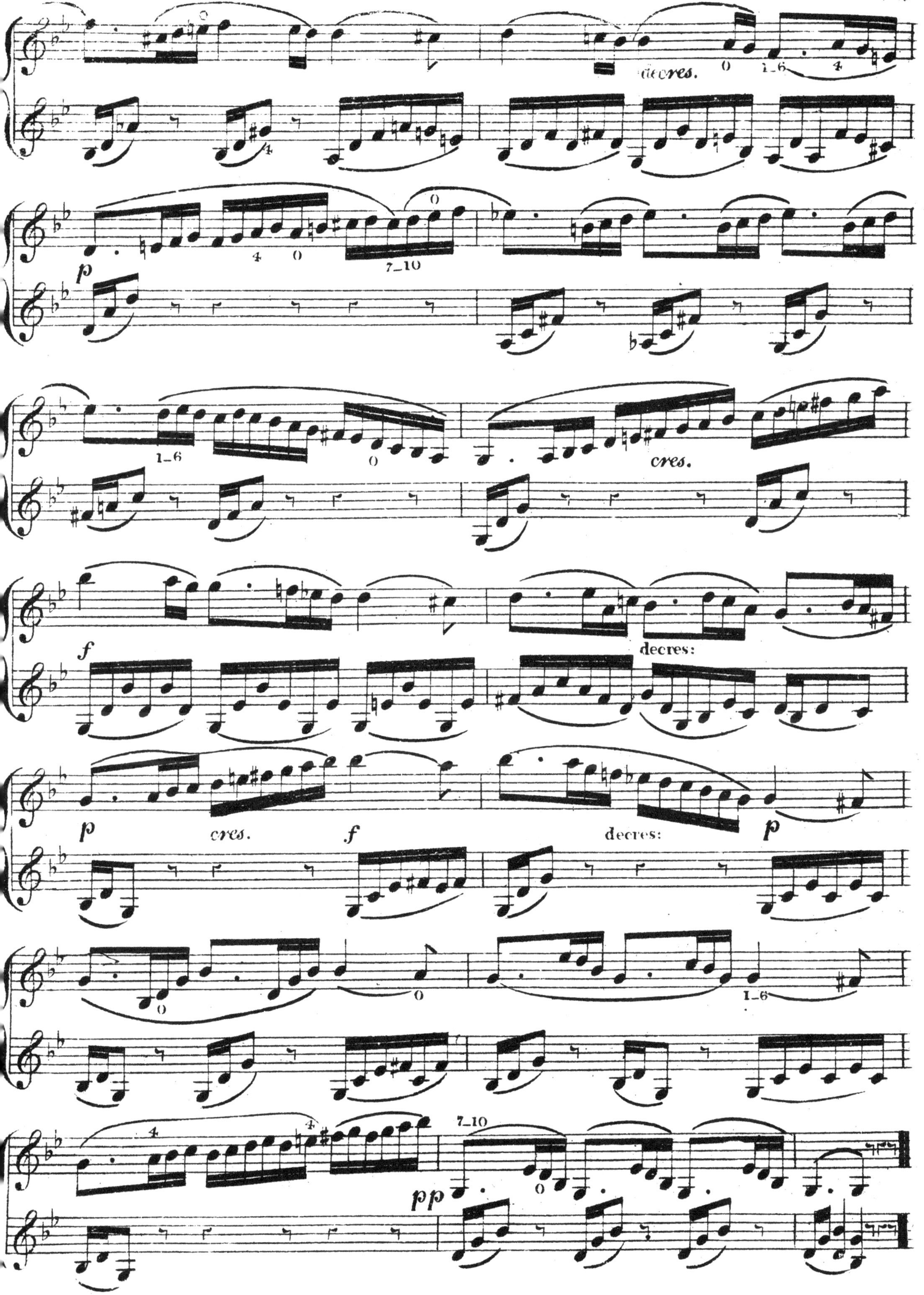
decres.
p
cres.
f
decres:
p
cres.
f
decres:
p
pp

68

In the 13th bar of the following Exercise appears a new Accidental, the double **Flat** (♭♭) serving to lower the E, already flattened by the simple ♭, still half a note more. The note with a double flat is called E double flat, B double flat &c. This double flat is contradicted by a ♮ with one flat attached to it,

Thus the Scholar has been made acquainted with the last of the five accidentals, viz: ♯, ♭, ♭♭, and ♮.

Allegretto. ♩ 108.
tiré.

Nº 34.

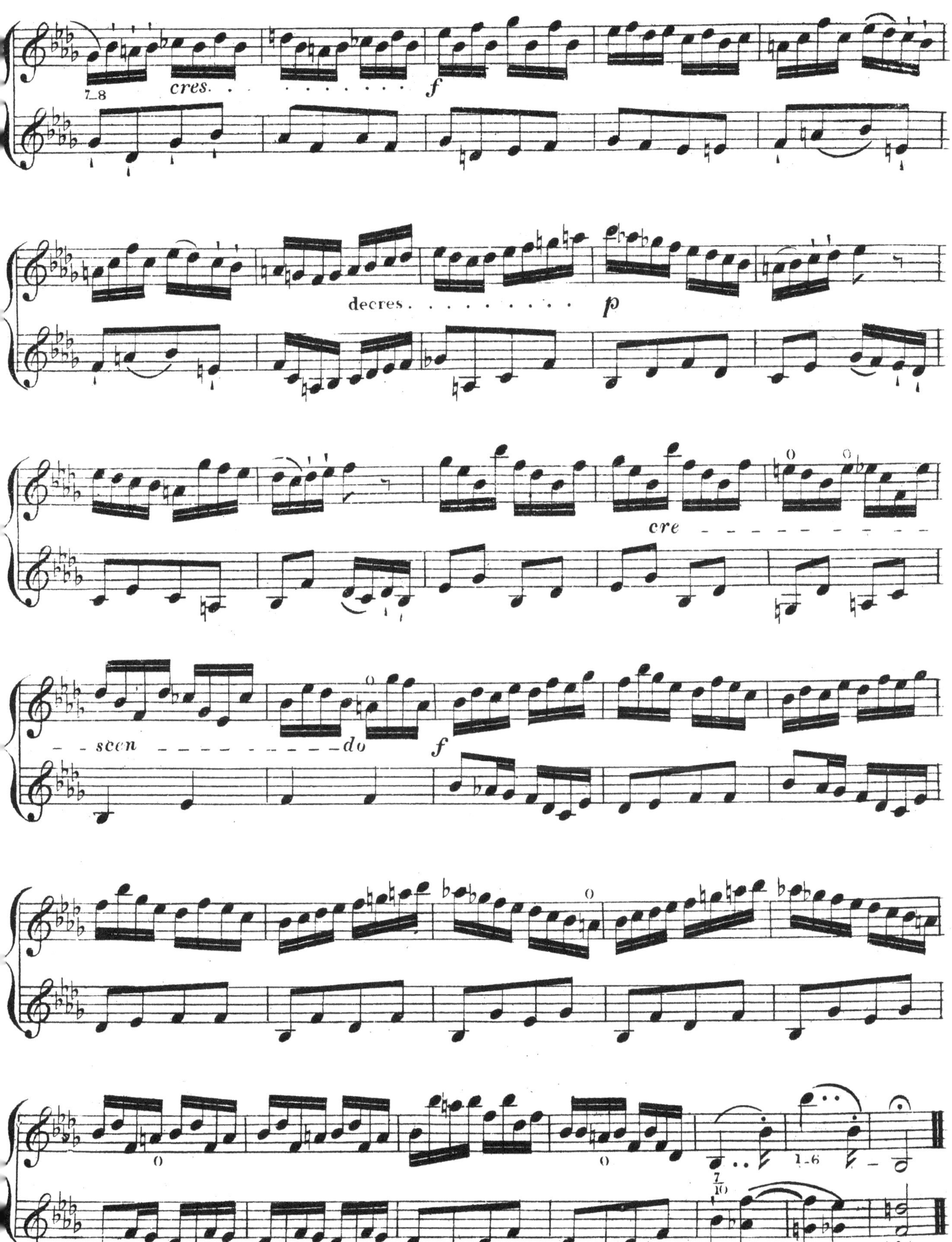
cres.
f
decres.
p
cre
scen
do
f

All major and minor_Scales, consisting of five whole and two half tones are called diatonic or natural scales. But there is another kind of major and minor Scales going through all the twelve half tones:

they are called chromatic, or artificial, and consist always of the same half tones, and are in major and minor, ascending or descending, the same to the ear though to the eye they appear different; i.e. written with other accidentals.*

The two following Exercises are intended for practising the chromatic Scales. If they are very quick, observe this rule, that with the little finger, because it is shorter than the others, and therefore less moveable, *never more than one tone is taken*, whilst to each of the other fingers two tones are appropriated. For the raised tone of the 4th finger, take therefore (as at 1.) the next open string, or (as at 2.) the first finger on the open string.

The E sharp at 2. is taken with the second finger, because *the same finger must never follow three times successively.*

As the open strings (particularly E and A) sound sharper than the same tones stop_ped on the preceding strings, they are avoided as much as possible in chromatic scales. In the 26th bar of the next Exercise, the E flat, (as if it were D sharp) is better taken with the third finger, so that the E need not to be taken on the open string, but with the fourth finger.

N.o 35.

* The Enharmonic Scale is not practically used.

cres.
poussé.
poussé.
tiré.
cres.
decres
cres.
decres:
cres.
decres:
poussé.
cres.
decres:

Allegro. ♩=112.

Nº 36.

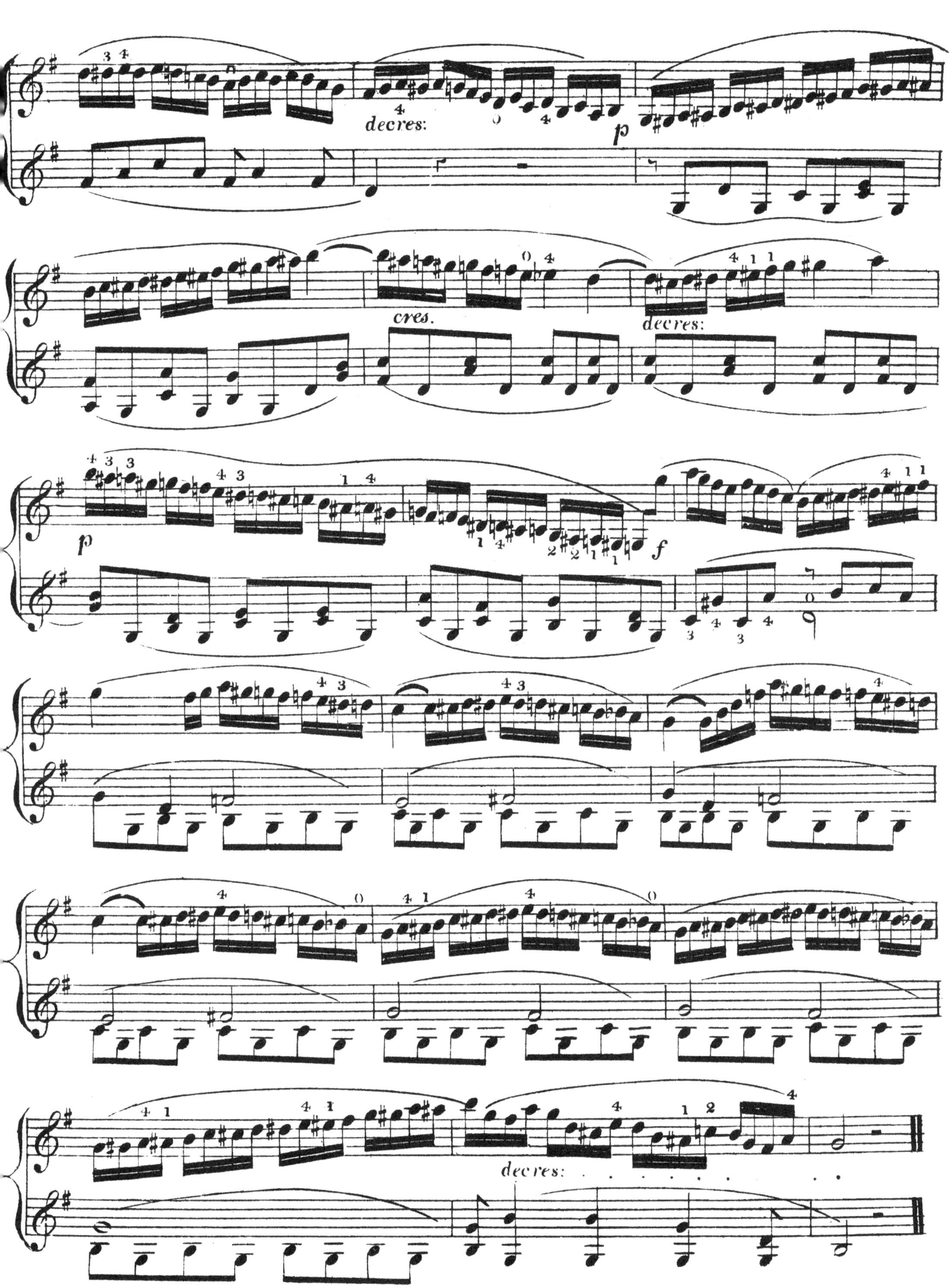
decres:
p
cres.
decres:
p
f
decres:

CHAPTER XVII

ON SHIFTS, THE EXTENSION OF FINGERS, AND THE HARMONICS.

Besides the tones from ♪ to ♪ to which all the preceding Exercises are confined, the Violin possesses an extent of Harmonic tones, of more than an octave.

C D E F G A B C D E

The highest tones of this scale, being difficult to read quickly, on account of their being placed so much above the ledger lines, the word Octave is generally writ_ten over them, and their higher situation indicated by 8va , as

If they are to be played again in the situation in which they are written, it is indicated by the word "loco," or also by the omission of the dotted or marked line.

OR

The tones extending above ♪ can only be reached and taken by the finger by moving or shifting the hand from its hitherto held position, more or less towards the bridge. These different positions are called Shifts. Formerly they were divided into half and whole Shifts A *half shift* was the position of the hand, which took the G of the E string ♪ with the first finger; a *whole shift* that which took the first finger on the A of the E string ♪ The next

position was again called *half shift*, the following again *whole shift* &c: To dis
tinguish the higher shifts from the lower, they were also called second half and
second whole shifts.

But as this denomination of shifts is intricate, I have here applied the French
manner, which marks the different positions of the hand, by *first Position*, se_
cond Position &c:

The lower position of the hand in which all the preceding Exercises have been
played is therefore called first position, by advancing the hand a little nearer the
bridge, so as to let the first finger fall on the G or G♯ of the E string,

we are in the second position; on in the third

position; on in the fourth position; on in the fifth;

on in the sixth; on in the 7th.; on

in the eighth position. &c:

In these higher positions of the hand, not only the notes of the E string, but
also the notes of the other three strings are played, altho' they may be
reached with the assistance of the E string in the lower position. But contin_
ually playing in this way would change the position of the hand too often, and
unnecessarily increase the difficulty. In fact, many passages really very easy,
in a quiet position of the hand could not possibly be executed.

In the new shifts of the following Exercises, the scholar will be careful not to
change the holding of the hand as hitherto used, and will see that the fin _
gers bent in both joints fall horizontally on the strings. In the second shift,
the wrist must not reach the ribs of the Violin, till the hand has advanced to the
third shift, where the ball of the hand adheres to the hollow of the neck.

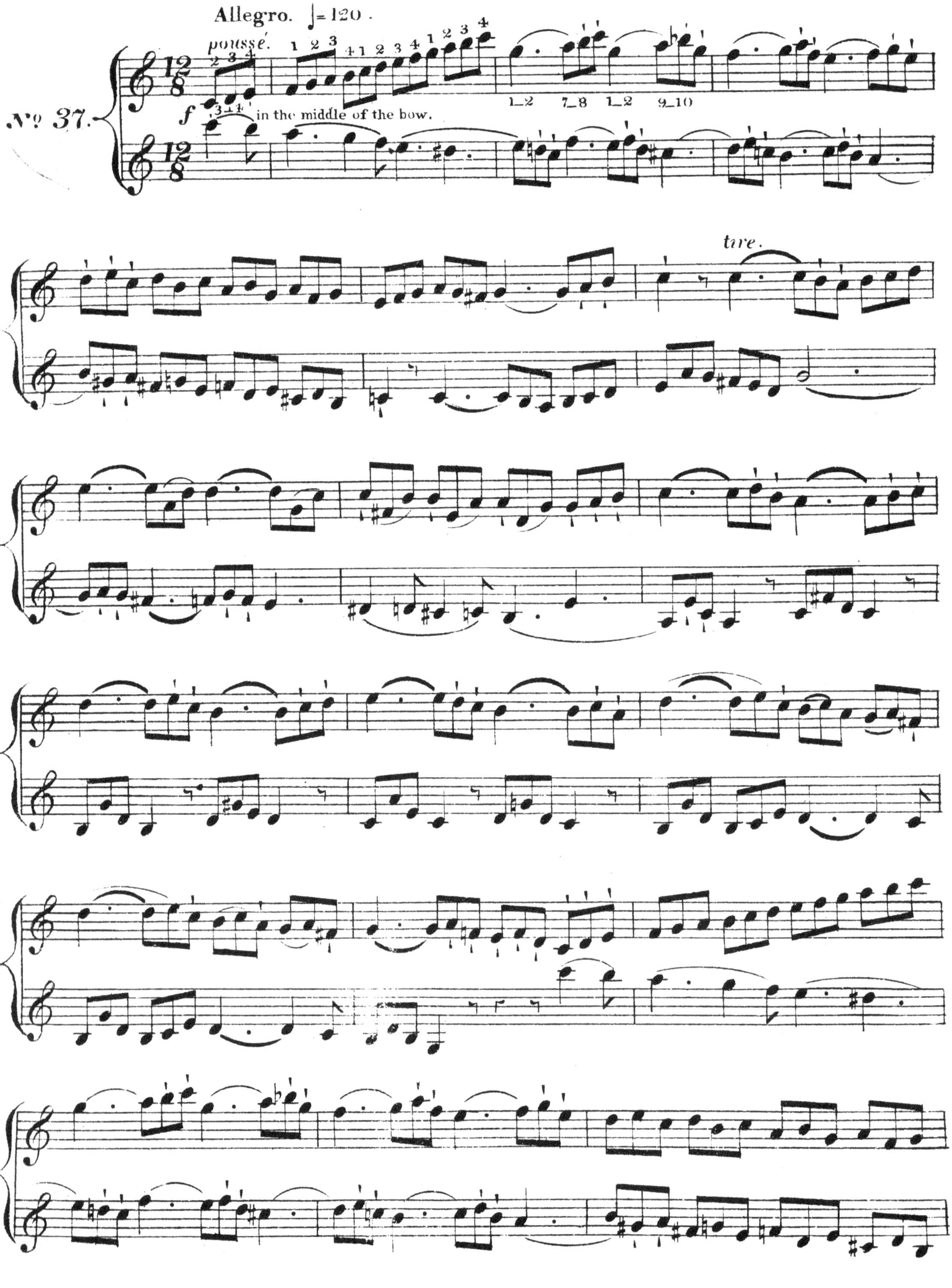
№ 37.
Allegro. ♩= 120.
poussé.
f
in the middle of the bow.
tire.

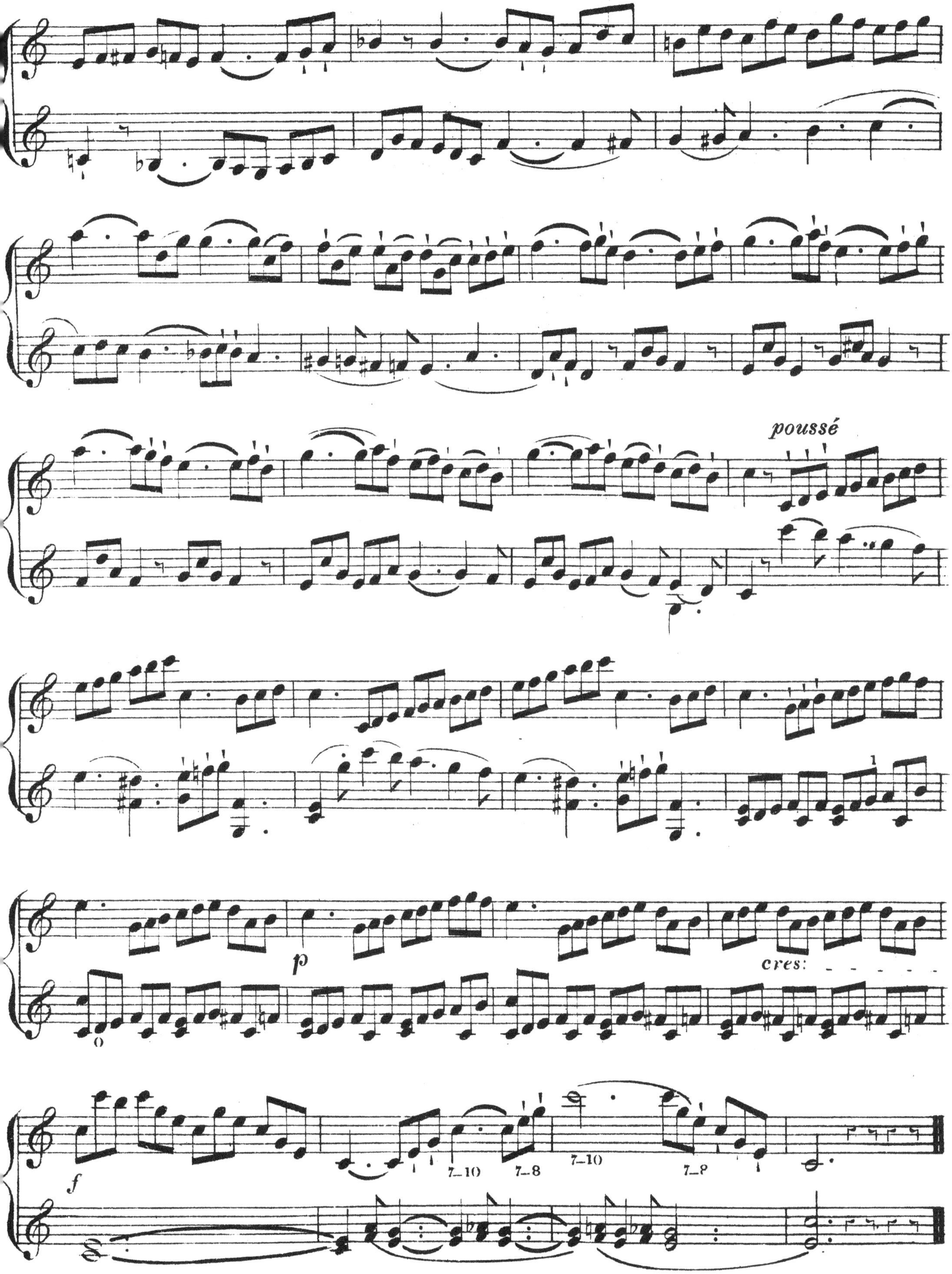
poussé
p
cres:
f
7_10
7_8
7_10
7_8
0
1

No. 38.

Allegretto. ♩-63.

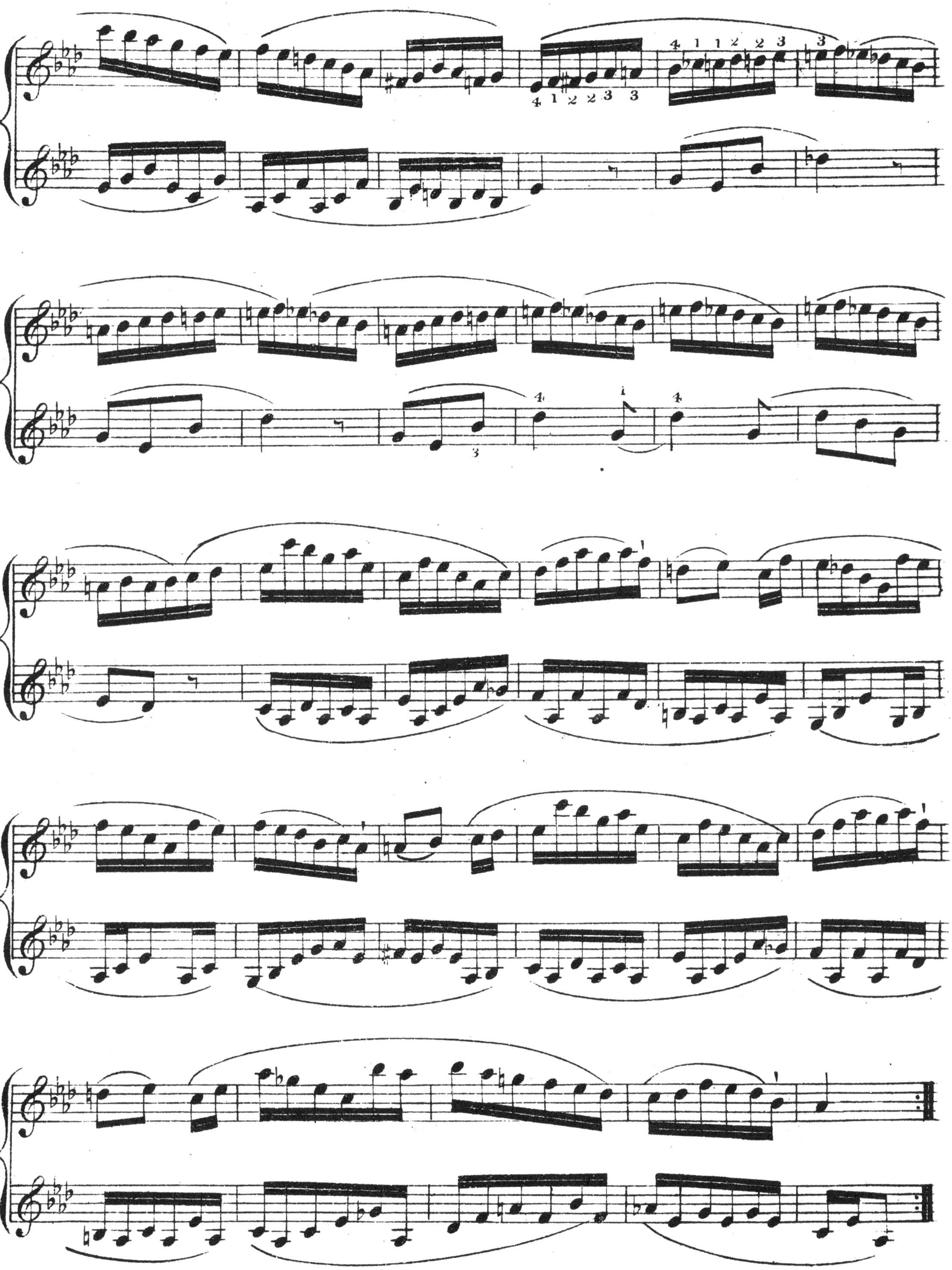

No. 39.

2nd Position.

Allegro. ♩-132.
tire.

f   sempre staccato.

tire.
7_10
11_12
11_14
13_14
1_6
7_10
11_12
11_14
tire.
13.14
1_6
7-8
7-10
11_12
11_14

Allegro. ♩ = 108.
3rd Position.
No 40.
tire.
pousse
tiré.
poussé.
tiré
poussé.

The following Exercise is intended to teach the Scholar, how to extend the finger to tones belonging to the next or preceding position. This is effected, either with the fourth or the first finger, without moving the hand, as:

To slur the extended tone in one bowing with the nearest tone, it must not be distant more than *half* a tone, as the *whole* tone, by drawing back the finger, produces an unpleasant effect, as:

But if the extended tone does not immediately follow the next nearest tone, then the *whole* tone, even with one slurred bowing, may be taken, as:

This extension of tones, not belonging to the position in which we are playing, avoids changing the position of the hand, on account of a single tone merely; but in the second case, where they are extended and might also, without leaving the shift, be taken on the nearest string it is intended to unite them with the other tones in a much more quiet bowing than otherwise could possibly be done.

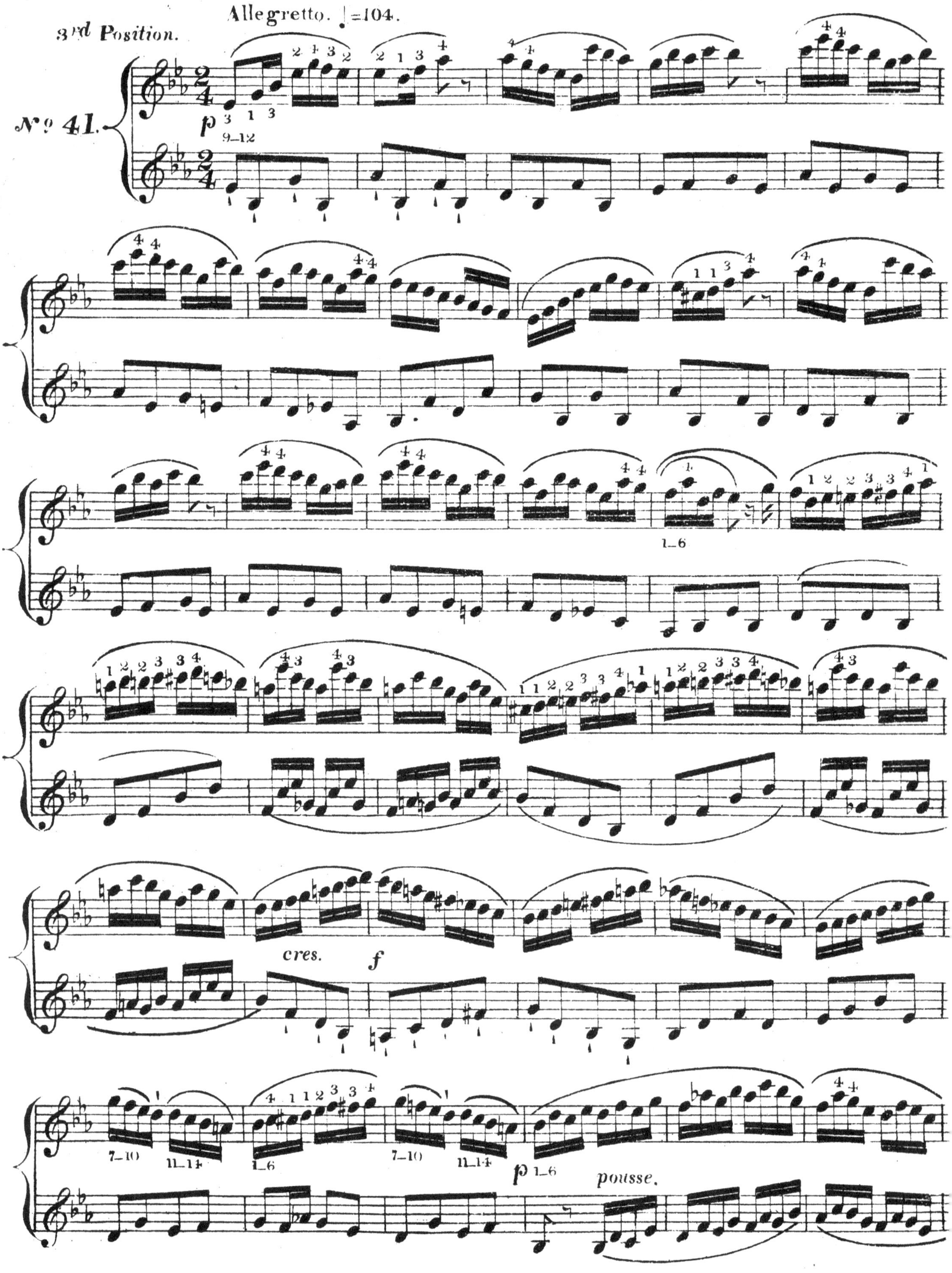
3rd Position.
Allegretto. ♩=104.
No 41.
p
cres.
f
p
pousse.

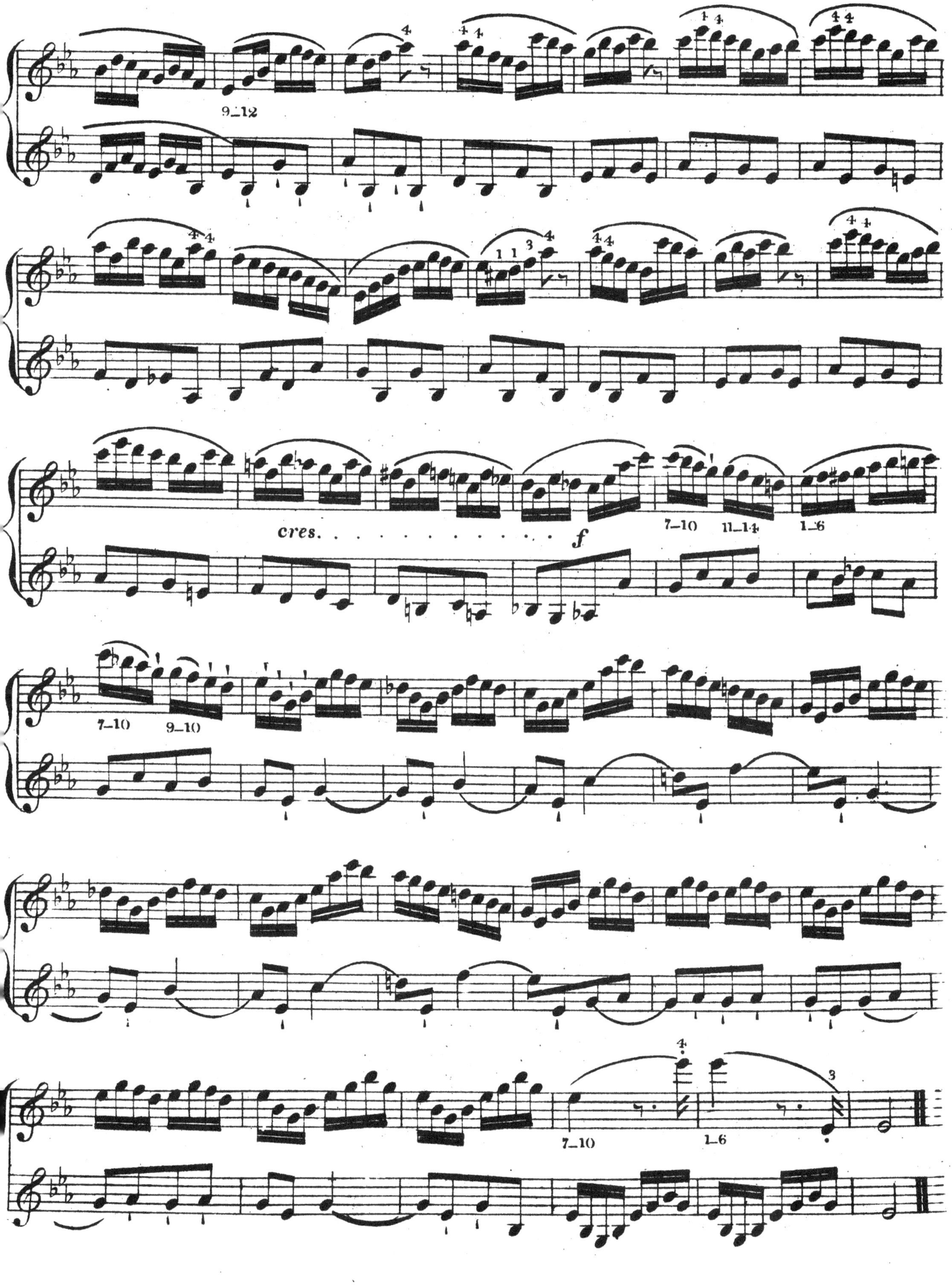
9-12
cres.
f
7-10
11-14
1-6
7-10
9-10
7-10
1-6

As the tones nearest the bridge lie always closer to each other, the Scholar's ear will also direct him to place his fingers from Shift to Shift more closely together, particularly the little finger, which, having to take the half tone, must closely adhere to its predecessor. In very high shifts it is necessary for the sure intonation of the half tone, that this be first removed before the other can be put down. It is not possible to determine in what position this shifting should begin, for a scholar with strong and fleshy fingers may find it even necessary in the lower posi tions, whereas thin and pointed fingers will not have this obstacle to encounter.

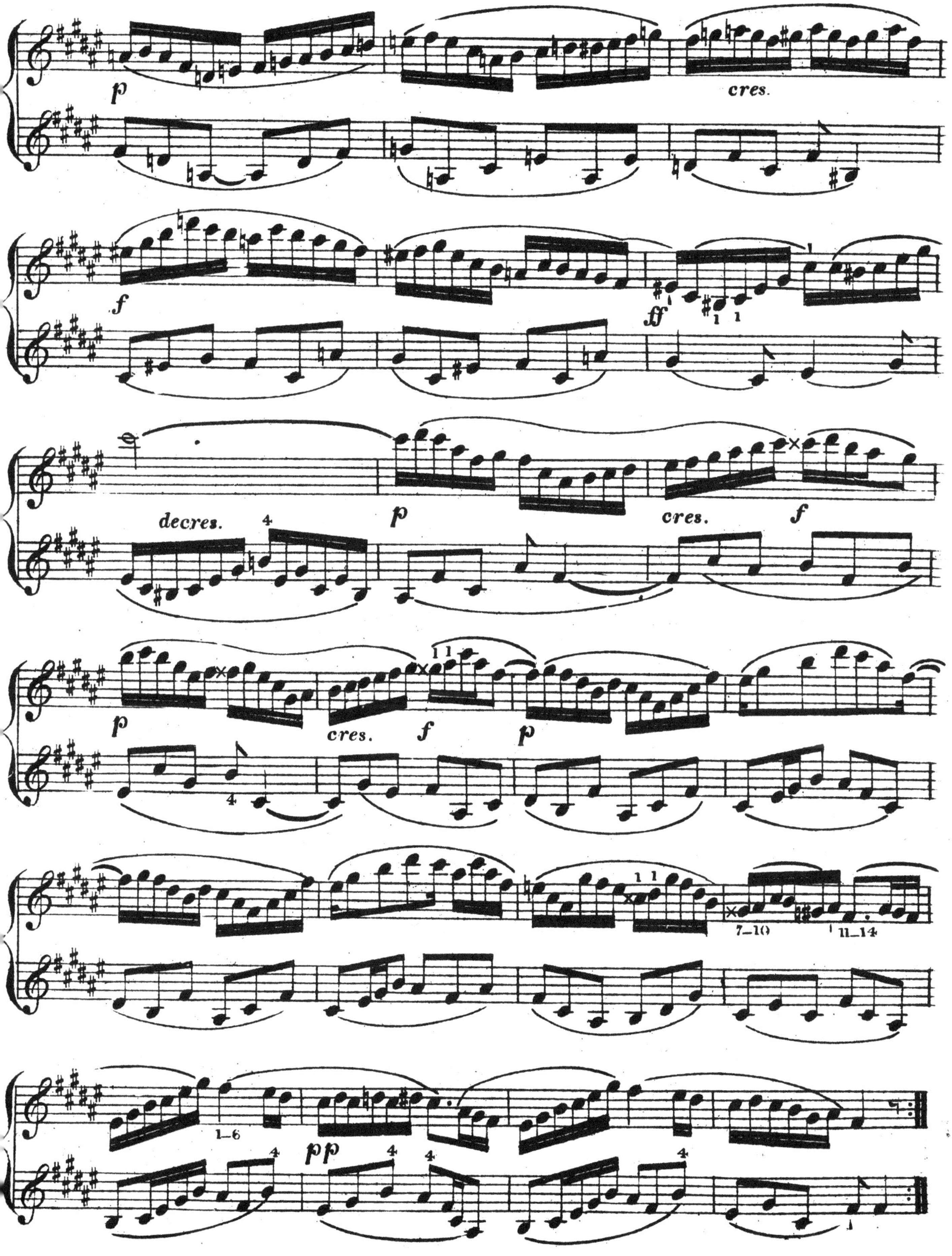
p
cres.
f
ff
decres.
p
cres.
f
p
cres.
f
p
pp

88

In the next fourth position, the left hand must be lifted a little more than hitherto, over the edge of the belly, to enable the fingers to reach the G string horizontally; at each succeeding position this lifting of the hand is gradually increased. The thumb by degrees is drawn round the back of the neck and the elbow moved more under the Violin. If the Scholar have a very small hand, he will be obliged in the highest positions to draw the thumb entirely from under the neck and even to rest it on the ribs; but then it is necessary to hold the Violin very tight with the chin, particularly in the sliding down of the hand to the lower positions.

In the 7th bar of the following Exercise, the hand in extending the A sharp, with the first finger, must by no means be moved from its position; nor the fourth finger in the 8th bar of the 2nd part at the A sharp.

4th Position.

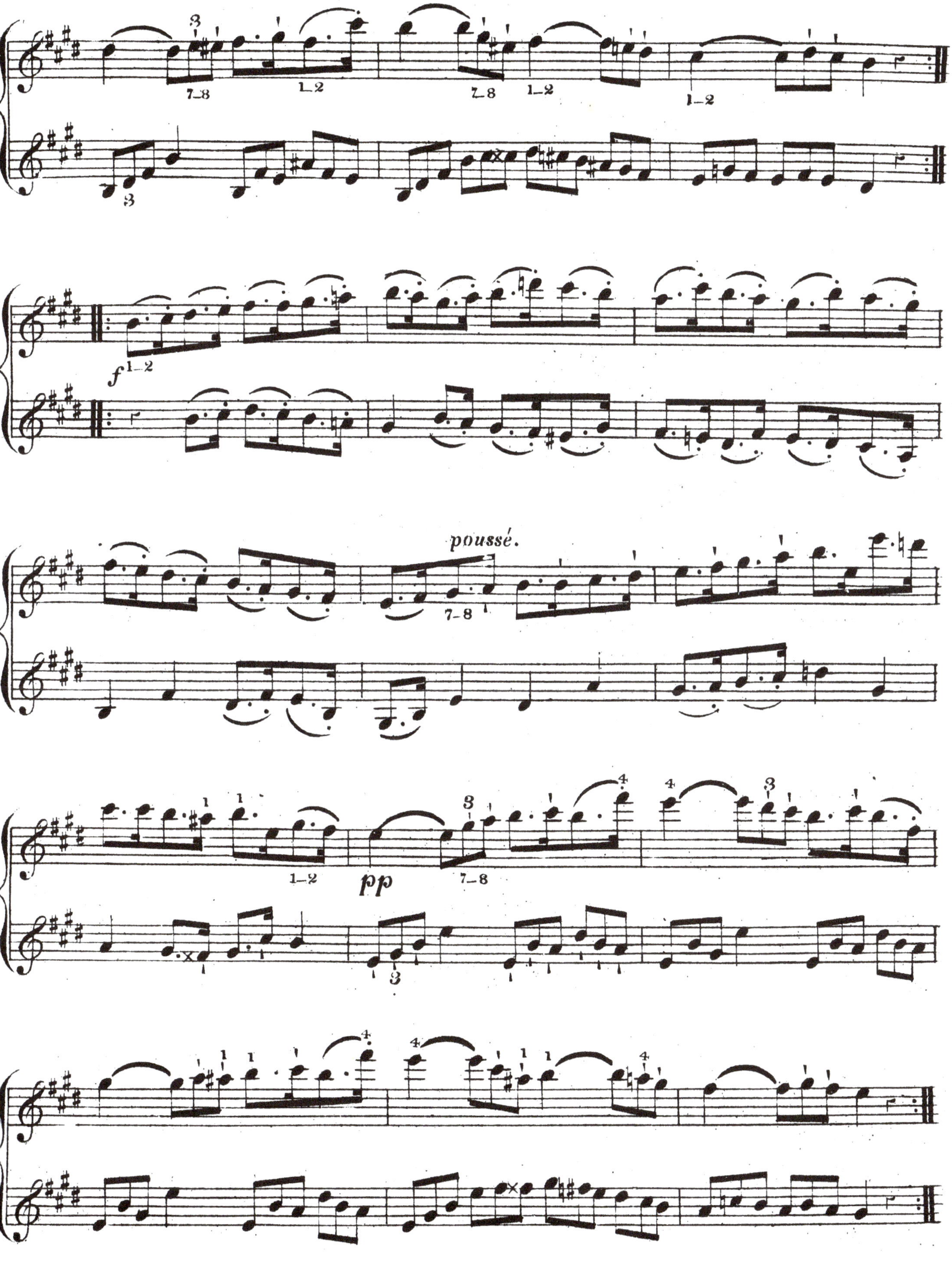
poussé.

The dotted notes in the following Exercise are to be bowed very short and darting

In the high positions of the hand, where the steps are very close, not only the tones of the nearest position, but also those of two or three higher positions can be extended. In the following Exercise there are such which appertain to the 7th and 8th position. I here again remind the scholar that in the extension of these tones, only the little finger should be stretched out as far as necessary, without moving the hand from its position.

Nº 43.

6th Position. Allegro. 𝅗𝅥 = 108.

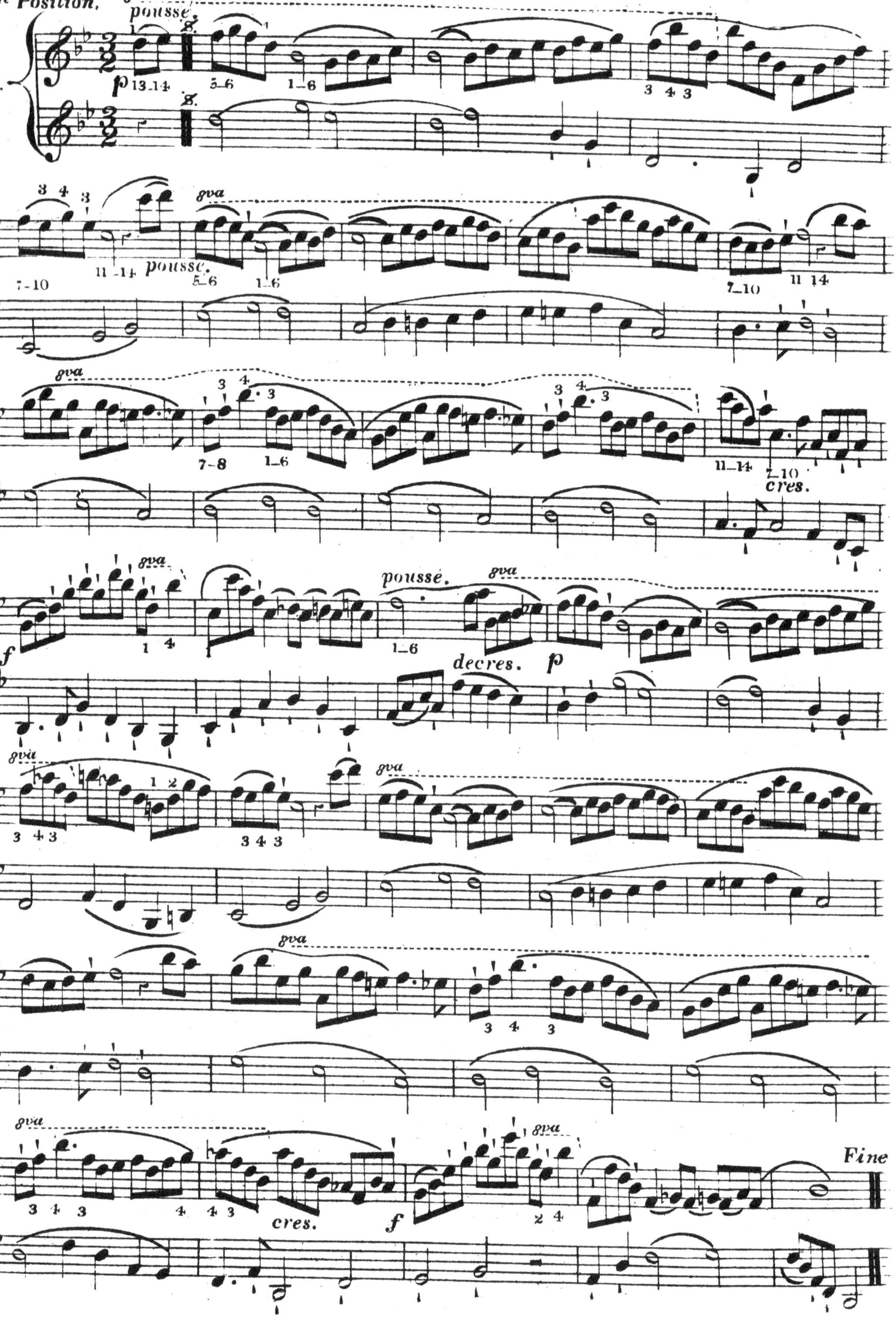

D.C. (da Capo) dal segno al
fine, denotes that the piece is
to be repeated from the sign
𝄋 and to end at the word
Fine.

After being sufficiently grounded in the different positions without moving the hand, the Scholar will then have to learn how to shift, or change quickly from one Position to another. For this purpose, the next five Exercises have been composed

In these, as well as in all the following Exercises, the ○ is often seen over notes, signifying that those notes when not played on the open strings, are to be harmonic-tones.

These tones are produced by lightly pressing the finger on the string without touching the fingerboard. They are on account of their clearer sound, particularly intended to render one tone more striking and predominant than the others, as for instance, the concluding note of ascending scales, or broken chords.

But as many of the harmonic tones which can be produced on the Violin, differ so much in sound from the natural tones of the Instrument that the ear will immediately recognise them as foreign and not belonging to the others, the good School only permits the use of such as do not transgress the above rule These are 1. the Octave, 2, the Fifth of the Octave, and 3, the double Octave, of each string, namely on

the G string: on the D string: on the A string:

and on the E string: The middle of the string gives the Octave, two third parts of the same, the fifth of the octave, and three fourth parts the double octave, whether measuring from the nut or the bridge. The harmonic tones must however always be taken on the side of the bridge, where they come out much easier than on any other part of the string Consequently all applicable Harmonic tones are taken on the same place as the like sounding *natural* tones.*

---

*The above named Harmonic tones, as not much differing in sound from the natural tones, have, intermixed with the latter, at all times been used by all good Violinists. All others, and particularly the ARTIFICIAL Harmonic tones must be rejected, because they so totally differ from the natural tones.
It would be degrading this noble instrument to play whole melodies in such childish foreign tones. The great sensation which the celebrated PAGANINI has created in recent times, by the renewal of the ancient and almost wholly forgotten Harmonic playing, and by his eminent perfection in it, however alluring such examples may be, I must nevertheless seriously advise all Young Violinists not to lose their time in such a study, or neglect what is more useful In support of this view, I quote the greatest Violinists of every age, for instance PUGNANI, TARTINI, CORELLI, VIOTTI, ECK, RODE KREUTZER, BAILLOT, LAFONT, &c of whom not one has ever played in the manner of PAGANINI. If even the harmonic playing was found to be an improvement in Violin playing, which good taste might justify still it would, in sacrificing a round full tone, be bought at too high a rate, for with this it cannot assimilate, as the Harmonic tones only speak with very thin strings on which it is impossible to produce a full tone.

Allegro. ♩ - 120.
N° 46
f
3d pos.
8va
4th pos
4th p
3d p
2d p
1st p
tiré.
5th p

8va
6th pos
8va
5th p
3d p
4th p
3d p
2d p
1st p
3d p
4th p
3d p
8va
5th p
3d p
1st p.
3d p
8va
7th p
3d p
1st p
4th p

8va
4th pos
3d p
2d p
1st p.
3d p
6th p
3d p
6th p
5th p
3d p
1st p
3d p
5th p
p
3d p
1st p
3d p
cres
5th p
f
cres
f
tiré

No. 47.

8va
3d p.
3d p.
6th p.
3d p.
6th p.
2d p.
8va
5th p.
1st p.
4th p.
3d p.
2d p.
1st p.
3d p.
1st p.
3d p.
1st p.

3d p. 5th p. 3d p. 1st p. 4th p.
8va
7th p.
2d p. 5th p. 2d p.
8va
2d p. 5th p. 7th p. 3d p.
1st p.
3d p. 2d p. 1st p.
3d p. 1st p.

The following Exercise contains passages in octaves. In no interval besides the unisons the smallest deviation from pure intonation so unpleasantly felt as in octaves; and the most careful stopping is required to produce them correctly. At present it will be doubly difficult, as with each new stop the position of the hand changes, and in proportion as it approaches the bridge, the fourth finger must gradually contract and approach nearer to the first finger. In passages of several octaves these two fingers are not lifted up, but firmly resting on the strings, are moved on together at the same time.

The moving of the bow from one string to another, is produced in the following Octave passages, by the wrist, and facilitated by an almost imperceptible raising and lowering of the elbow.

Where two notes are to be slurred in one bow, an even division of the 16 semiquavers is particularly requisite, in order to avoid their sounding alike.

Nº 48

Allegro. ♩= 126
f
1st p
4th p.
1st p.
decres.
p
1st: p.
cres.
f
4th p.
3d p.
8va
f
1st p.
5th, 1st p.

8va
8va
6th p.
1st p. 4th p. 3d p. 1st p. 3d p. 6th p. 3d p. 1st p.
decres.
p
1st p.
cres f
4th p.
3d p.

104 Likewise in passages of tenths, as they appear in the next Exercise, the fingers
remain on the string and glide on together.

(*) This lowest position of the hand close to the nut is best denominated half position, also sometimes called the back position

A still more frequent and rapid shifting of the positions than in the pre_ceding is to be found in the next Exercise, there are even leaps from the lowest to the highest positions. It is very difficult in these leaps to get a firm stopping of the high tones, with an intonation both pure and harmonious, without considerable practice. The distance of the leap which the hand has to make, must be most exactly measured, so that the finger can at once stop the right tone, without seeking for it, and then remain firm and immoveable.

If two tones lying at a distance are to be drawn together in one bowing, (as in the 9th 10th and 11th bars of the following Exercise) the leap from one tone to another cannot be made without the sliding of the hand being heard. This unplea_sant howling can however be avoided, by moving forward the first finger of the first tone, untill the finger of the second tone can fall on its place; in the 9th bar of the Example therefore, move the first finger from E to B.

5th Position.

and then let the fourth finger fall on the second E; the same is done in the 11th bar, with the second finger, from E to B.

7th Position.

after which the little finger falls on the high B. But this gliding upwards must be done so rapidly as to make the passing from the small note to the highest note imperceptible, (in the first Example a fourth, in the second an octave,) and so to deceive the ear, that it appears to have passed the whole space from the lowest to the highest note uniformly, by the sliding finger. Many Violinists, (in opposition to this rule) certainly do in such leaps, slide with the finger of the high tones, and play the passages in this manner

But this method, as the unpleasant howling is possibly not to be avoided must be rejected as faulty.

Only in case where the highest note is to be taken in Harmonics, (as in the 5th and 6th bar of the following Exercise) it is allowed to use the little finger for sliding on to the highest tone. During the clear vibration and distinct intonation of the Harmonic tone, the howling can then be avoided by the rapid gliding on of the finger. To produce the Harmonic, the finger must be gently raised at the last mo_ment of the sliding, so that the string may not touch the fingerboard, and then both fin_ger and bow should be elevated from the string to give a bell·like after-sound.

But if the concluding note of such a broken chord is no Harmonic tone, a totally different Position must be chosen. Suppose for instance the given two bars (5 and 6 of the Example) stood half a tone lower, they would require the following finger_ing.

* The Scholar will already have observed that such passages (and all those, similar to the four preceding and following examples, in which the shifting frequently changes) might also be played with other fingering Reasons might be stated why the given fingering has been chosen in preference, but it would lead me to diffuseness, and be superfluous, as the Scholar will soon perceive why the prescribed shiftings are pre ferable to others. I may give the preliminary assurance that I have always chosen either the most commodious or (if not so) then those shifts, with which the marked passages can be produced in the most clear and harmonious manner. When the Scholar has once mastered the fingering, systematically carried through this School, he will have no difficulty in applying it also to other compositions.

No 50.

tiré
8va
loco
h.p.
1st 3d 7th 6th
1st 2d 4th 6th p.
1st 3d 5th 8th p.
1st 4th 7th p.
3d 6th p.
2d 4th 7th p.
1st 4th 8th 4th 7th 11th
3d p. 1st p.
2d 3d 5th 6th 7th 8th p.
1st 11th 3d

In addition to the remarks in the 16th Chapter on the execution of the Chromatic Scales. it must be here stated, that, if,(as at the end of the preceding Exercise) it ex_ tends over the position of the hand, the first and second finger must alternately change to higher positions, until the four fingers serve to finish the scale.

CHAPTER XVIII.

ON THE MANAGEMENT OF THE BOW, AND ON THE DIFFERENT BOWINGS.

The preceding Exercises were principally intended to form the left hand, but the Scholar will also have made some progress in the management of the bow, provided he has strictly attended to the rules before given. He must now proceed to perfect himself in this important part of the mechanism of Violin playing. A correct and agile management of the bow is indispensable, not only for the production of a fine tone and neatness of execution, but is also the first requisite necessary for producing a feeling style. It is in reality the soul of playing.

Correctness of bowing, the Scholar will already have obtained, if he have strictly follow- ed and mastered the rules laid down in Chapter X, for the holding and moving of the right arm, as well as for the holding and moving of the bow.

Facility of bowing, namely: moving the bow in long and short bowings, slowly and quickly; close to the bridge, or at a distance from it; piano or forte; at the upper, middle, or lower part; and with an equal case, the Scholar will acquire by learning the following Exercise.*

In the first Exercise the bars are fingered to serve as references. The Scho_ lar will also find new signs and words, which relate to the increasing and decreasing of power in tone.

---

* Before the Master proceeds, he will do well to examine, whether the Scholars management of the bow is not irregular and faulty, and if it should be so, he ought to repeat the former rules and Exercises in bowing, until the Scholar has returned to a correct management of the bow.

Bar 1. This sign, under the note shows that the tone is to begin *piano* or weak, and increase gradually, having in the middle of its duration the greatest force, and in the same way return to the piano. The bow is placed close to the nut at a little distance from the bridge, and quite loose on the string, by which at first only a small portion of the hair touches it; its motion is in the beginning as slow as possible, but, as the tone increases in force, the bow must bo pushed quicker, approach the bridge and be pressed more on the string, so that in the end the whole width of the hair is spread over it. On the decrease of the tone, the pressure and rapidity of the bow gradually slackens, and also by degrees moves farther from the bridge. Here a good division of the bow is principally necessary, that the *middle of the note* may meet the *half of the bow,* and the *end of the note* the *end of the bow.* The swelling from piano to forte should be strong, but the tone must be as fine and full as. possible. The delicate placing of the bow on the strings (near the nut), and the slow drawing of it, requires therefore, diligent practice.

In bar 3, the bow must be drawn from the nut to the point with gradually increasing force and rapiditiy; therefore to preserve a sufficient length of bow, scarcely a third part must have been used on beginning the second half of the bar. As the bow has but little weight at the point, the pressure with the first finger of the right hand must be very strong at the conclusion of the bar. Likewise at the beginning of the following 4th bar, which must be begun with the same force, as the ending of the preceding bar. At the *decres.* of this bar, the bow is gradually to be raised, and pressed lighter upon the strings, as, (near the nut) even the weight of itself would be too heavy for a *piano.* In moving it slowly on, guard against standing still, for a breaking of the tone might be thereby observed.

From Bar 5 to 8, the same remarks are applicable.

Sopra la 4ta, (quarta) Bar 9, means: that this and the following bars as far as the dots . . . . . . go, are to be played on the fourth, or **G** string.

The **G** string, as it is more difficult to be put in vibration, requires a greater pressure of the bow; it also requires the bow to be quicker drawn, and therefore the following 4 bars, (9 to 12,) are more difficult to execute than the similar passage at the beginning of the example, so as to keep a sufficient length of bow, and yet to produce the required shades of increasing and diminishing power, united with a fine tone. A careful division of the bow, which has already been taught, together with diligent study, will gradually lead to a correct execution of the passage.

Hitherto we had only *one* bowing in each bar; in the 13th and 14th bars, and afterwards oftener, there are however two. In these likewise the whole bow is taken, but it is pressed on the strings much lighter, to give these bars no more tone than the preceding.

The Violin possesses among other advantages, the power of closely imitating the Human voice, in the peculiar sliding from one tone to another, as well in soft as in passionate passages. This is exhibited with good effect by the slurred notes in the 13th and 14th bars, either upwards or downwards. The last Chapter showed how this was to be done. Move the second finger from D to F, after which the fourth falls on A flat, and downwards the third finger from G to D, after which the first falls on B. The sliding must be made so quick (as already stated before) as not to make a vacancy or break, appear in the slide, between the lowest and highest note.

The 14th bar is played like the preceding.

For the B of the 16th bar, because it is marked *piano*, half a bow must only be used. The second half is, however, during the pause pushed up, and the bow then at the beginning of the 17th bar, is again placed close to the nut. The F in this and the following bar must be as much brought out as possible in order that the *pianissimo* of the 19th and

20th bars may be more contrasted. For this reason also the passage is first played on the E string, and then repeated on the softer A string. The bow at the forte is pressed strongly on the string, and drawn near the bridge, and in the *pianissimo* it is drawn over the end of the fingerboard, and pressed lightly on the string.

In the 22^d bar in sliding the harmonic A, with the lower C, the fourth finger at the moment of the sliding must be firmly pressed on the string, and drawn down to the E, after which the 2^d finger falls on the C

The five last notes of the 24th bar, in the downbow, are played with a soft *staccato* and *diminuendo*, i.e. with decreasing power.

In the 26th bar, the first finger is pushed up on the A-string to the F and then the high F is taken *forzando*, (*fz*) i.e. with increased force and tone. As the pas sage moreover is marked *forte*, it requires the sliding upwards to be done with the utmost rapidity and force. By this means only, the leaping over of the octave from will be hidden to the hearer, and make it appear to him as if the sliding from one tone to another had been done without interruption.

The bars 26, 27, and 28, require the utmost force the instrument is capable of.

In the second half of the 29th bar (played with a down-bow) the force gradually diminishes, and in the beginning of the 30th bar, (because two notes only are to be played with a whole bow), the bow must be gently carried over the string. The second of these two notes is besides marked under the slur with a dot, which signifies, that it is to be played distinct from the other. Therefore the sliding of the second finger on the F, must not be heard; but at the moment of moving on the bow, a short stop or rest is to be made.

The period or passage from bar 32 to 38 is to be played like the beginning of the Exercise. On the E string, (being thinner) the bow in the crescendo of the tone, may be brought still nearer the bridge.

At the beginning of the 40th bar, the F is to be taken with the third part of the up‑bow, the B however with a very short down‑bow.

The leap from B to A flat, bar 41, is played by moving the first finger on the A string to the A flat, exactly in the manner before stated.

In the 42^d bar the bow must be only drawn two thirds of its length, then the last note of the bar obtains a very short up‑bow, after which, for the B flat of the following bar the remaining third part of the bow is used. In the same manner the 44th bar is played

and also the beginning of the 45th. In the second half of the bar, two notes are slurred by a separate slur and the fingering shows that the passage is to be played on the D string. The two slurred notes F, D, are therefore connected by gently sliding the finger, which for the second F, during the momentary rest of the bow, is so placed, that the drawing back of the hand is not heard.

The last bar but one is to be played *morendo* i e dying away, a decreasing to a hardly perceptible tone.

One advantage which stringed Instruments have over all others, consists in the great diversity of bowings, whereby a variety of tone and a richness of expression is gained, which so eminently distinguishes them from all others. Every Violin Player ought therefore to possess a great flexibility and power in the various bowings. The next Exercise shows the most effective bowings generally in use. Each line has two bowings one *above*, and one *below* the notes. the latter to be played at the repetition of the phrase The bowings are numbered to serve as references in the text.

At N? 1. each note requires one bowing. This bowing (french detaché) is made with a stiff back-arm, and with as long bowings as possible, at the upper part of the bow. The notes must be equal in duration and force, and join each other without letting an unequal stop, gap or rest, be observed at the changing of the Bow. At the pause in the 4th bar, the bow is raised from the string and replaced with the down bow. This bowing is at all times understood, when no marks for bowing are given.

N? 2 is also made with the upper third part of the bow, and with a steady back-arm. The two first slurred notes obtain the downbow to the point, then follow two very short bowings, for the staccato notes, then again one long bow for the slurred notes, to which now, more towards the middle of the bow the two following short bowings join, so that alternately, the two short bowings are made, once close at the point, and once more towards the middle of the bow

N? 3, begins with two short bowings; the rest is played like the preceding, with this difference, that now the notes 3-4 and 7-8 quavers in the bar, are marked by longer bowings, and accented. whilst at N? 2. the accented notes were 1-2 and 5-6

No. 4, is begun with a down-bow, as is always the case, if not expressly stated up-bow or pousse.) The bowing of 3 notes in the up-bow, (only one of which is to be taken in the down-bow with an equal length of the bow,) requires that the down-bow should be drawn very quickly.

At No. 5, the reverse case takes place. Here the down-bow is slow and the up-bow quick. There the first of four notes is stronly marked or accented and quickly played, here it is the last.

At No. 6, the second of the slurred notes is every time strongly marked by a pressure of the bow, represented by the mark   under the note.

At No. 7, the first note is sharply accented. Both styles of bowing are like the former, made with the upper third part of the bow, and a stiff back-arm.

At No. 8, for the first four slurred notes, however a longer bow (from the middle to the point) is taken, then four short bows at the point, then a long bow to the middle of the bow for the 4 slurred notes of the 2d bar, then again four short bowings in the middle of the bow, and so alternately at the point and the middle. In these half bowings, the back-arm cannot now remain any longer perfectly stiff, but on the bow approaching the middle, must be a little pushed after.

At No. 9, commences with four short bowings in the middle of the bow, and is then played like the preceding number.

At No. 10, a *whole* bow is taken for the first seven notes; then two very short bowings at the point, then again for the six slurred notes a whole up-bow, then two short bowings near the nut, and so on, alternately at the point and nut.

118

No. 11 and 12, are played in the same manner, but only with **half bow**, from the middle to the point.

At No. 13 and 14, the upper third part of the bow is again only used with a stiff back-arm. The second of the two notes is strongly marked by a pressure of the bow.

At No. 15, a third part of the bow; at No. 16, a half; and at No. 17, a whole bow is taken. At No. 15, a good effect is produced by pressing upon the last of the four slurred notes, which allows the taking off of the bow to be heard. At No. 16, however the change of bowing must not be heard, and all tones should be equally powerful. The same should be done at No. 17, by an equal division of the bow.

At No. 18, the bow is placed close to the nut, and by applying about one eighth of its whole length every time to three slurred notes, and to the single note a very short and sharp up-bow, it is gradually drawn down to the point.

At No. 19, the contrary motion takes place, by beginning with a short down bow at the point, and in that manner gradually reaching the nut.

At No. 20, and 21, the bow must be very sparingly used, in order not to end with a weaker tone than at the beginning. The second of the slurred notes, must, by shifting the bow a little be played off abruptly.

At No. 22, begins the bowing called *Staccato*. It consists in a short and distinct marking of the tones in one bow.

The Staccato, if done well, produces a brilliant effect, and is one of the principle orna-ments of Solo Playing. The capability for it, is, in some degree, a natural gift, for expe rienee has shown that the most distinguished Violinists, though giving it the most diligent practice, could never attain it, whilst much inferior artistes acquired it with little or no practice. Yet even with natural qualifications, nothing but a constant practice will enable you to master it.

The Staccato is made with the upper half of the up-bow, more than that it must not reach, even if twenty, thirty or more notes are to be played in one bow. You should therefore accustom yourself from the beginning to use as little bow as possible, i.e. only as much as is actually required for the clear intonation of tones. The pushing on of the bow is done with a steadyfore and back-arm, and solely with the wrist. Every note obtains as much pressure with the first finger of the right hand, as to lay the whole width of the hair on the string. For the distinct separation of the tones, the bow is lifted after every push, but not so much as to cause the edges of the hair to rise off the string.

The beauty of the staccato consists principally in an equal, distinct and clear separation of the tones in the strictest time.

At first practise it slowly, and when it is acquired distinctly and strictly in time, a quicker time may gradually be taken.

At N° 22, two very short bowings are taken; at the following five numbers, third part bowings and at the two last, half bows. The length of the downbow is regulated according to the number of tones, which in the up-bow are to be played *staccato*. **In N° 23** it ought therefore to be as short as possible, because five tones in the downbow and only three in the up-bow are to be taken; in N° 27, however, it must be as long as possible, because for two tones in the down-bow, there are six tones in the up-bow.

Nº 53.

This Exercise begins with three introductory notes, consequently according to rule with an up - bow. Exceptions to this rule are marked by the word *tiré*.

At the *detaché* of Nº 1, I observe again, that all tones must be equal power, and that it is a bad (yet frequent) style of playing, every time to accent the first of three notes.

For No 2, and 3, see the explanation of similar bowings (Nº 2, and 15,) of the preceding exercise.

At Nº 4, the three slurred notes in up - bow, are to be made with the short bow, so as not to move too far from the point.

At Nº 5, the same is to be observed at the two slurred notes, because also in this bowing the position must remain near the point. The first note is sharply accented.

At Nº 6, the three introductory notes are likewise taken with a short up - bow, and then for the single note, marked with ⎯⎯⎯ , an equal portion of down bow is used.

At Nº 7, for the slurred notes, half bows are used; consequently the two short accented tones are alternately in the middle and at the point of the bow.

At Nº 8, whole bow; therefore the accented tones are near the nut and at the point alternately.

At Nº 9, and 10, the Scholar will remember what has been said of the Staccato in the preceding exercise.

There is also a staccato with down-bow, but it is more difficult than with the up-bow, and in quick passages sounds rather dull: For this reason it is less calculated for a brilliant display in the *Allegro;* but in melodious passages for the portamento and soft accenting of tones, it has a good effect. It is executed like the up-bow. At N.º 11, the bow is placed in the middle and drawn, in short, sharp strokes to the point.

At N.º 12, the bow is placed near the nut, and in using it to the two slurred notes, it is every time drawn to the point.

The second half of N.º 12, at poussé, is made close at the point, sharply marking each third note.

At N.º 13, arises a new kind of Staccato; staccato and slurred notes alternately in one bow. It is exceedingly difficult, because the staccato run of the bow is constantly checked by the two slurred notes. I recommend a diligent practice of it, as it gives great command over the bow.

In the last bars of N.º 13, the bow, after the two slurred notes, should every time be raised a little.

At N.º 14, the fz (forzando) marked note, is to be accented as much as possible by a longer bow, and sharp pressure of it; but the bow must not be prolonged beyond the upper third part.

Nº 54.

The first five parts of this exercise must not be played too quick, as some of its bowings can only be well executed in moderate time.

The ten first numbers of the above different kinds of bowing, are all played with a stiff back-arm, with the upper third part of the bow, and with still shorter bowings.

The rocking on the strings at Nº 1, is produced by moving the wrist.

At Nº 2, the two first notes of each bar are sharply marked.

The bowing of Nº 3, has already appeared in the last exercise but one; it serves as an introductory exercise to

Nº 4, which is called Viotti's, (coup d'archet de Viotti) either because it was first employed by that great Violinist, or what is more probable, was beautifully and effectively executed by him. Of the two notes tied in one slur, the first is given quite short and soft, but the second with a longer bow, and strong pressure, is marked or accented as much as possible.

The bowing at Nº 5, is called in the French School *martelé* (hammered.) It consists in a sharp, smart, quick stroke or push with the upper part of the bow; however, the bowing should not be too short, as then the tones would sound dry and rough. The separation of the tones

 is made by resting the bow, after each tone a moment, thereby instantly checking the vibration of the smartly accented string. In time and power, the tones must be perfectly equal. The word *segue*, denotes that the kind of bowing here indicated in the first bar, is to be continued throughout the following bars.

The bowing Nº 6, is much like that of Nº 4, and is played in the same manner; but the effect is different, as in Nº 6 the unaccented, in Nº 4, the accented part of the bar is strongly marked.

The bowing of Nọ 7 and 8, might, analogically with the *hammered*, (martele) be called the *whipped*, (fouette) as the string at the notes with the > is in some measure whipped with the bow. The bow is lifted over the string, and in bowing up, thrown with force on it, and as close to the point as possible, to prevent the trembling motion of the stick of the bow. After the beat it is pushed on quietly about 3 inches, and then for the next note, is drawn back in a bow equally long. At Nọ 7, every third note of the bar. and at Nọ 8, the first and third note is whipped in like manner. The difficulty of this bowing consists principally in moving the bow, so that the beat may be always equally high over the string, and the bowings of equal length. If well done, it is of most unex — pected and imposing effect.

At Nọ 9, of the four notes in one bowing, three are slurred, and the last sharply, and strongly marked. This last note requires as much bow as the three first conjointly.

Nọ 10, is executed in like manner, with only this difference, that the former slurred notes, are now, both in the down and up – bow, alternately played staccato.

The two latter parts of the exercise are taken a little quicker.

Nọ 11, is played with a half–bow; Nọ 12, with third part bow; and Nọ 13, with still short er bow.

In Nọ 14, the Scholar learns another new bowing, which is called *R. Kreutzer's*, from its being first met with in that celebrated Violinist's compositions. It gives two notes to each bowing, of which the two first are dotted, the two latter slurred. The second of the marked notes must have a long bow and strong pressure.

All these bowings the Scholar should practise diligently, and perseveringly, singly at first and slowly, then by degrees quicker, and each of them should be equally studied, till he has perfectly mastered the whole.

Only then will it be advisable to proceed to the next Chapter.

CHAPTER XIX.

ON DOUBLE STOPS, BROKEN CHORDS AND ARPEGGIOS.

The Violin has another advantage over Wind Instruments, in giving two, nay even three and four notes at once, and in rapid succession, so as almost to sound simultaneously. Two notes are called double stops, 3 or 4 notes broken chords, or if the single tones are distinctly and successively articulated, Arpeggios.

The greatest difficulty in these various stoppings is *perfect intonation*. To this the master must attend strictly from the commencement, for from the increased difficulty both for finger and ear, if the Scholar have contracted bad habits, there may be great difficulty in correcting them. It is not uncommon to hear Violinists play single tones perfectly in tune, but double stops, without their perceiving it, most intolerably false. The perfect intonation in these stoppings is not only difficult, requiring both ear and finger to pro_duce several tones at once, but, because the position changes so frequently. Sometimes the fingers are unusually stretched out for one stopping and for the next instantly drawn close together.

Another difficulty is the equality of tone to be used in the different degrees of *piano* and *forte*. It is obtained by an equal pressure of the bow on both strings and thus giving them an equal vibration.

It is equally difficult to connect the double stops, as the changing of the stops and shifts requires always to be executed in a rapid, firm and unhesitating manner.

Be careful to avoid the habit of first "seeking" for the right stops.

My former instructions for the division and management of the bow generally, must be most carefully attended to.

The word *Maestoso* (majestically) in the following exercise, refers as much to the style of playing as to time. The first is stately and dignified, the latter, slower than the ordinary *Andante*.

If the Scholar can play the upper part of the above Exercise without mistake, the Master should then change with him, and try him in the accompaniment, as it offers stops of a new difficulty, equally calculated to improve the Scholar's ear and hand.

The like should be observed with the following Exercise.

126

Larghetto, is the diminutive of *Largo* (slow, heavy, extended) and originally was called a little *Largo*. *Larghetto* is therefore a movement somewhat quicker than *Largo*.

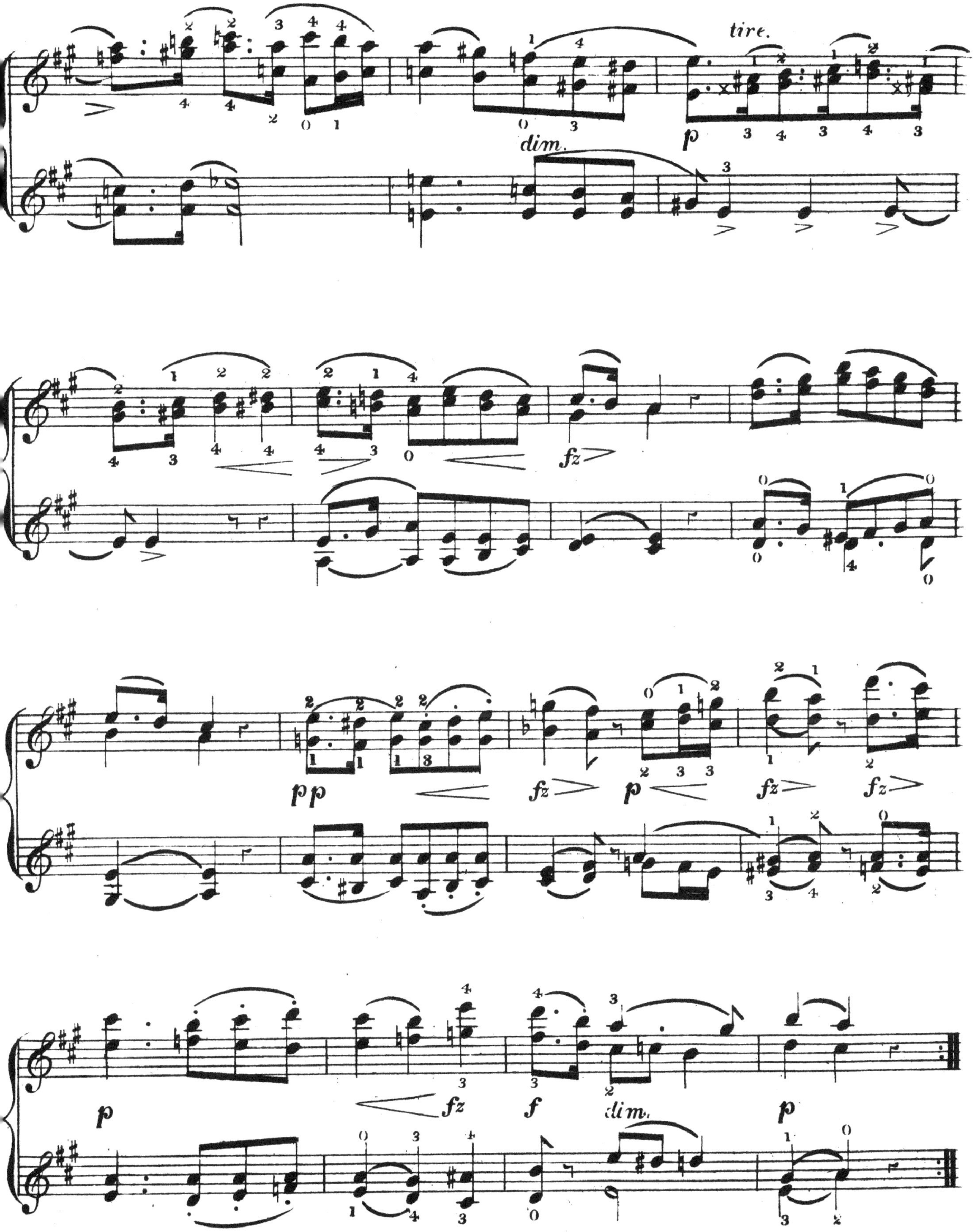
tire.
dim.
dim.

In the following piece, the *Rondo*, (i.e. a lively, pleasing Musical piece the theme or sub-ject of which is often repeated) we proceed to more difficult double stops.

As positions, bowings and nuances (or shades) of *piano* and *forte*, are carefully marked, they should be strictly attended to; but above all do not neglect true intonation.

RONDO.

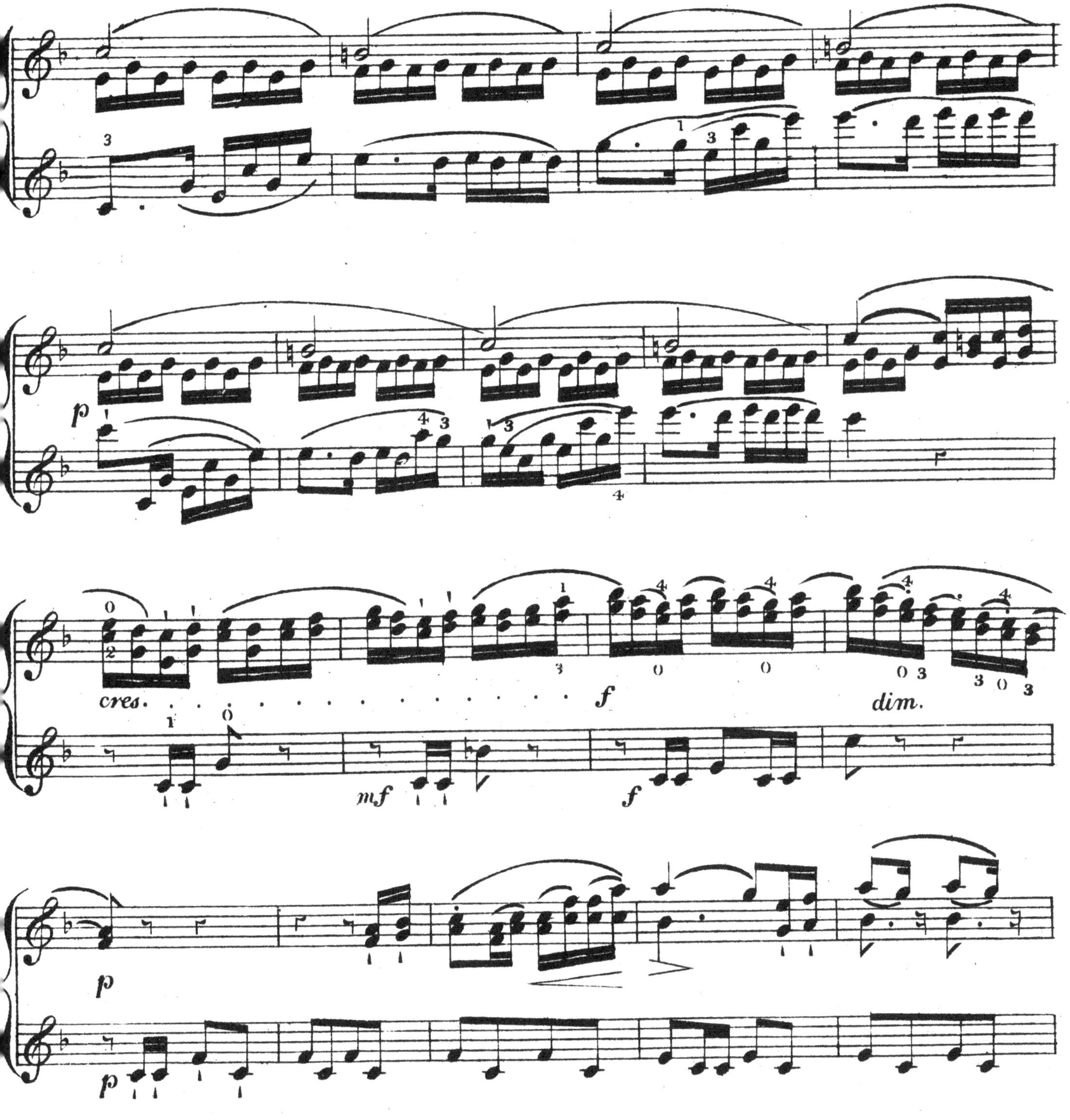
p
cres.
f
dim.
mf
f
p
p

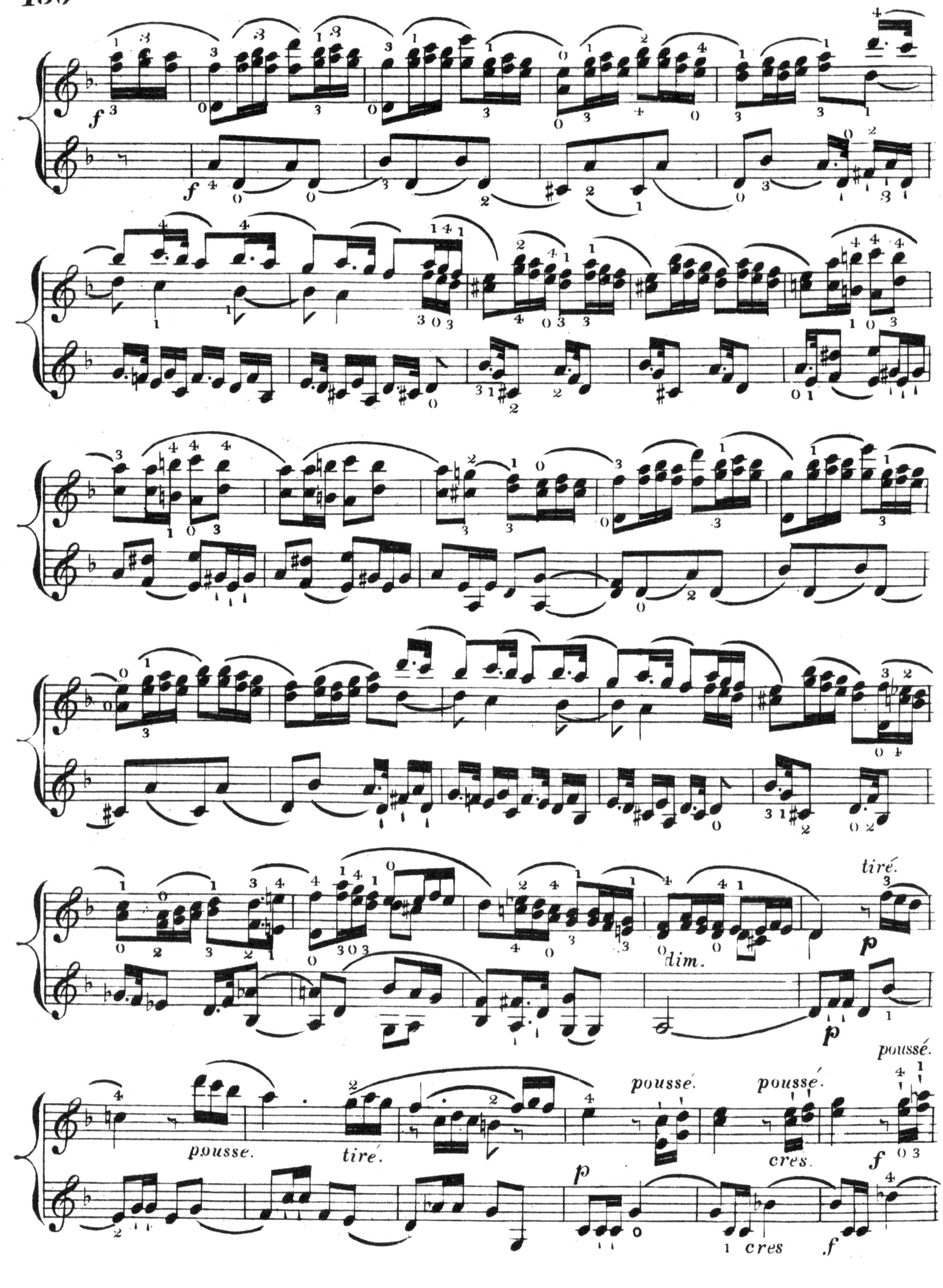
dim.
tiré.
pousse.
tiré.
pousse.
pousse.
pousse.
cres.
cres

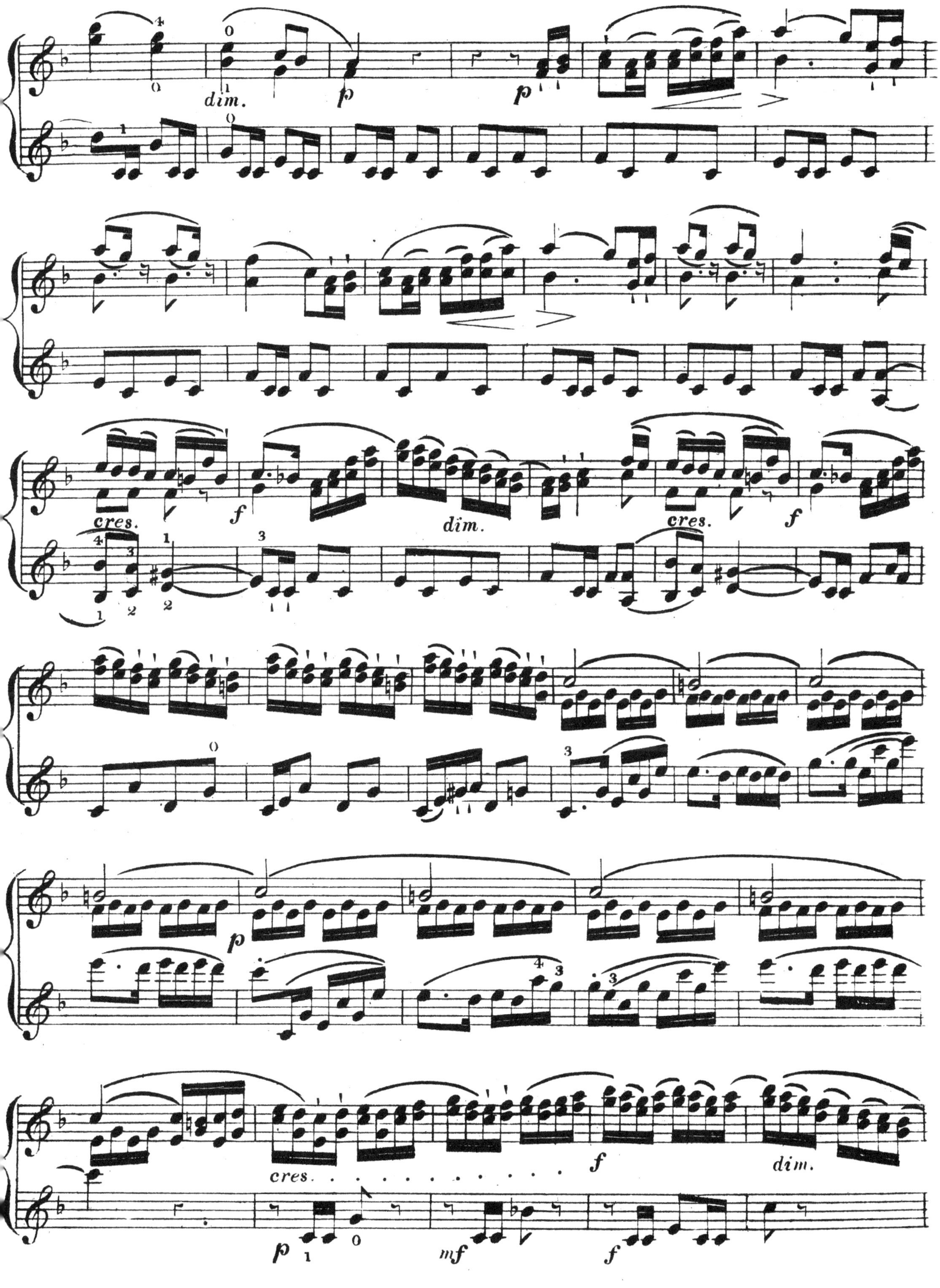
dim.
p
p
cres.
f
dim.
cres.
f
p
cres.
f
dim.
p
mf
f

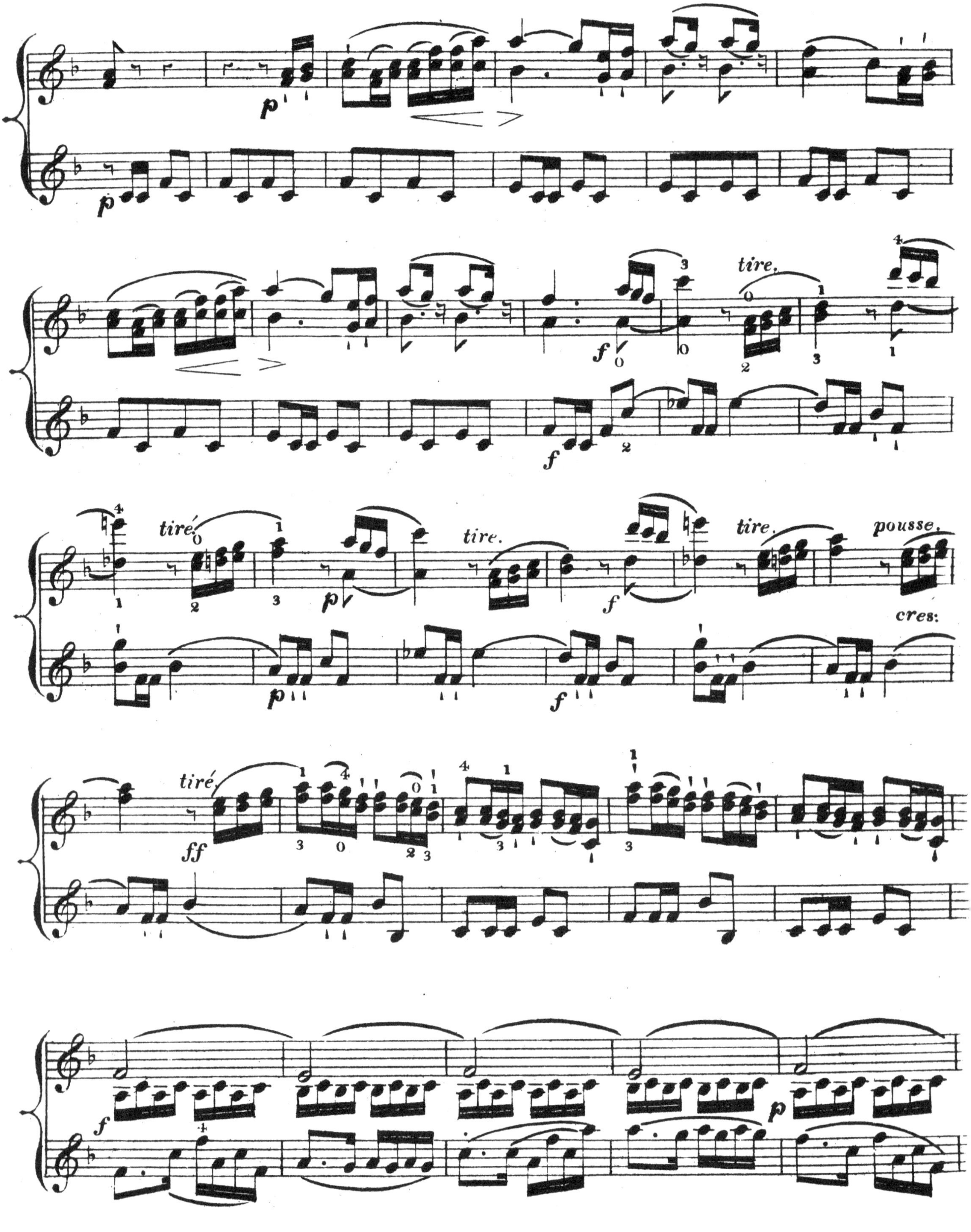
p
p
tire.
f
f
tiré
tire.
tire.
pousse.
p
f
p
f
cres:
tiré
ff
f
p

The following Exercise is a Minuet, a stately, serious, yet graceful dance, consisting of two parts and a Trio, after which the Minuet *da capo* i.e. from the commencement to the *Fine,* is played over again. The name Trio for the two last parts is of ancient usage, when it was customary to write them in three's, or for three obligato parts. The Trio is generally written in a major or minor, relative to the principal key.

In Symphonies and quartetts, the second or third movement generally consists of such a Minuet. Latterly however, the original character of the Minuet has been lost sight of, and it is now more properly denominated *Scherzo.*

At the four-part chord of the first bar, the bow is placed close to the nut, firmly on the two last strings, then with a strong pressure pulled across the two highest, and quietly drawn down to the point. Although the two lowest notes are written as crotchets, the bow must not remain on them the full time, for their duration at farthest must be only that of a quaver.

The second bar is played like the first, but with an up-bow; the third again with a down-bow.

In the same manner, the four first bars of the 2nd part are alternately taken, with down and up-bow. The chords in crotchets in the 5th and following bars, are all played with the down-bow, laid on close to the nut, with strong pressure of the bow and wide extended hair, and sounding together as much as possible; after which, the bow is pulled off very smartly. At each chord, the bow should be placed afresh; the bowing must however not be too short, as then the chords would become sharp and dry.

At the double stops of Octaves in the Trio, the tones must be distinctly separated; rest therefore with the fingers on each tone as long as possible, and then move on to the next, very quickly.

134

Minuetto da Capo.

The following Exercise consists of Arpeggios on three strings. The Scholar, after acquainting himself thoroughly with the stops, should carefully practise the eight different kinds of bowings He has principally to attend to true intonation; to an easy and pliable management of the bow, the motion of which, with a quiet position of the body, should only proceed from the right arm; to an equal division of the notes, and lastly, to the strict observance of all former stated shades of *piano* and *forte*, in the various kinds of bowing.

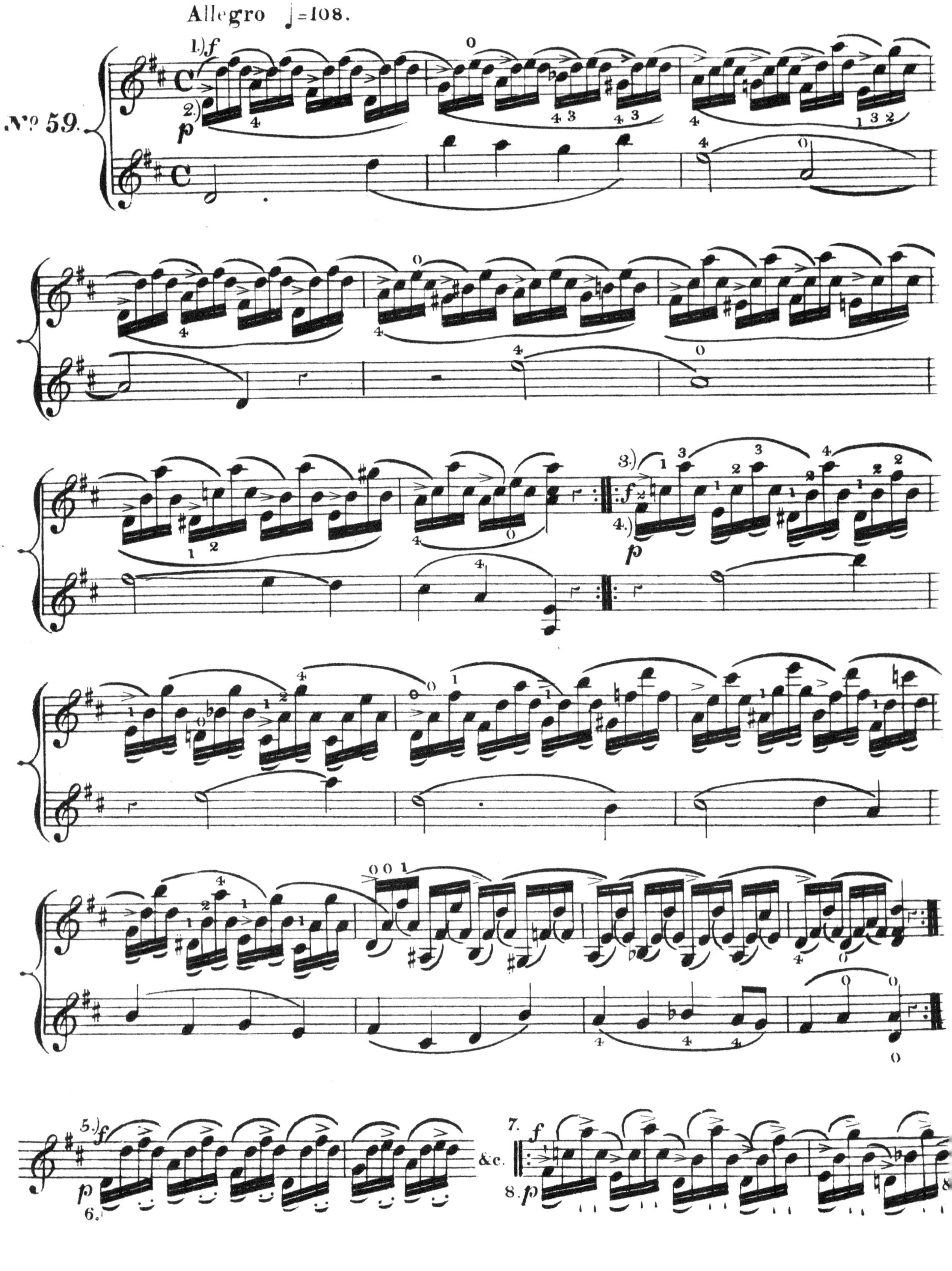
Allegro ♩=108.
№ 59.
&c.

After the foregoing eight bowings are well practised, the Scholar should repeat the Exercise *Piu moderato,* (i.e. a little slower in time) in triplets of 16 semiquavers with the following four kinds of bowings.

This being well practised, play this Exercise for the third time *Allegro molto*, (very quick) in triplets of quavers, with the following four kinds of bowings. It is to be here observed, that the 3d kind of bowing is all made with the down-bow close to the nut, the 4th however, must be at the point of the bow, alternately with down and up-bow.

Next follow Arpeggios on four strings, with ten different kinds of bowing. As the four tones of which the consist are not always in one position,(as for instance immediately at the beginning of the 2d bar, where the two first tones appertain to the second, and the two succeeding ones to the third position) a perfect intonation is here doubly difficult. The Scholar should therefore play this Exercise at first quite slow, to familiarise his ear with the chords and his fingers with the unusual stoppings. When this has been done, then practise all the different kinds of bowing, with due regard to the given rules of the last Exercise.

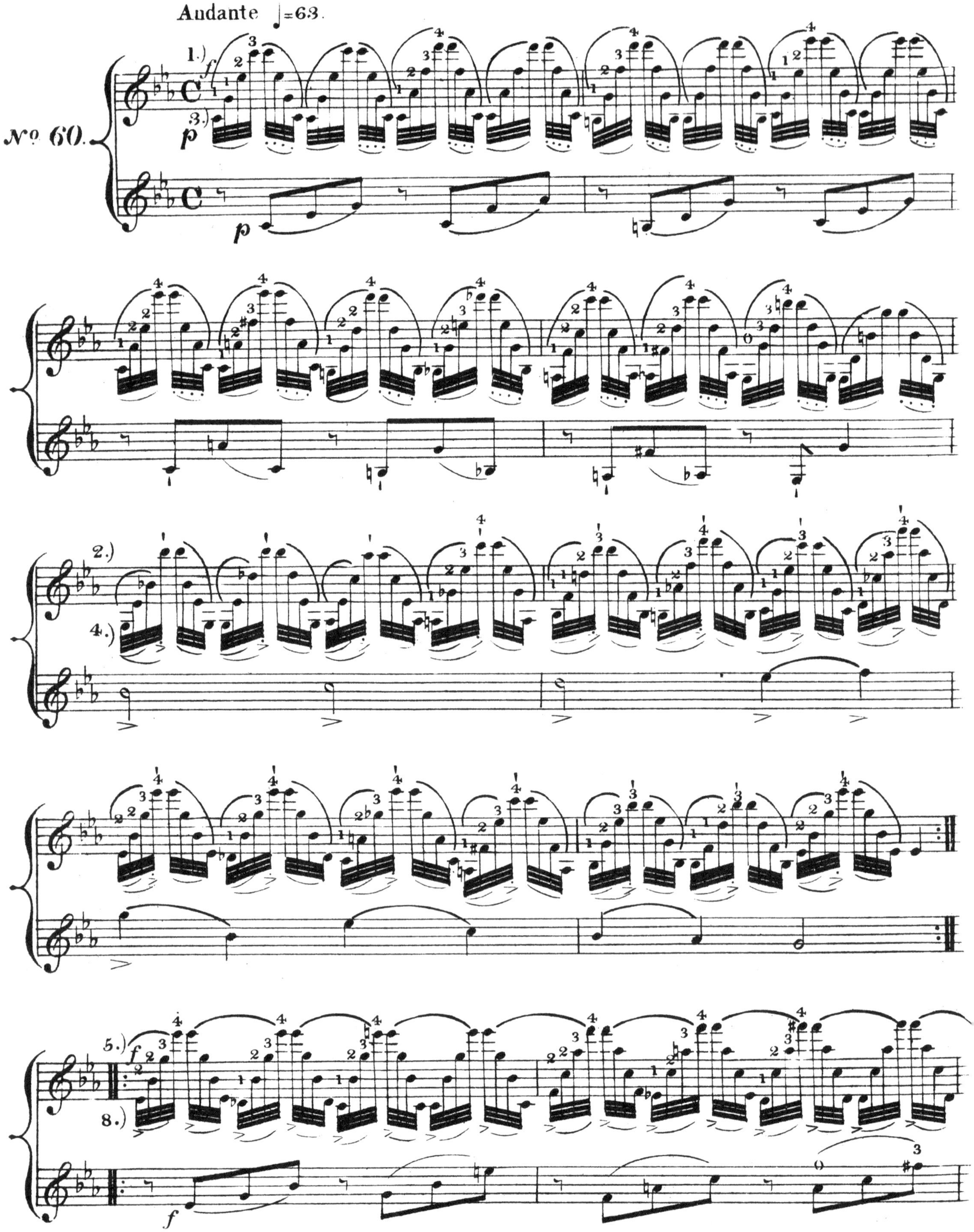
Andante ♩=63.
Nº 60.

*) The different kinds of bowing, in the preceding arpeggios, as well as in the Exercise 52, 53, and 54, might easily have been increased in number; But I have purposely confin'd myself to the above as the most easy and effective, because a greater number fatigues the Scholar, and would perhaps have prevented him from practising them with perseverance and precision. The above contain more examples than are likely to occur in practice.

CHAPTER XX.

ON GRACES, ORNAMENTS OR EMBELLISHMENTS.

They serve to animate the melody, and to heighten its expression.

Formerly, it was usual for the composer to write the melody as simply as possible, and leave the ornamental part to the player or singer; thus a variety of ornaments or graces were gradually formed, for which names were invented, and which one player learned from another. But as every one tried to improve on his predecessors, and to add new inventions of his own, it at last caused such irregularity, confusion, and consequent tastelessness in the ornaments, that composers found it necessary to prescribe limits to their embellishments: at first, it was done with smaller notes, the division being left to the performer, and afterwards, with large notes, and a strict division of the bar.

Of all the ornaments of former times, the following only have been retained, some of which are represented by signs, and others by small notes. To the former belong the Shake (tr), the Pralltriller (⌁), and the double turn, or Mordente (∿ or ↶). To the other, the long and short Appogiatura, and some others without name.

The Shake is the repeated trilling of two notes lying close together, namely, of the tone over which the Shake sign is placed, and its minor, (a.) or its major second, (b.)

The duration of the Shake is determined by the value of the note, the number of its beats, and by the greater or less rapidity with which they are to be made.

Every Shake generally begins or ends with the principal note, i.e. the one which is noted down.* If the Shake is to begin with the appogiatura, or with the lower note, it must be expressly written down, as for Example:

---

* This rule J.N.Hummel first advanced in his Piano-forte School, and has properly exemplified it by examples.

The Shake ends by the under - appogiatura or turn, connected with the following note. This consists of the lowest note and is followed by the principal note.

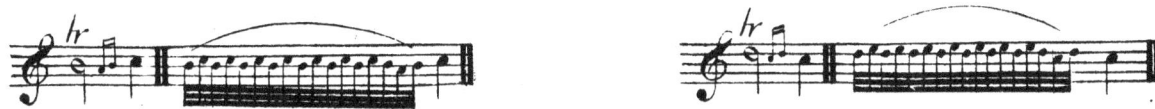

In concluding a Cadence or shake, sometimes the following inferior and superior turn is made.

Generally the Turn, (at least in modern compositions) is written with small notes, where this is not the case, the Scholar has to supply them; but there are also Shakes, which on account of their shortness, or on account of the succeeding passages, do not admit of a concluding turn.

To the Violinist the Shake is the most difficult of all Ornaments, and to perform it well, requires like the staccato, a natural capability for it. Yet this by great practice, is more easily to be conquered than the staccato.

The Shake must be perfect in the intonation; the Scholar has therefore to observe. whether the Appogiatura with which it is to be beaten, lies a half or a whole tone from the principal note, and then try at each beat of this interval to stop always perfectly true.

It is not unfrequent even with Violinists, otherwise possessing a perfect intonation, to beat the Shake with the half tone too high, and particularly towards its close, to extend their trilling finger too far from the principal note. Sometimes the shake with the whole tone, especially in the higher and close positions is often played too high; i.e. instead of the interval of a second, the minor or even major third is used, which sounds execrably disgusting to every well educated ear. Again therefore, I strongly urge the acquirement of a *perfect* intonation in the shake.

The beats must be equal, so that neither of the two sounds of which the shake consists, is heard more than the other.

To obtain a brilliant shake, the Scholar should from the first accustom himself to lift the trilling finger high, (i.e. to the first joint of the fixed finger,) and let it fall with force. In endeavouring to beat at once a rapid shake, this point is often overlooked by learners; the consequence then is, that in long shakes, the finger as if lamed, sticks to the string, and a fine and powerful shake is never obtained.

The Scholar has also to guard against too great exertion in forcing a quick and powerful shake, by an unnatural extension of the sinews; the free motion of the trilling finger would only be more obstructed, and much sooner be fatigued. Avoid also the rubbing of the.

trilling fingers against the fixed one, but give them at once the requisite firm and free position.

Each finger requires diligent practice in the shake, but the little finger most, on account of its shortness and weakness. For altho' with every perseverance, it will never be equal in power and rapidity to the second and third finger, (therefore in long and quick shakes. one of these is taken in its stead, by changing the position,) its perfection must not therefore be neglected, as in double shakes and in many successions of shakes, the use of it cannot be dispensed with. Even the first finger, which is never used in simple shakes, (as no shakes are made on open strings,) cannot be spared in some double shakes.

In regard to the quickness of the shake, the following general rules are adopted. In the *Allegro*, and generally in musical pieces of a spirited character, the shake is quicker and more powerful than in the *Adagio*, and in the soft and expressive Cantabile. In all Cadence-shakes, i.e. such as terminate a period, (see bar 11 and 25 of the next Exercise) the beats throughout should be *equally quick*. In the *Adagio*, and in shakes serving to embellish the melody, it has often a good effect to begin slowly, and gradually to increase in rapidity. This shake may either be united with a *crescendo* or a *decrescendo*. A shake must never begin quick and terminate slow.

The beats of the shake with the half tone, are generally taken a little slower than with a whole tone, as the ear cannot so easily catch the rapid change with the small interval, as with the large one. Likewise shakes on the lower strings (as they vibrate slower,) must not be beaten so quick, as on the A and E strings.

The tones of the after-beat or turn, have the same rapidity as the shake, and must, even in the shortest shake, be distinctly heard.

Each shake inclusive of the after-turn, must obtain the full duration of the note over which it stands. It is therefore faulty to terminate the shake too soon, and thereby cause a vacant space between that and the following note.

After the Scholar has well noticed the above, proceed to:

The first six shakes are all with a half tone. The trilling finger has to fall therefore always quite close to the fixed one. The execution of the first bar is:

The 6th Shake on D♯, is beat with the little finger, & to make it as distinct and powerful as the others, requires a separate study.

In the 7th bar, begins a shake with a whole tone in the 2^d position, in which the beginning note or appogiatura, is written down. It is played thus:

The shaking note E, should be always perfectly true. As the shake is too long for one bowing, change it at every bar. To do this unobserved to the ear, see that the trilling finger continue its beats uniformly at the changing of the bow, and in the same motion; that the new bowing commence with the same power with which the preceding one ended; and that the change take place on the principal note, consequently here on the D.

In the 9th bar, the second finger moves on to the D sharp, without increasing or slackening the beats of the third finger. To the beginner, this will be rather difficult, and must therefore be practised with perseverance. This shake in moving on to the D♯, was hitherto beaten with a whole tone, is now beat with half a tone; observe therefore that the trilling note E, must remain constantly true and free.

Bar 13, commences with a chain (continuation) of shakes, which hang together without intermediate notes. Generally the afterturn is given only to the last shake; but in cases where shakes are as long as these, it has a good effect, to terminate each shake with a turn. At shorter shakes, as in bar 22, and 28, it is better omitted. Each shake in such a chain begins with the principal note, whether its predecessor has an after-turn or not.

Before the *tr* bar 14, is a ♭, showing that the trilling note is not to be B but B flat; and consequently is beaten with the half tone. In the same way the ♯, before the *tr* in bar 16, changes the trilling note into G♯, the beat is therefore with a whole tone. The after-turn of this shake is written out in large notes, and cannot therefore be played quicker than semiquavers. Consequently the rule, that the after-turn should be of equal quickness with the tones of the shake, is not applicable here. In the shakes without an after-turn in the chain, bar 22. the trilling finger must not be disturbed or retarded in its regular beat, by the moving on of the hand.

The shakes bar 26, belong to the class which do not admit of after-turns During the pause, the bow should rest on the strings without being raised.

In the chains of shakes bar 28, progressing by half notes, particular attention should be paid to the intonation of the trilling note, and endeavour to keep the trilling finger in equal and uniform beats, no matter how often and quick the hand may change its position.

This last succession of shakes is however very difficult, requiring the most diligent and persevering practice.

The 62d Exercise (alla Polacca; i e. in the style of a Polish National dance) is intended for practising the short shake without after-turns. On account of the shortness of the trilling note, no more than two, or at most three beats can be made, which, however, must be powerful and distinct.

146

The Scholar should accustom himself from the first, not to remain longer on the shake-note than its value prescribes; the neatness and beauty of these shakes consists, in fact, in throwing them with ease into the melody, without destroying its rhythm. The execution of this shake is:

In the 11th bar, is found the second kind of shakes, the "Pralltriller," it is a shake with one beat and is played as follows:,

The beats must be powerful, and made with a high lifted finger.

In the 16th and following bars there are four shakes, whose trilling note is augmented by a ♯, and in the 23^d, a shake whose trilling note is lowered by the sign ♮, before the *hr*.

In the Trio we have short shakes in slurred notes; here the effect depends on not remaining too long on the shake note, nevertheless both beats should be distinctly heard. The execution, is:

To the shake for the little finger, on A, in bar 4, the Scholar should give a diligent practise.

The five short trills (Pralltriller) in the last bar but one of each part of the Trio, are executed in the manner already stated.

In the 63.^d Exerc. are the other shakes, namely, the Double shake. in thirds, Sixths, and Octaves; the simple shake in Double stops, and the accompanying shake, or the shake with an accompanying part.

The former remarks on the simple shake are also here applicable, to which I may add, that in double stops the beats of the trilling finger must be perfectly equal. The second finger must therefore not outstep the little finger, and the beats of the former should be corresponding to those of the latter; neither should this double shake be attempted to be played quick, until the little finger has obtained as much power and flexibility as may be wanting to cope with it.

Sometimes in Double-shakes, one is beat with a whole, the other with half a tone, (as in bar 3 of the Exercise) and requires a pure intonation in the falling of the trilling finger. The after-turn, in order to be in two parts, has often to be made in a different position to that of the shake itself (see bar 2 and 4.) The sliding down of the hand should therefore be as quick as possible, (to join the after-turn without resting) and in equal rapidity with the beats of the shake.

In the 5th bar, commencing with simple shakes in double-stops, the scholar should endeavour to let the sustained note of the shake vibrate unbroken. For the rest, the former remarks on short shakes are applicable, with only this difference, that here in the prolonged duration, more beats (3 or even 4) are made. The second and fourth shake can only be made with the little finger, showing the necessity of giving it incessant practice

In the 9$\underline{th}$ bar begins the most difficult of all shakes, namely: the one with an accompanying part. The great difficulty in this, is, that neither the shake finger in its beating, nor the bow in its bowing, are stopped or disturbed by the putting in of the accompanying part. In order to stop the C in the accompaniment with the 2$\underline{d}$ finger, without raising the shake note G, place the finger in such a manner on the G, as almost to touch the A string, that with a slight motion forward, it might also cover the string The bow during the pauses in the accompaniment, must only be raised a very little above the A string, so as to fall again quickly upon it without much motion, when the accompaniment recommences The change of the bow is always to take place during the pause in the accompaniment; this shake consequently divides into four bowings, of which the first (a down-bow) is of the length of four crotchets, the second of three, the third again of three, and the last of two crotchets How the change of bow can be done unobserved to the ear, has been mentioned before. This accompanied shake, well executed, should sound as if played by two persons.

The first bar of the 2nd part contains a shake of a sixth, in which the first and third fingers can be practised in equal beats. The B♮ is taken by the second finger, because the first finger is wanted for the shake on the open D string. The afterturn of this shake allows for the two notes of the upper part only one appogiatura in the lower part.

For the Octave shake in bar 6, the first and little finger can be exercised to produce equal beats. The change of the bow takes place at the fourth crotchet as imperceptibly as possible.

In the accompanying shake of the 2nd part, the second finger on C is at first to approach the E string, to be able to take the G of the accompaniment without disturbing the shake; but in bar 18, the D string, in order to reach the F. This shake likewise begins with a down-bow divided into four bowings.

In the accompanying part of the preceding Exercise stands several times: *pizzicato* (abbrev: *pizz.* or *pizzic.*) i.e. pinched. It signifies that the tones are to be produced by pinching or pulling of the string, (as on the Harp or Guitar,) instead of using the bow. This continues until recalled by the word *coll'arco* (with the bow.)

The *pizzicato* being often used in the **Orchestra and Quartett**, the following instruction how it is to be played, will not be out of place.

If only a few tones are to be played *pizzicato*, and the *coll'arco* following quickly after it, the Violin is to remain in its ordinary position. The bow then is taken in the full hand, and held at the nut by the three last fingers of the right hand; but the thumb is placed with the ball of the hand against the lower edge of the finger board, when the string is pulled with the point of the first finger.

But if the *pizzicato* continues for a time, or if a pause precedes the *coll'arco*, it is better to take the Violin down. It is then placed with its back against the right side of the body and supported with the right back arm. The bow is to be held in the above stated manner; in lieu of the thumb, however, the first finger is placed against the fingerboard, (yet a little distanced from the edge,) and the string pulled with the thumb.

This method, in long passages, is preferable, as the *pizzicato* with the thumb produces a fuller and clearer sound than with the first finger.

The third of the above named embellishments, (generally written by signs and seldom by notes) is the Double-turn. (Mordente) It consists of three successive tones, the middle one of which, is that tone, over which the sign is placed, and sometimes begins with the upper, sometimes with the lower note. Latterly we have begun to show by the sign the particular ornament which is intended to be applied. *That* sign therefore, which has the first hook or notch bent upwards shews that the double turn is to begin with the upper note, thus:

the contrary way shews that it is to begin with the lower note:

If the Mordente does not stand *over* but *after* the note, to serve as a link to connect one note with the following, then the principal note is again added as a fourth note. and executed only just before entering on the following tone, thus:

Played.

Is the Mordente over a dot, then this dot is its fourth note, and sustained according to its value:

Played.

With two dots, the Mordente is made just before the second:

Played.

An accidental sign above or below the Mordente, either raises or lowers the upper or the lower tone..

 Played.

or  Played.

Accidentals above and below, affect the superior and inferior Notes of the turn.

 Played.

or  Played.

The Mordente is always played rapidly, whether in quick or slow time, and very distinct and perfectly equal in its 3 or 4 Notes, both as regards quickness or power. Perfect intonation is the first requisite here, and in its practice requires the greatest attention to the essential signs of the Key, as well as to the accidental signs added to the Mordente whether the sign be upon the note or after, it is always played with one bowing.

Among the Ornaments or embellishments written out with small notes, the most frequent in use are, the *short* and *long* appogiatura. In modern compositions they are generally written out in large notes and with regular divisions of time; but as in old, and sometimes in new compositions, we find them in small notes, it is necessary that the Scholar should understand and be able to execute them.

If the appogiatura stands before a note which can be divided into equal parts, it obtains the half of its value, thus:

Before a note with a dot, it obtains the value of the note, which then begins only at the dot:

Where there are two dots the appogiatura obtains the value of the note and this then begins with the first dot:

In double stops, when an appogiatura stands before one note only, the other note and the appogiatura begin together:

As the appogiatura always falls on the accented part of the bar, mark it more strongly than the note before which it stands, and always in one bowing, because as an appogiatura, it belongs *to* the note, and in it only, finds its resolution.

The short appogiatura distinguish'd from the long appogiatura, by a cross cut $\left(\begin{smallmatrix} \ast \\ \flat \end{smallmatrix}\right)$ lessens the note before which it stands, very little of its value. It is quickly and lightly united with this in one bowing:

The following Exercise will facilitate the Scholar in the reading and execution of the different double-turns, as well as the long and short appogiaturas.

12.
13.
14.
15.
p
cre - - scen - - do.
f
dimin - - - - en - - - do.
pp
Bar 12.
Bar 13.
Bar 14.
Bar 15.

cres.
f
pp
8va
p
f
dim.
28
p
29
f
30.
31.
p
32.
pp
morendo.
Bar 28.
Bar 29.
Bar 30.
Bar 31.
Bar 32.

Other ornaments used by modern composers are generally written out in large notes, and in regular divisions of time, which prevent all misconception; But sometimes they are written in small notes, and where the time-division is left to the performer, it is necessary to add the following observations in regard to their execution,

Most of these embellishments are played very quickly, in order that the note, before which they are placed, and to which they are added as grace notes, may lose but little of its value. It is often difficult to guess, from which note (whether the preceding or succeeding) the time, requisite for the execution of the grace note, is to be taken. A general rule cannot be given, but I have written out the mode of playing some of those ornaments which occur most frequently.

In Adagios or any other slow and cantabile pieces, these grace notes must be proportionally slower, according to the character of the composition.

Amongst the embellishments may also be classed the *tremolo*, and the changing of the fingers on one tone and on the same string.

The singer's voice in passionate passages, or when he forces it to its most powerful pitch, has a trembling which resembles the vibrations of a strongly struck bell. This, the Violinist can imitate very closely, as well as many other peculiarities of the human voice. It consists in the wavering of a stopped tone, which alternately extends a little below or above the perfect intonation, and is produced by a trembling motion of the left hand in the direction from the nut towards the bridge. This motion must however be slight, and the deviation from the perfect intonation of the tone, should hardly be perceptible to the ear.

In old compositions the *tremolo* is indicated by points . . . . or by the word *tremolo*; in new compositions it is generally left to the performer. Avoid however its frequent use, or in improper places. In places where the *tremolo* is used by the singer, it may also advan. tageously be applied to the Violin. This *tremolo* is therefore properly used in passionate passages, and in strongly marking all the fz or $\succ$ tones. Long sustained notes can be animated and strengthened by it: if such a tone swells from p to f, a beautiful effect is produced by beginning the *tremolo* slowly, and in proportion to the increasing power, to give a gradually accelerated vibration. Also by commencing rapidly, and gradually dropping the tone to a sound hardly perceptible, a good effect is produced. The *tremolo* may be di. vided into four species, viz: into the rapid, for strongly marked tones; into the slow, for sustained tones of passionate cantabile passages; into the slow commencing and increasing tone; and into the rapid commencing and slowly decreasing of long sustained notes. These two latter species are difficult and require much practice, so that the increasing and decreas ing of the vibrations may at all times be uniform, and without any sudden change from slow to quick, or the reverse.

By changing the finger on one tone, something similar to the effect produced by a human voice is likewise imitated, namely: by the sounding of a new syllable upon the same note, which causes its division into two parts, the latter being sung with the same breath, and having it slightly accented.

When the Violinist causes this division of two equal tones to be made by the taking off, or changing the bowing, he does it with a continued and quiet motion of the bow, and by substituting one finger for another. The hand is thereby so far drawn back or pushed on, till that finger, which is to relieve the first, can fall in its place, as:

Consequently, the 2nd finger from E ($+$) to E, is drawn back, that the 4th may fall on the second E; the 3rd is pushed on from D (✻) to D, that the first finger may take the 3rd fingers place; and lastly, the first finger is drawn back from E (✻) to E, to enable the 4th finger to fall on the second E.

This sliding on to the above mentioned notes should not be heard, nor the phrase be played ·as in the following:

The changing of the finger on the contrary, must take place so rapidly that the quitting of the finger on the first note is hardly to be perceived by the ear.

In the following Exercise, the above, as well as the *tremolo*, are intended for practice.

The quick *tremolo* is indicated by 〰 the slow by 〰 the gradually increasing 〰 and the gradually decreasing by 〰

In changing the fingers, I beg again to remark that the finger which relieves the other, must not fall down until the hand has assumed that position by which, without being stretched or drawn back, it can command its proper place.

The Exercise begins with a *staccato*, hitherto not used by the Scholar, namely the one in broken chords. It is played like those running in scales; yet it requires still greater care than those, to avoid the leaping of the bow.

The grace notes in the 4th and 8th bar, are played in the manner before indicated, the first in demisemiquavers, the second in semiquaver triplets.

In the last 4th of the 14th bar, the 2^d finger is taken for the last note but one, as in this manner the Major third from G♯ to E can be stopped much easier than with the 3rd finger. The hand remains stationary in the 2^d position In the 15th bar the two D Sharps are separated by the change of finger. The first begins *p* and with a slow *tremolo*, increasing in time towards the second D Sharp

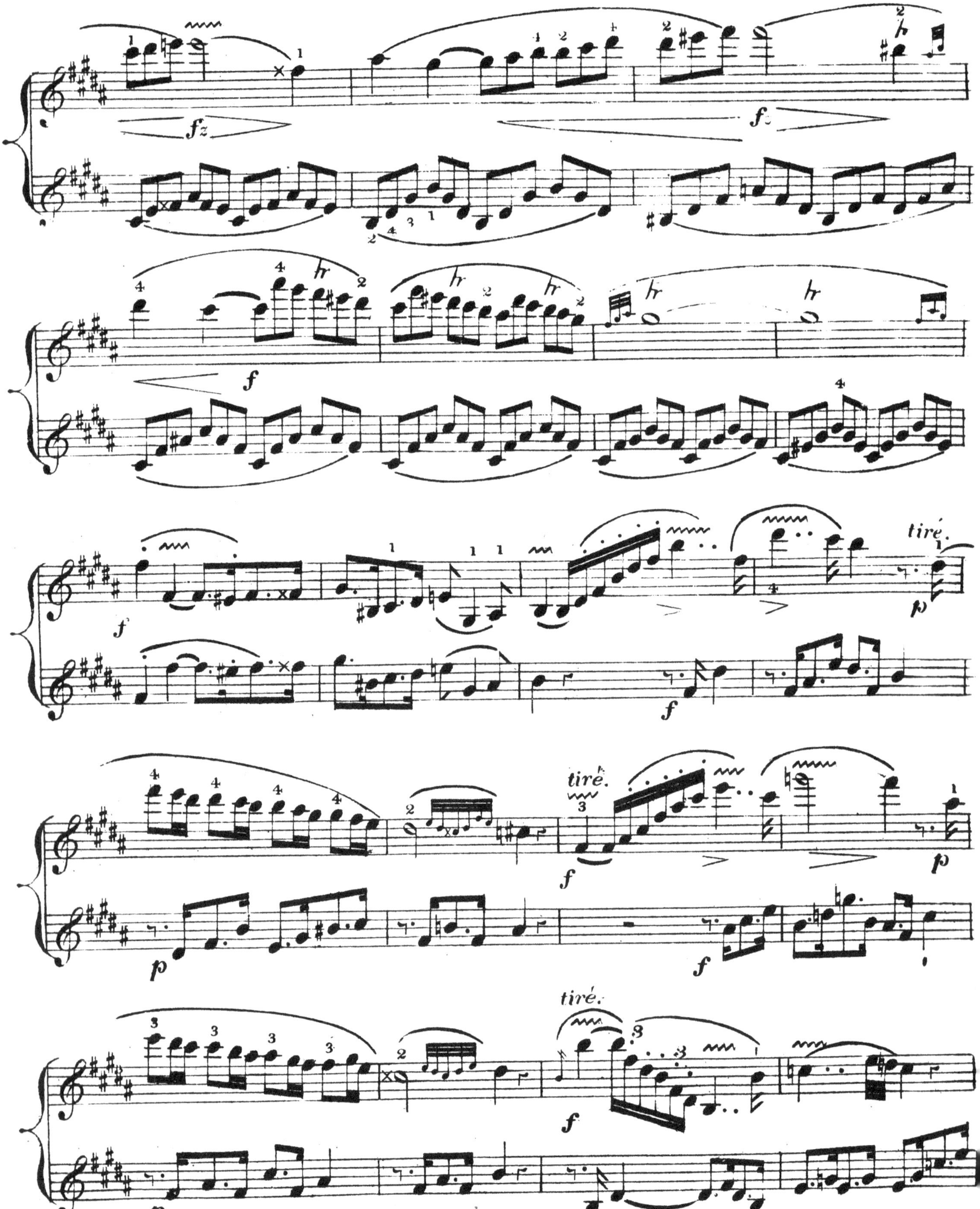
tiré.
tiré.
tiré.

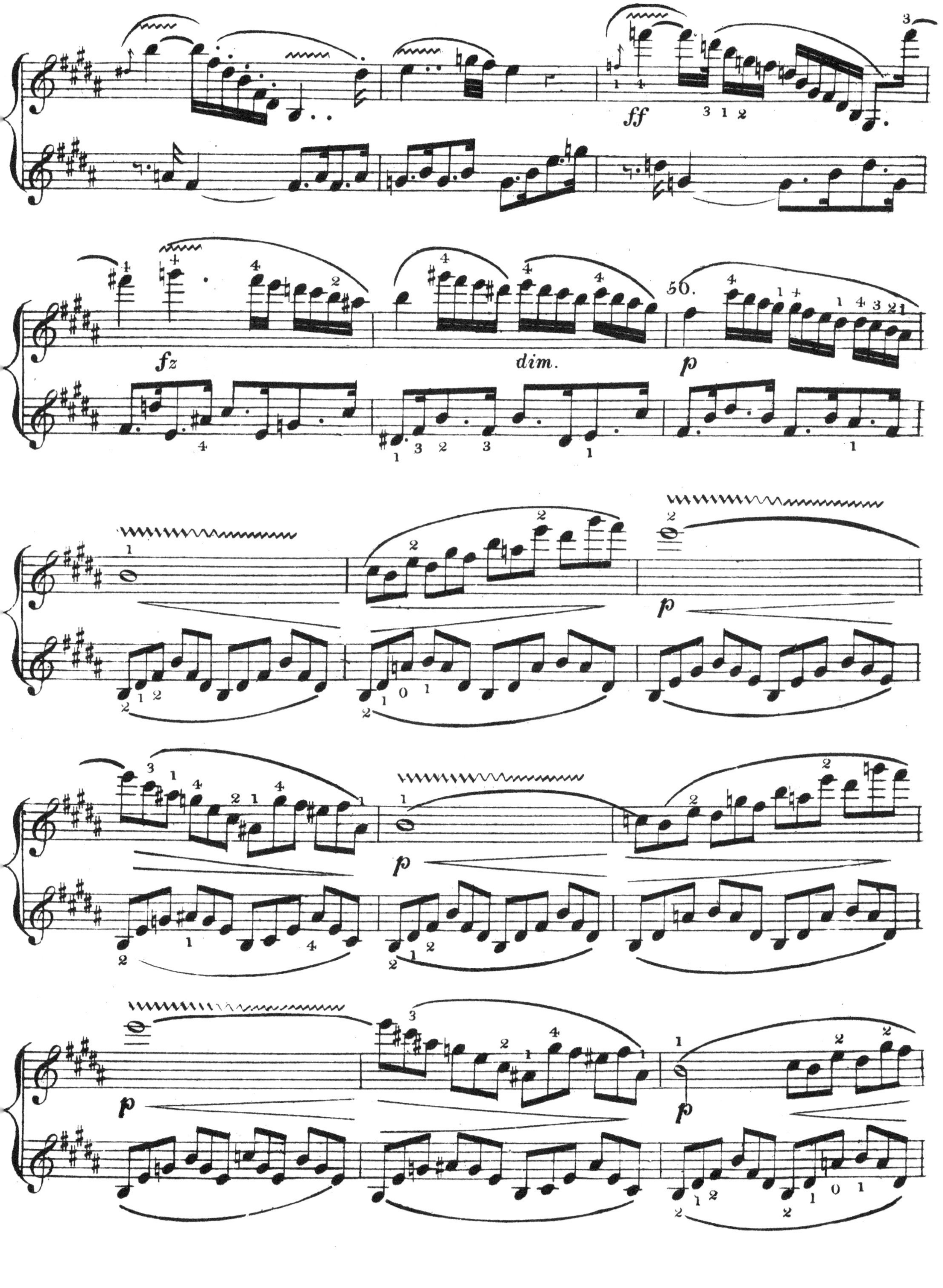
ff
fz
dim.
50.
p
p
p
p
p

In the 60th bar at the change of finger, the hand is moved down every time one shift.

The B of the 65th and 66th bar, receives in the first half a *cres.* with a gradually increasing *tremolo*, and in the second half a *dim.* returning gradually to the slow *tremolo*.

Finally I must still name an embellishment, frequently used by Violinists, but only in order to dissuade from it, or at least to warn against its frequent use, namely the beating of the finger on a vibrating string in sustained tones. The Scholar will have observed, that the open string also vibrates, if the Unison, the Octave or the Fifth of the same is played. When this vibrating string is touched by one of the fingers, the vibration ceases; lift it up and it recommences. This repeated several times, causes the beating, against which I have already warned. It very easily becomes a habit, and is then very unpleasant.

Perhaps it may be used on the three harmonics as these cannot be affected by any *tremolo*, On these it is produced by touching the lower open string.

In the next Exercise, the *Thema con Variazioni* * is again reproduced, all that the Scholar has been taught, and practised separately in the preceding Chapters, here united in the manner usual in brilliant concerto pieces

The unusual bowings (taught in Chapter 18) are here applied in more difficult passages, and offer to the Scholar at first, fresh difficulties, which however, by diligent and thoughtful practice and attention to the former and present remarks, he will soon overcome.

Where two different bowings are marked in the Variations, the one *above* the notes is played first, and at the repetition the *lower* one

Bowings, Shifts, tremolo's, and other signs of expression, must be carefully attended to.

THEMA CON VARIAZIONI.

In the first bar of the Theme, the bow is placed close to the nut, and for the two first notes drawn down to the middle; then the third note obtains a short, but soft upbow, and the last note, the second half of the downbow, This refers also to the upbow of the 2d bar, and to all other similarly marked bars. The theme should be played *dolce*, soft and engaging.

---

* A simple melody with variations, which at every repetition, is more richly embellished, without ever losing its resemblance to the Original Melody.

The first Variation requires a whole bow throughout, with the exception of the last bar but one, in which the three slurred notes are taken with third-part bowings. In the 2nd species of bowing the slurred and dotted notes are to be well distinguished.

Respecting the three species of bowing required in the 2d Variation, I have to refer to Nos 4 5 and 6 of the 54th Exercise.

The third Variation must be played with ease and elegance. For the staccato in every case, as little bow should be used as possible.

The 2 first bars of Var: 4 are smartly marked. *(martellé)* The slurred notes of the following bars must be strictly uniform in the division, with the due resting on the first note, such as has already been taught in the lesson on Octave passages. The bowing of the first bar at the repetition of the part, sounds better *p*, than *f*, as you cannot prevent the moving on of the hand from being heard. In the following (Viotti's) method of bowing, it may, however, be avoided very well, and is therefore applicable to all degrees of power. The first bowing is made with very slight motion of the hand. The 2d Part is for the first time played with the kind of bowing taught in the 51th Exercise under No. 8; at the repetition, which, on account of the varied notes, has been written over again. attend strictly to the fingering.

Var: 5. is to be played slower. The first six notes are easiest taken on the half shift. At the leaps in the 3d bar, remember the former rules on sliding from one tone to another. In gliding down from the high harmonic E, to the G♯, the little finger should press the string firmly on the fingerboard. ___ That this gliding from one note to another should never degenerate into a howl_ing, I have already mentioned.

Var: 6. *Allegro Moderato* (moderately quick) must be played boldly and powerfully. The triplets in the first bar not being accented, are in general taken with the up-bow; here, however, they are marked with the down-bow, because with this, the finger ascending, the tone is more distinct, and at the same time more powerful. An up-bow is taken in commencing with the 2d part, where the passage is descending

In Var: 7. part 2^d, another double Shake is introduced, in which the shake of the accompanying part begins later. In addition to the former observations on the Double shake, commence the shake of both parts with the principal note, and not disturb the shake of the upper part, in its uniform beat, by the commencement of the second shake.

Var: 8. consists chiefly of passages in tenths, the bow leaping over one string. It is very difficult to do this distinctly,& requires persevering practice. Begin it in the slowest time. The bow must not jump over the string, but should sink or drop down over the intermediate string, from the lower to the upper, without setting it in vibration, during the standing still of the bow,) as has before been taught, and takes place at the *martellé* after every note. At the place, where this leaping over the intermediate string ceases, and a quieter motion of the bow begins, I have particularly to caution the pupil against hurrying

Var: 9 is played *con espressione*, with expression This notification might here appear

superfluous, as a Solo should never be played without its due expression, but in this instance
it applies to a heighten'd expression, to a performance full of soul.

This *Adagio* requires a correct and feeling delivery, and the nicest shades in the manage
ment of the bow. The Scholar should again refer to the notes of the 51ˢᵗ Exercise and pay
the greatest attention to the changing of the bowing, as a single misapplication of the up and
down bows must destroy all ___ The *p* and *f* the length of the bow, and the rapidity with
which it should be drawn, are to be strictly observed; it is also necessary to keep the most
correct time, when the accompaniment, as is the case here, consists in uniform notes and figures

The 10th Var: has *tempo* 1°; *(primo)* it consequently returns to the **first time** of the *Andante*.

Var: 11 and 12, offer less difficulty in bowing, but more for the left hand. The frequent changing of the shifts makes it very difficult to play all the notes perfectly equal. The attention of the Scholar ought therefore to be particularly directed to this, the Master always accompauying in the strictest time.

Whole bowings are always taken, whether 8, 16 or 32 notes are to be played in one bow.
Observe again the most equal division of the bow.

CODA.

Coda, (addition) is the free conclusion of a Musical Piece; with Variations, as here, it is one which is not composed on the Theme. Generally the principal melody of the last Variation is more developed, & consequently a more satisfactory conclusion given, than the end of the Variation itself would have permitted.

END of the SECOND PART.

THIRD PART.

CHAPTER XXI.

ON DELIVERY, OR STYLE IN GENERAL.

Style, is the manner in which the Singer or Player performs the Music noted down by the Composer. If it be confined to a faithful delivery of that written down by notes, Signs, or words of art, it is called a *correct style* or *delivery;* if the Performer adds ideas of his own, and if he be capable of intellectually animating the subject so that the hearer may discover and participate in the intentions of the composer, it is called a *fine style,* in which correctness, sentiment, and elegance are united.

The *correct* Style or Delivery naturally precedes the *fine style.* To this therefore are applicable the instructions given in the preceding chapters; and as they contain all the techni cal means requisite for a fine style, I need only point out their application.

Fine style is however confined within certain limits. The capability of discerning the charac ter of the Musical piece, elevates the *correct* to the *fine* Style and enables the performer to participate in the sentiment displayed, and reproduce it; this is a gift of nature, which may be strengthened & improved, but cannot be taught.

A recapitulation of that belonging to a *correct* style may be useful to enable the Scholar to judge, whether he has perfectly understood it, and thereby obtained the capability of attain ing the *fine* style.

A correct style or Delivery requires: perfect intonation, exact division of the notes in a bar, according to their duration, a strict observance of time, of light and of shade, & also of the different kinds of bowing, slurs, doubleturns, shakes &c.

A fine style or delivery besides the preceding, requires the following technical expedients 1st, the finer shades of the management of the bow, as regards the character of tone; viz: strong, even, rough, soft, fluty, or, in the accentuation and separation of Musical phrases 2d The artificial shifts which are not used merely on account of any easier mode of playing, but for expression and tone, to which belongs also, the gliding from one note to another, and the changing of the finger on the same tone; 3d The tremolo in its four degrees. 4th The increasing of time in furious, impetuous, and passionate passages as well as the retarding of such as have a tender, doleful, or melancholy character.

But all these means of expression lead to a *fine* style or delivery only, when good taste watches over their application, and when the soul of the performer guides the bow and animates the finger. When, therefore, the Scholar is so far advanced, as in some measure to command the mechanism of playing, it will then be time to cultivate his taste and to awaken his sensibility. The best way probably is to let him often hear good Music and distinguished singers and performers, pointing out to him the beauty of the composition as well as the method used by the Singer or Performer to heighten the expression and give effect to the piece.

CHAPTER XXII.

ON DELIVERY, OR STYLE OF PLAYING CONCERTOS.

The Concerto being generally produced before an Audience in a large room, and with the accompaniment of a numerous Orchestra, requires, above all, a full and powerful tone. This does not necessarily exclude the more delicate Shades of playing, as the Violin possesses the peculiarity of making even its softest tones be heard at a considerable distance. Consequently the Performer can develope, in a Concerto, the whole extent of the different degrees of light and shade of which the Violin is capable.

The intention of Concerto playing is to show the skill of the performer, and presupposes the most complete command over all technical difficulties. The Scholar should not risk a public performance of a Concerto or other Solo piece, until he has so thoroughly overcome all difficulties, that its success cannot be affected by outward circumstances, such as great heat in the room, the trepidation of a first appearance before the Public, or by an unyielding accompaniment.

It is not enough to conquer difficulties, they must also apparently be done with elegance and without exertion. Then only will the hearer have an undisturbed enjoyment of the fine science of the Artist.

To the highest mechanical perfection in Concerto playing must be added a sentimental delivery, as without it the most brilliant playing gains only cold admiration, and never intimate participation.

To cause this participation requires the composition to be full of feeling and sentiment. ____ The Scholar should therefore for a Public performance look to a composition which will display not only his capabilities, but which also possesses sufficient intrinsic merit to satisfy the most cultivated ear, without taking into consideration the merits of the performer.

The application of the means of expression in fine style or delivery, enumerated in the preceding Chapter, cannot be taught by rules and precepts, but only by examples; in order to give them to the Scholar, I have shown the style of performance in the two following well known Concertos, as near as could be done by notes, signs, and words, and where this does not suffice, I have supplied an explanation,

By Strictly following all these signs and precepts, the Scholar, if he only possess the capability of a fine delivery, will, without doubt, attain the expression requisite in these two Concertos.

An accompaniment has been added for the master.

Before the Scholar commences, he should observe, that every period beginning in the full bar, or with an accented part, is, after the general rule, begun with the down bow; such periods however, commencing with introductory notes to a bar, or with an unaccented part, must be with an upbow. The exceptions to this general rule, are noted by *tiré* or *poussé*. In other respects the bow, according to the marked kinds of bowing, is regularly drawn backward and forward. The turns are all short, and the long ones found in the Original, are here written down, according to their value, in large notes.

SEVENTH CONCERTO by RODE.

First Allegro. First Solo.

The first *Allegro* of this Concerto has in the subject and its repetition a serious, elevated, and somewhat melancholy character. It requires to be played with a grand, full tone, and in many parts with a passionate, yet on the whole, with a tranquil dignity.

The first 15 bars, with the exception of the concluding notes of each period of four bars, are played with the longest possible bowings. At the *forte*, the bow is carried with equal pressure from one end to the other, close to the bridge, and is so rapidly changed, that neither a slackening of the power, nor a space between the tones can be heard. Where the power is to be diminished, the bow is carried farther from the bridge. The concluding notes of the 3 first periods obtain only half bow; this, therefore during the pause, is lifted above the string, then moved upwards and replaced close to the nut. At the 6 first notes of the 14th bar, the bow is pushed up half, then for the last note a very short down bow is taken, and the remainder of the bow for the two first notes of the following bar. — The passage in crotchets, commencing at bar 16, is played with the upper half of the bow. The bowings are taken as long as the stiffness of the backarm will allow.

In order to produce the shakes full and brilliant, the half of the value of the preceding note has been taken and added to the shake note. The last four notes of the 19th bar obtain again the whole bow. The shake in bar 23, begins slowly and increases gradually. The division of the bow in bar 25, is similar to the one in bar 14. The second half of the 28th and 30th bar is to be so played, that the first notes obtain a little longer duration than their value warrants, and the loss of time may be regained by a quicker playing of the following note. (This manner of delivery is termed rubato.) This increasing of time must be gradual, and harmonize with the decreasing of the power. For the first notes make use of much bow, in order that the latter may be the more delicate.

The shake in bar 31 must have a full tone; but do not rest too long on the shake note, which would oblige you to hurry the two following notes. The G sharp of the 32nd bar, with the $>$ should be strongly marked. Bar 36 is played *poco ritardando* (kept back a little) i.e. the time gradually decreases. To every note of bars 38, 39, 46, and 47, give equal strength and sustain them well, without leaving any space between.

Play the **53.rd** and **2** following bars as powerful as possible, but only with half bow and a quiet backarm. Play the dotted notes in bar 54 very smartly and with a downbow, to give a greater con_trast with the *PP* of bar 56. In bar 58 and 60 prolong the 9 th note (G) a trifle, and make the loss of time good again, by the increased rapidity of the following notes. The Semiquavers of the 61 st and 62 nd bars must be very smart and short. Remember what has been said about the *martele*. The tones of the scale of B, in bar 63 must equalise in power and rapidity.

The *cantabile* from bar 65 to 84, requires much expression, and by following strictly the signs, the Scholar will not fail to produce it. The 4 first bars of the passage, commencing at bar 80, are to be marked with the greatest force, to contrast the more with the *piano* of the 84th bar. The 6 notes of the broken chord must be distinctly heard. Prolong the two last quavers of the 81st and 83rd bar a little, without disturbing the time. At the triplets in bar 85 the bow is gradually drawn close to the nut, in order to give a whole downbow to the 86th bar.

SECOND SOLO.

SECOND SOLO. —— The introductory note is played, close to the nut, and the three min_
ims are separated by short rests. At the third B only, draw the bow down to the point, and
for the low G♯ replace it quickly close to the nut. To the 3 last notes of the broken chord take
a whole bow, at the first double stop draw it down half, afterwards the short upbow and the remainder for the third double stop. Let the first note of bar 9 be moderately increased, so as to avoid
the succeeding staccato becoming too loud.

The greatest force is required for the 1st note of the 10th bar. At the commencement of the staccato, guard against giving the preceding note a pressure, which certainly assists the run of the bow in the staccato, but is completely erroneous. Play the *pp* of the 12th bar, like all *pp*s, as far from the bridge as possible. The period from 17 to 20th bar, play the first time sharp and strong, but at the repetition as delicate and soft as possible. The passage from bar 29 to 39 is played with half bowings and as forcibly as possible, At the four F sharps of bar 38, raise the bow a little over the strings, and throw it on with force close to the point; it must not however cause a trembling of the stick.

The Cantabile commencing in bar 40, should be played with force and passion. Play the semiquavers in the 55th and three following bars with flat bow and with bowings as long as the fixed backarm will allow. The *martele* of bar 59 can be then so much shorter and sharper.

At the semiquaver triplets of the 61st bar. rest a little on each of the first notes, and unite them again without causing the least pause.

To the following may be applied the remarks on similar passages in the first Solo.

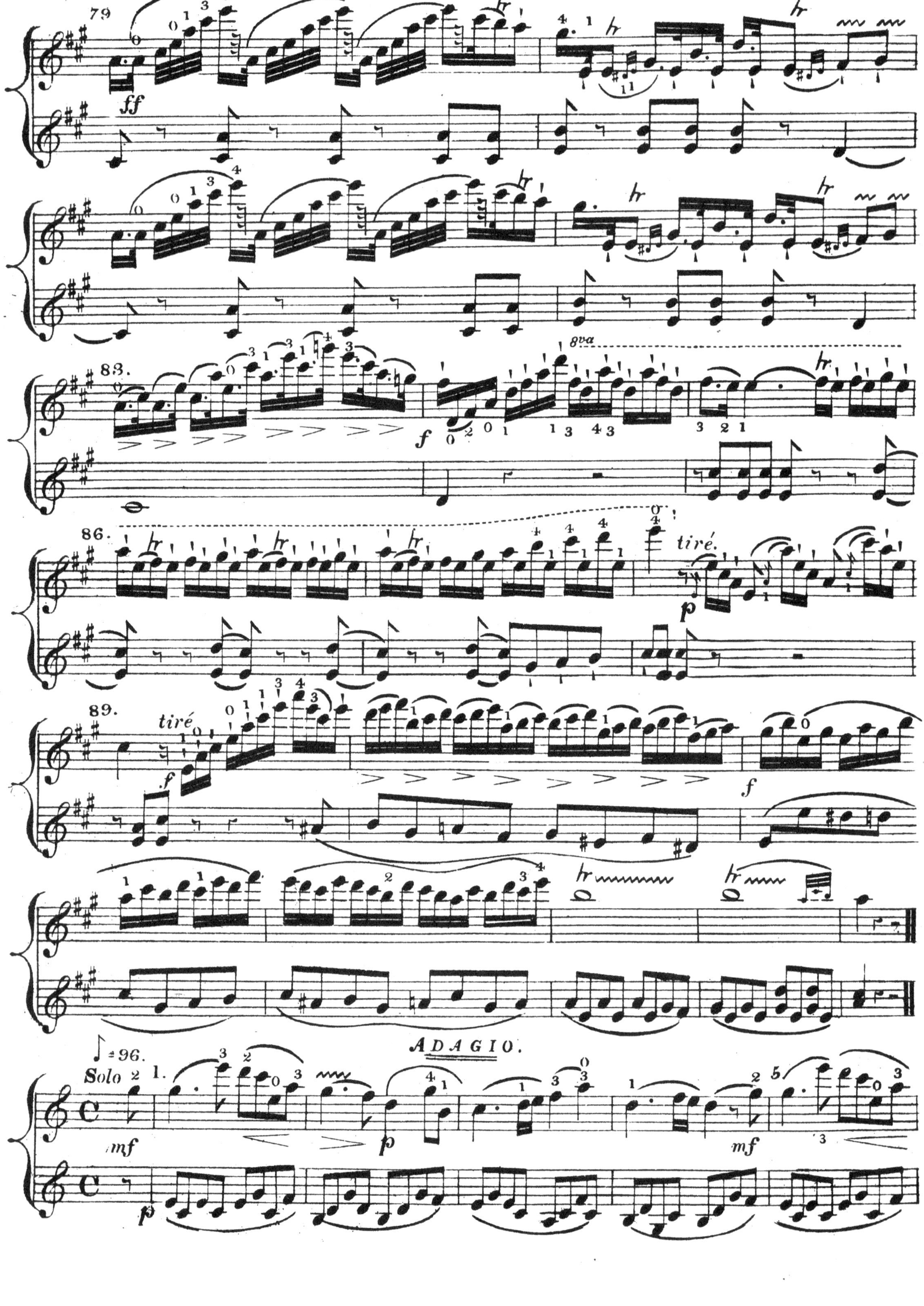
79
ff
83.
f
8va
86.
tiré
p
89.
tiré
f
f
ADAGIO.
♪ = 96.
Solo
mf
p
p
mf

THE ADAGIO,

In the maggiore, consists of a graceful Melody, to be played in a simple, unpretending yet feeling style. The Minore being performed throughout on the 4th string, partakes of a more passionate character; here then, the delivery must be augmented proportionably by a grander tone and increasing tremulous passion.

The soft gliding from one note to another, must not only be upwards, as in the first bar from G to E, but also downwards as in the same from C to the open E, and in the following one from G to B.

All the Introductory notes require little bow, which is placed on the string near the nut.

The Shake, bar 26, commences slowly, increasing gradually in quickness.

THE RONDO,

Has a spirited character, fanciful and melancholy in its Theme, and must be delivered with vivacity and energy, but also with elegance. The introductory notes commence with a down—bow close to the point of the bow. For the 3 first slurred notes of bar 1, the half of the bow is taken, then for the C, a short down bow; after which the second half of the bow is used for the 2 quavers. The 2^d bar is played the same, except with a down bow, the 3^d again as the first.—The last note of each of these bars, having < and a tremolo, is to be marked as strongly as possible. The sliding from E to A in the 4th bar should not be done too quickly, and in the *dim.* the bow is gradually distanced from the bridge. Bars 5. 6. 7. should be played with a soft, engaging tone, but the < less marked than in the 3 first bars. marked with f.

At the 3 slurred notes bars 17 and 18, keep the bow back, as much as possible, to enable you to return again, in the succeeding short (staccato) notes, quite to the point. The gliding up and down of the finger in bars 28,29 and 30, must be distinctly heard. Mark the 4 semiquavers in bar 31, very smartly. For the next three bowing use "whole bow," but in the 34.th bar only "half." To the first note of every triplet in bar 38, give a strong pressure. On the F♯ of bar 39 retard a little and regain it on the five following notes. In the 44 and 45 bar, the last of the 3 slurred notes is strongly marked, using little bow, to enable you to return, in the 3 dotted notes, as much as possible to the point. The Scales in bars 46,47 and 48, should fluently roll along, and increase to great force in the latter tones.

The Melody commencing after the Pause, play in a light and elegant manner, but the passage
(bar 66) with a powerful flat bow, and with bowing as long as the fixed back-arm will permit.——
On the Shakes bar 71 and 73, retard considerably, and regain it on the following notes of the bar.
Observe the same on the four F sharps of bar 78 and 79, in which the tremolo must also be
predominantly heard. To the tones with > in bars, 83 to 86, use much longer bowings than to the.

other unaccented tones, so as to play alternately in the middle and at the point of the bow.

The crotchets in bar 88 and 89, with the ⌄ must be strongly accented. With the *ritardando* of bar 90 commence also the *diminuendo*. The former Tempo recommences with the 3 introductory notes of the Theme.

The Major is played a little slower and very melodiously, consequently with flat and long bowings. At the *poco piu lento*, particularly, produce a very grand tone.

Bars 31 to 38, play very delicately with the bow distant from the bridge.

The passage in bar 38, requires again quicker time.

At the 3 slurred notes of bars 40 and 41, and particularly on the first, retard a little, and play the three following notes so much the faster.

Distinguish the 42^d bar from the 38th, by giving the accent to the second note, instead of the first.

The slurred notes **G♯** and **A** in the 46th and following bars, are to be strongly accented, and use for that purpose as much up-bow, as was required for the 4 first notes of each bar in a down-bow. In like manner accent all the tones of this passage, marked >

At the *pp* bar 57, distance the bow as much as possible from the bridge.

From the 65 th bar, the former remarks are applicable, with this difference between the 66 th, and 86 th bar of the first Solo, that now only two instead of four notes are to have the the strong accent and a longer and stronger bowing. As these longer upbows succeed each other (bar 67.) therefore reaching the middle of the bow or even beyond it is unavoidable at the conclusion of the passage: consequently at the following pause the bow must be drawn back over the strings and replaced close to the point.

NINTH CONCERTO (Op: 55.) by L. SPOHR *

The Character of the first Allegro is serious, yet impassioned; that of the Adagio gay and soft; of the Rondo, strong and agitated.—— The first part must be played with a grand tone and persevering force; the melody very legato and the passages with much spirit; the Adagio with tranquil mildness, except in the passionate passages; the Theme of the Rondo melodiously, the following Solo (B Minor) and the similar one in (F Major) very animated, almost wild; the middle part however soft and engaging.

The technical execution, of the prescribed signs of expression in *Rode's* Concerto and several of the Exercises have been amply shown by explanatory notes, and it may be reasonably supposed, the Scholar is now enabled to find them out, in this Concerto: explanations have therefore been entirely omitted. The Scholar's diligence must now also be increased, that he may not miss any of the prescribed signs of expression, nor any of the fingering and shifting.

The time in each part of this Concerto remains unchanged. The compositions of the Author seldom require the time to be increased, or decreased, to heighten the expression. Generally, only such compositions demand it which are not composed in one form, or imagined in equal measure of time. The Scholar should rarely, and with moderation, if his feeling should induce him to it, use the means of expression already mentioned, as by any alteration in the measure of time, the whole character of the composition might be destroyed.

* Chosen on account of several difficulties which the Scholar has not encountered in Rode's Concerto, as for instance: chromatic Scales, Double stops, staccato &c. &c.

NINTH CONCERTO BY L. SPOHR.

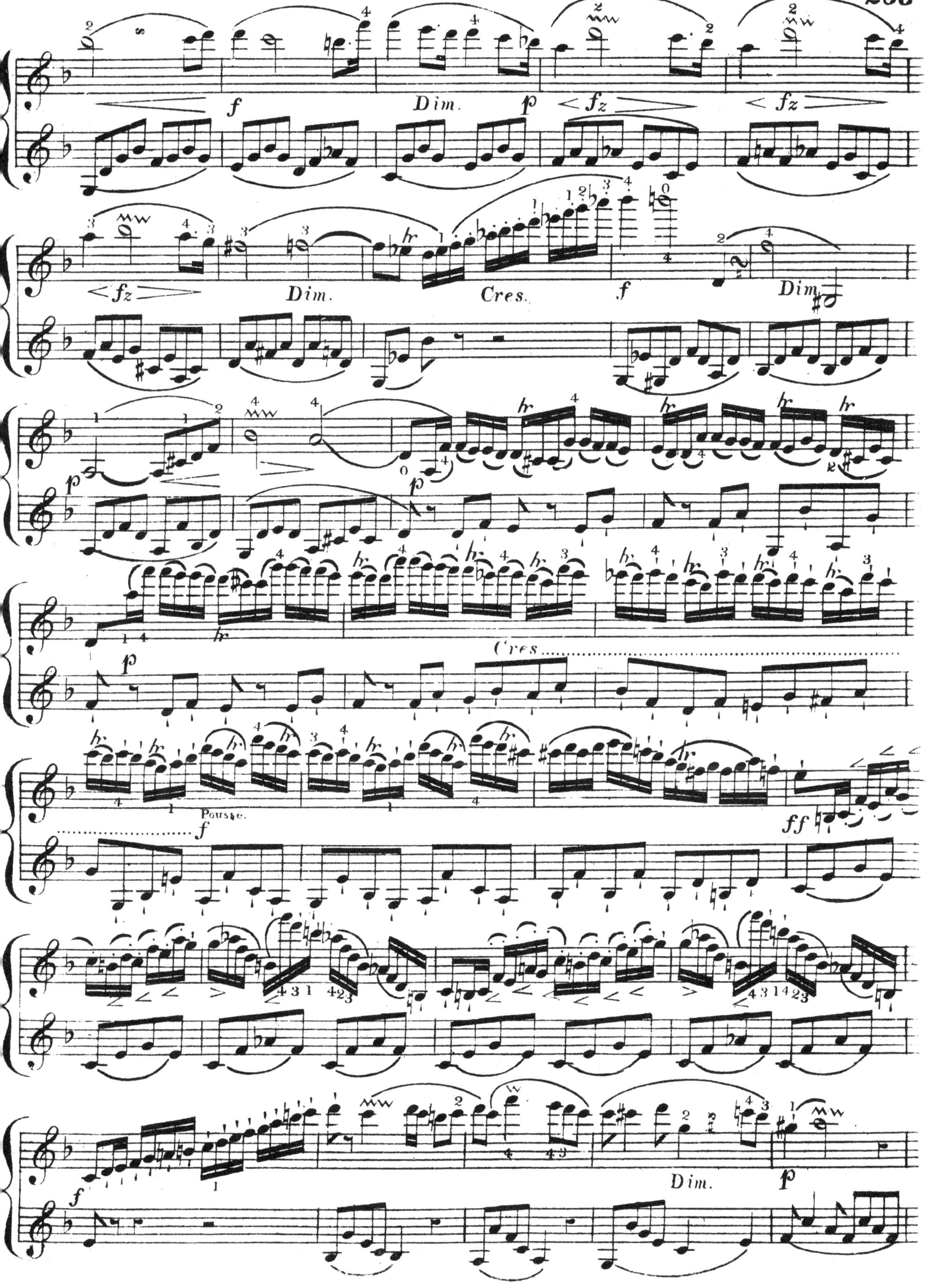
Dim.
Cres.
Dim.
Poussé.
Cres.
Dim.

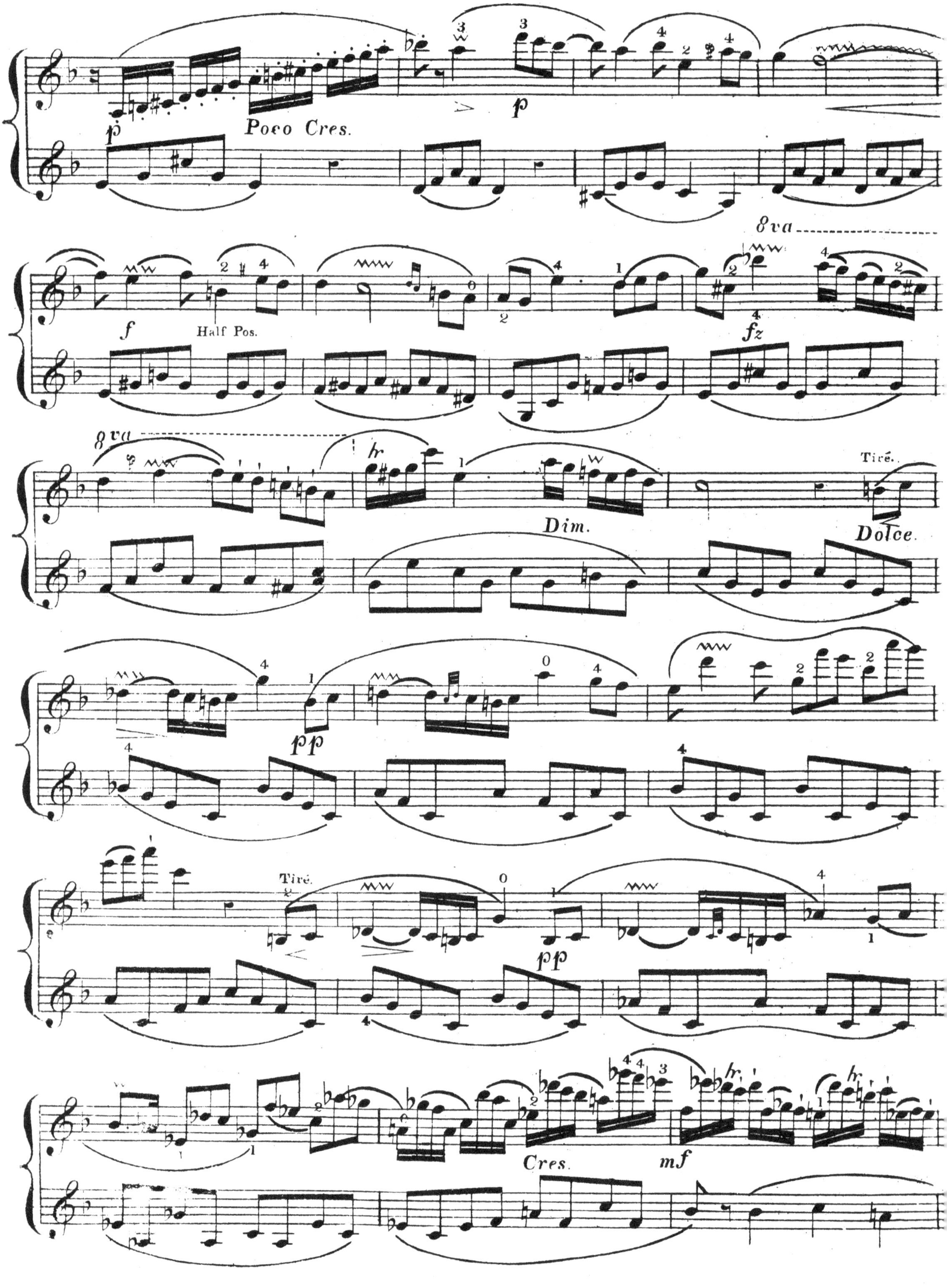
Poco Cres.
Half Pos.
8va
Dim.
Tiré.
Dolce.
Tiré.
Cres.

Cre scen do ff
Diminuen do.
p Cres ff
mf
8va loco.
Cres.
f p
p Cre
scen do f

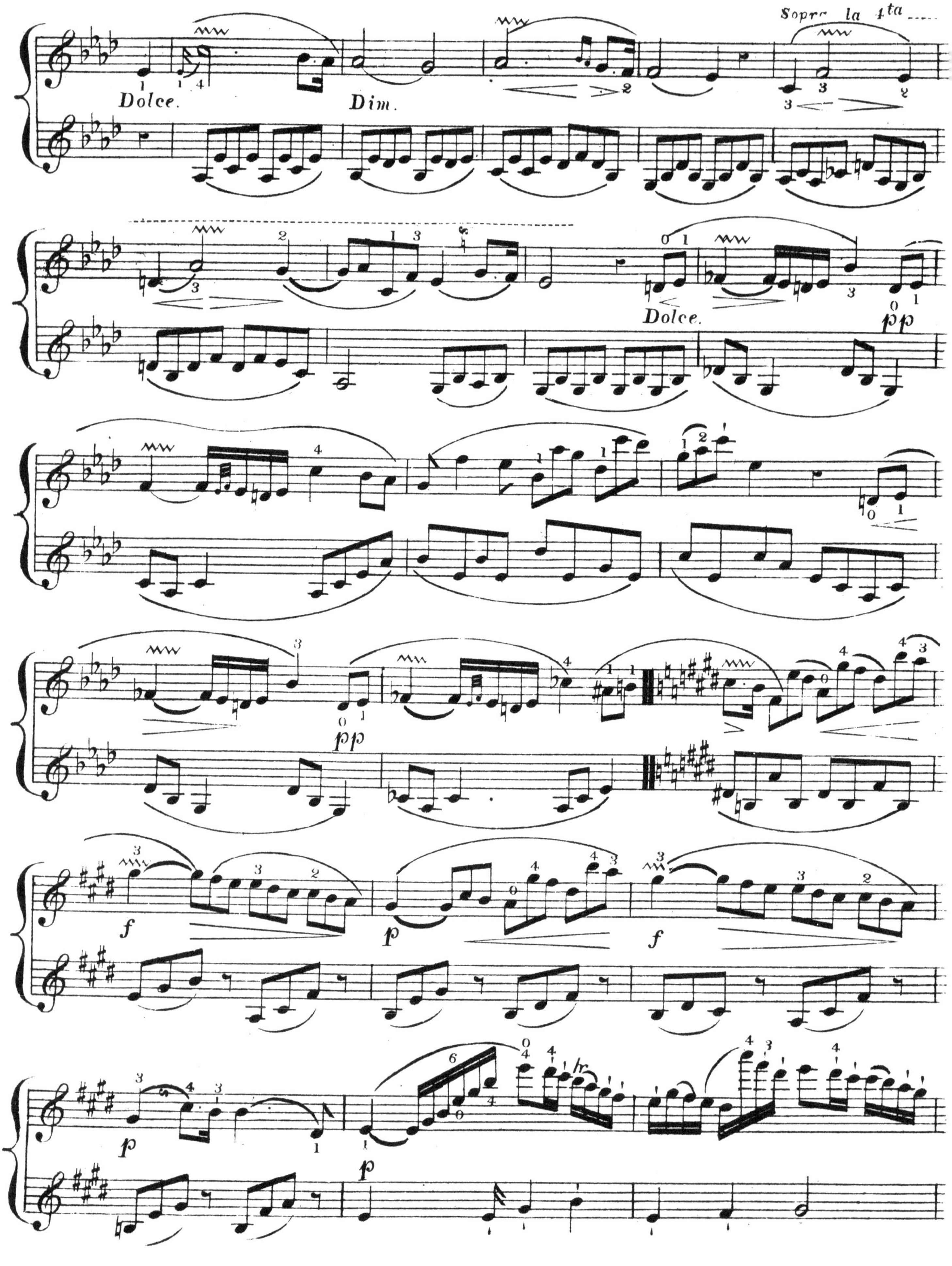
Sopra la 4ta
Dolce.
Dim.
Dolce.
pp
pp
f
p
f
p
p

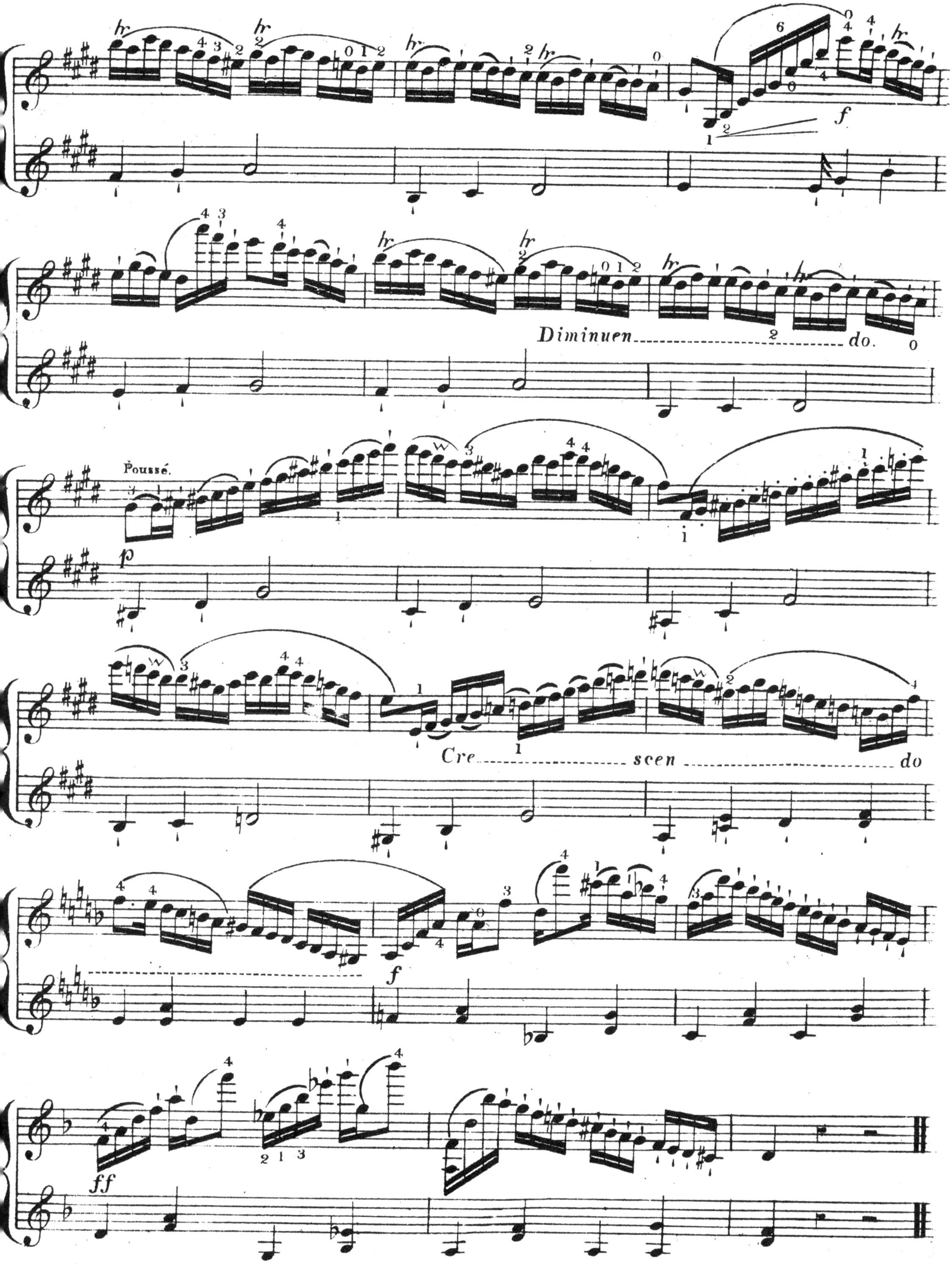
f
Diminuen do.
Poussé.
p
Cre scen do
f
ff

Tiré
p
Cre
scen
do
f
Dim.
f
Dim.
fz
fz
Dim.
pp
f
Dim.
fz
fz
fz
Tiré
f
Diminuen
do.
p

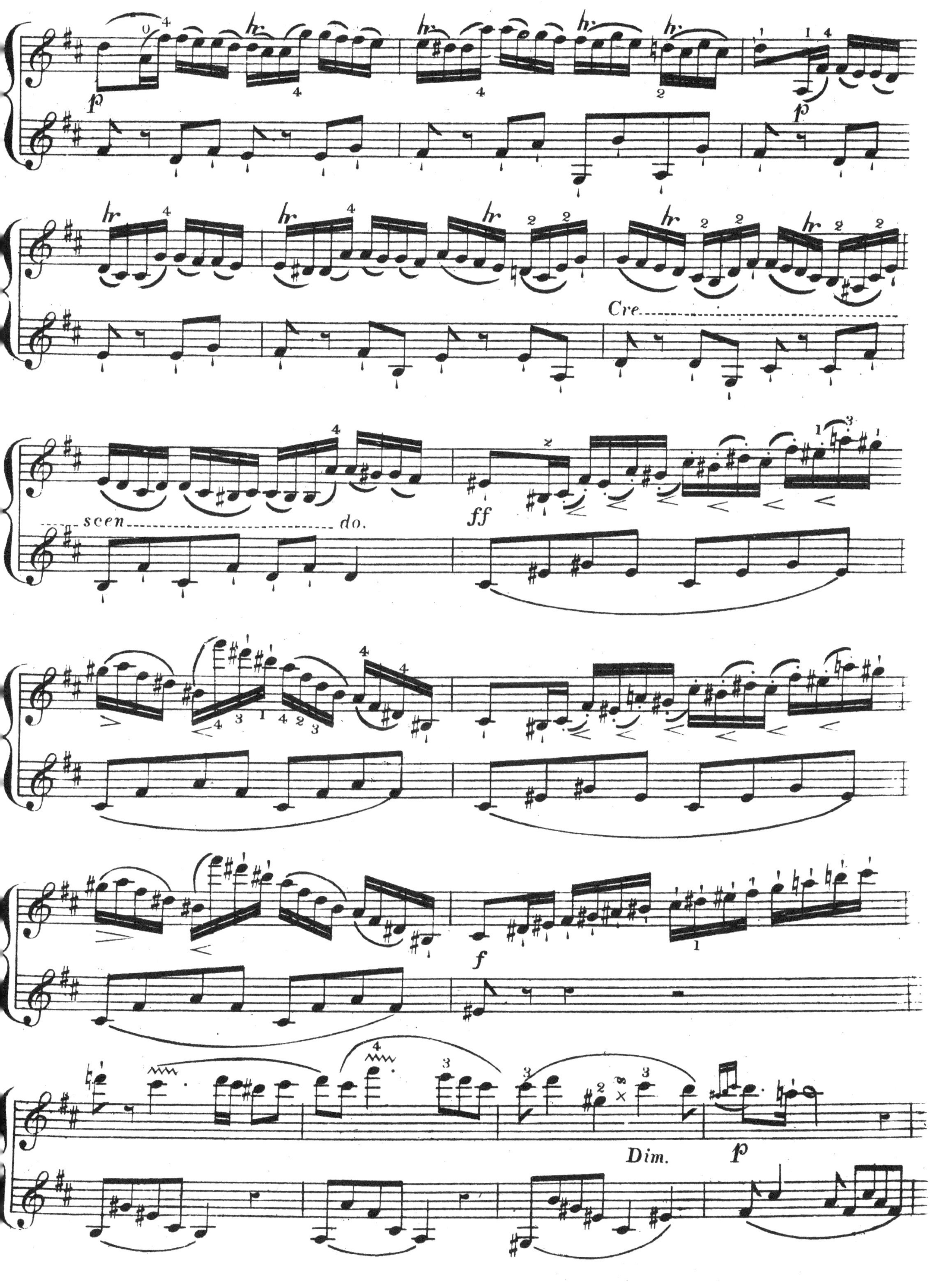
p
p
Cre
scen
do.
ff
f
Dim.
p

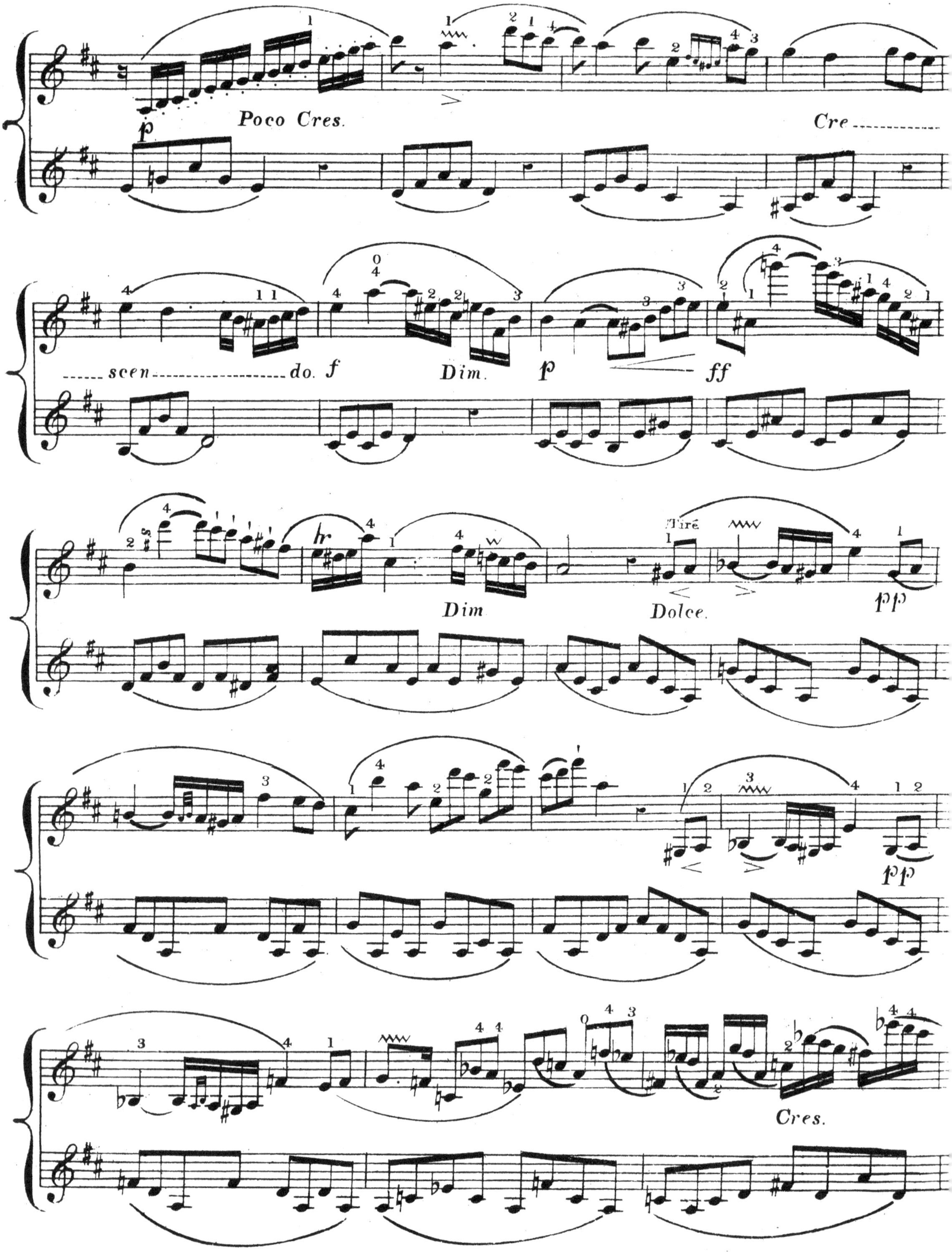

Poco Cres.
Cre
scen
do.
Dim.
Dim
Tiré
Dolce.
Cres.

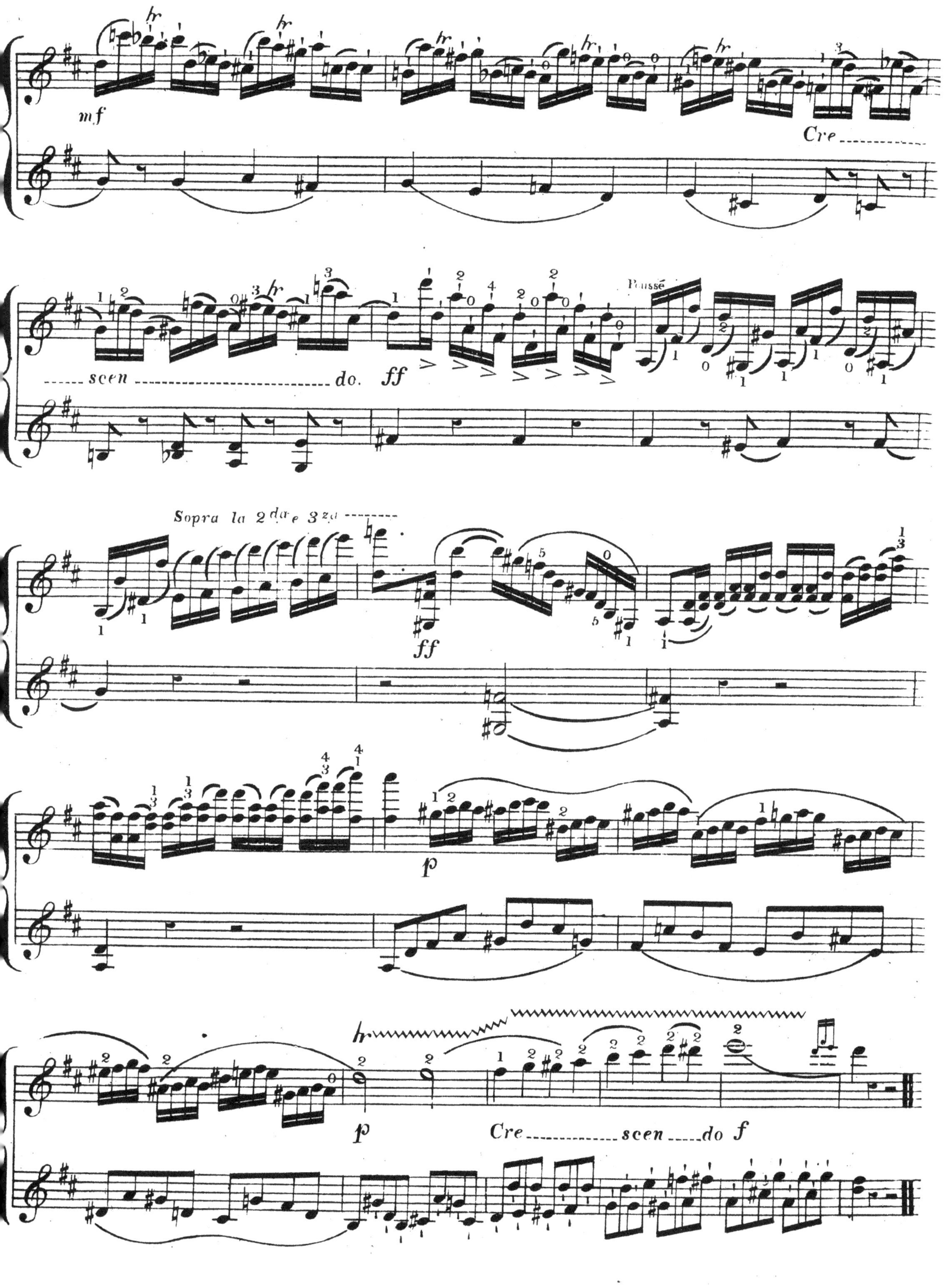
mf
Cre
scen
do.
ff
Poussé
Sopra la 2da e 3za
ff
p
p
Cre
scen
do
f

ADAGIO.

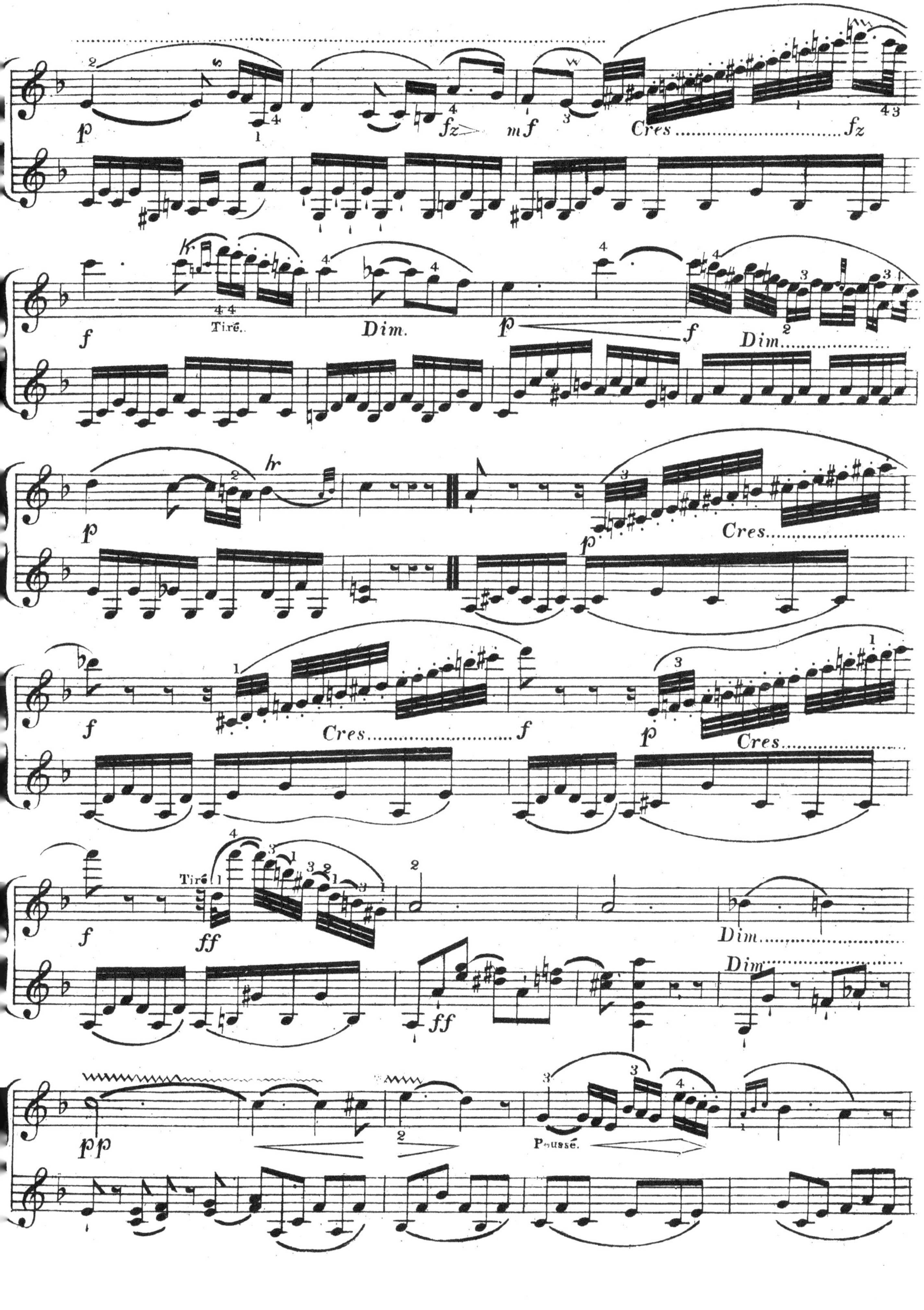
Cres
Tiré
Dim.
Dim
Cres
Cres
Cres
Tiré
Dim
Dim
Poussé

f
Dim.
p
Tire
Ist. Pos.
pp
Cres
fz
1st Pos.
Cres
f
Dim.
p
Poussé.
f
segue.
Cres
f
Dim
p
Cres
f
Dim.
p
Cres

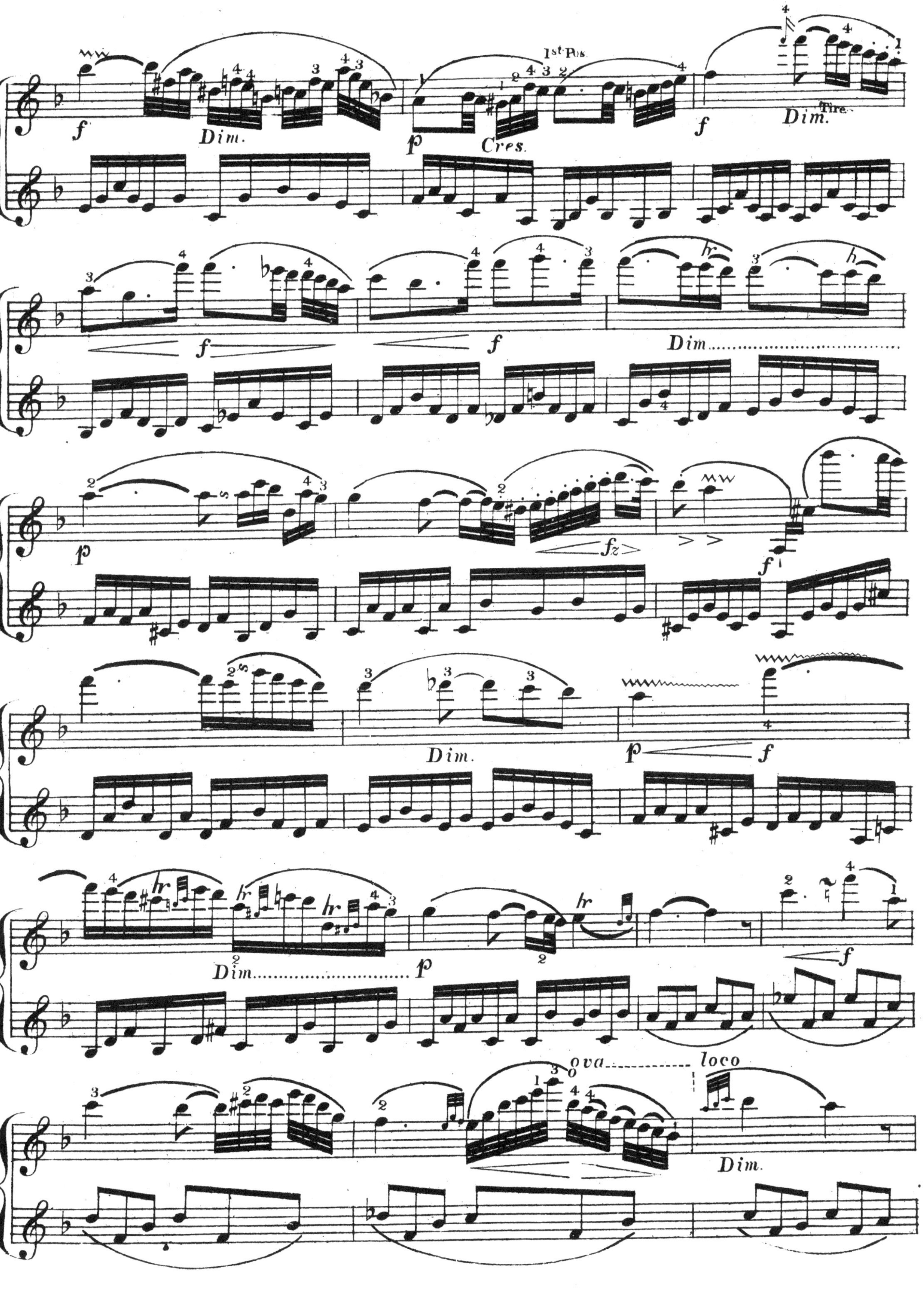
1st Pos.
Dim.
Cres.
Dim. Tire
Dim.
fz
Dim.
Dim.
ova
loco
Dim.

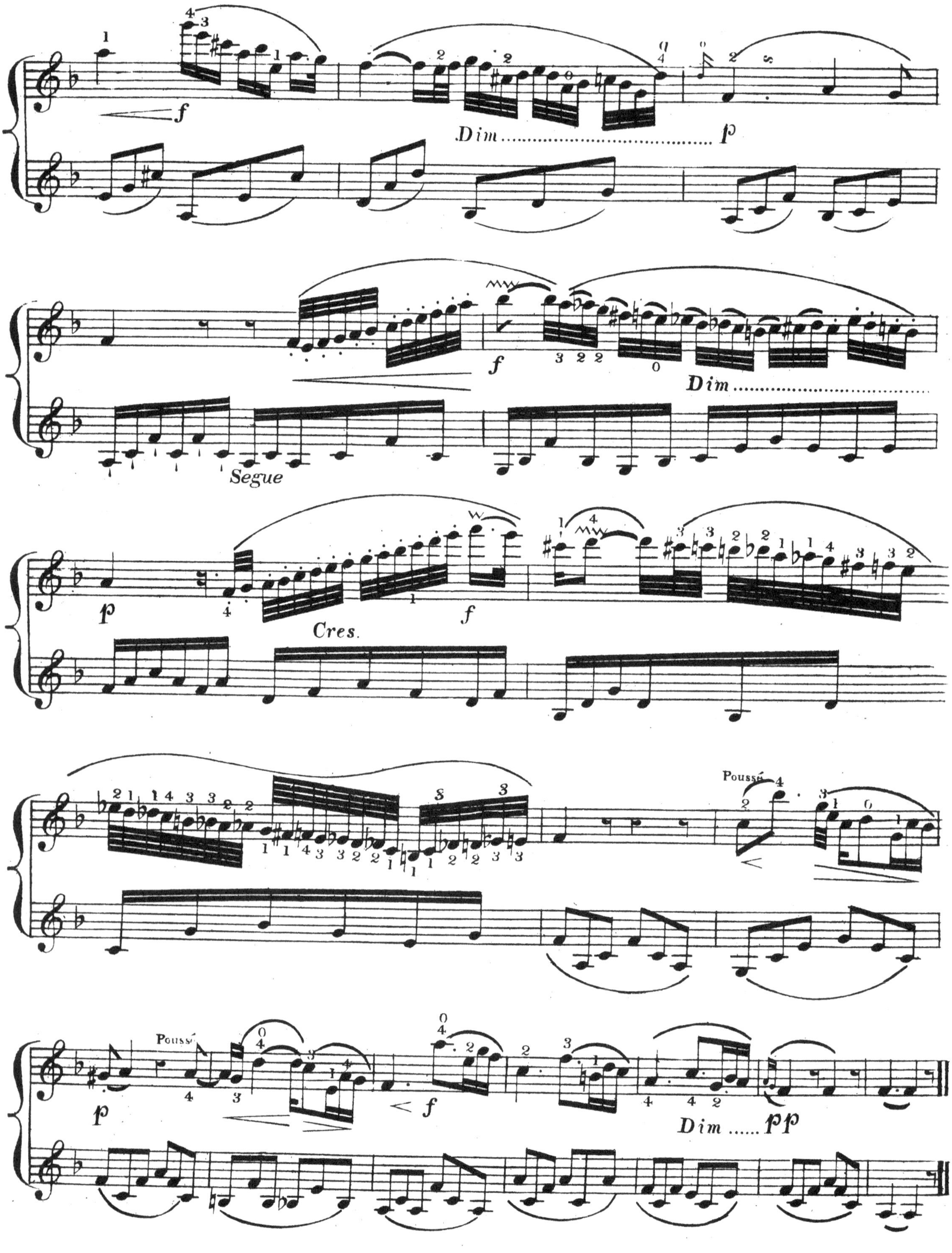
f
Dim .... p
f
Dim ....
Segue
p
Cres.
f
Poussé
p
Poussé
f
Dim ...... pp

RONDO.

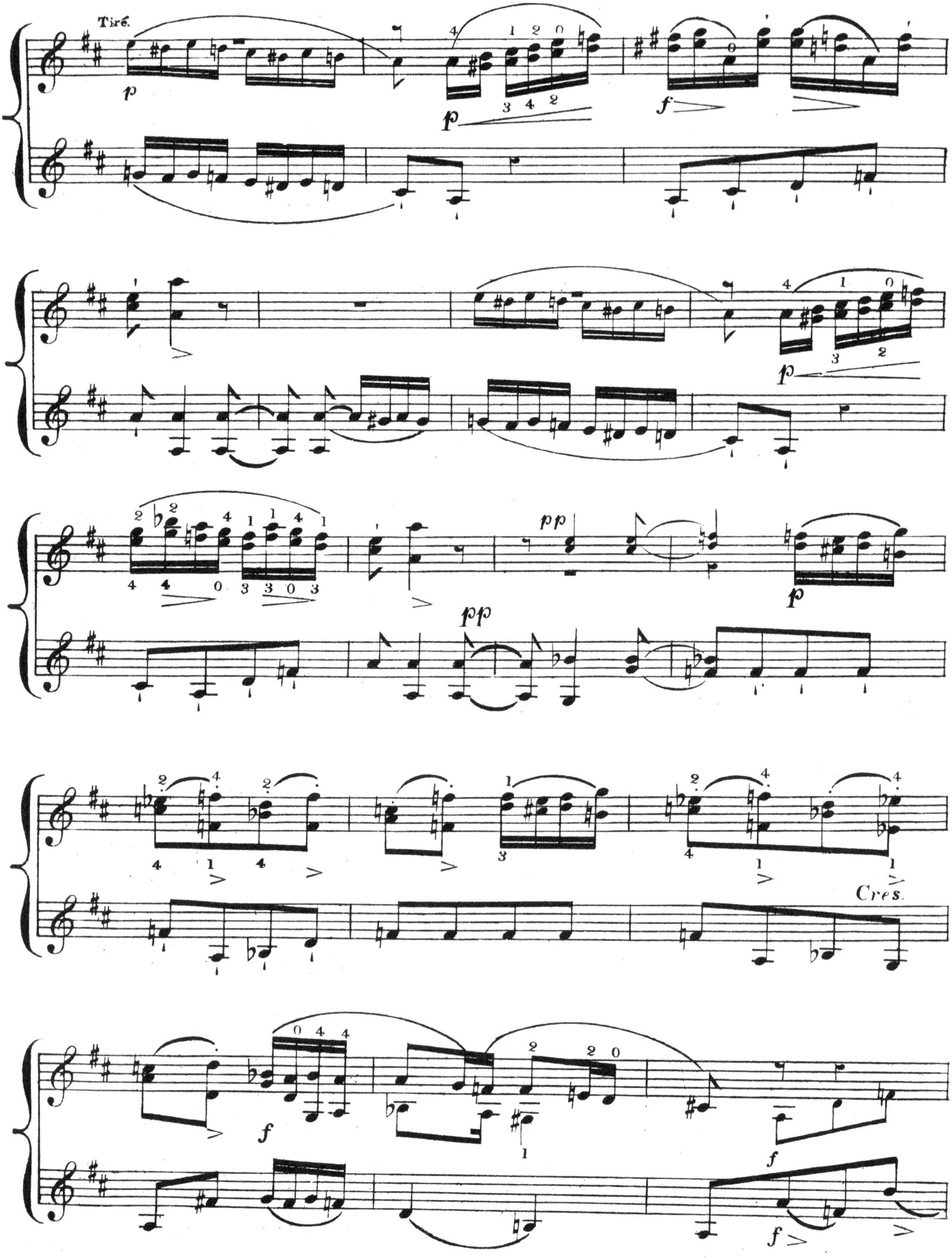
Tiré.
Cres.

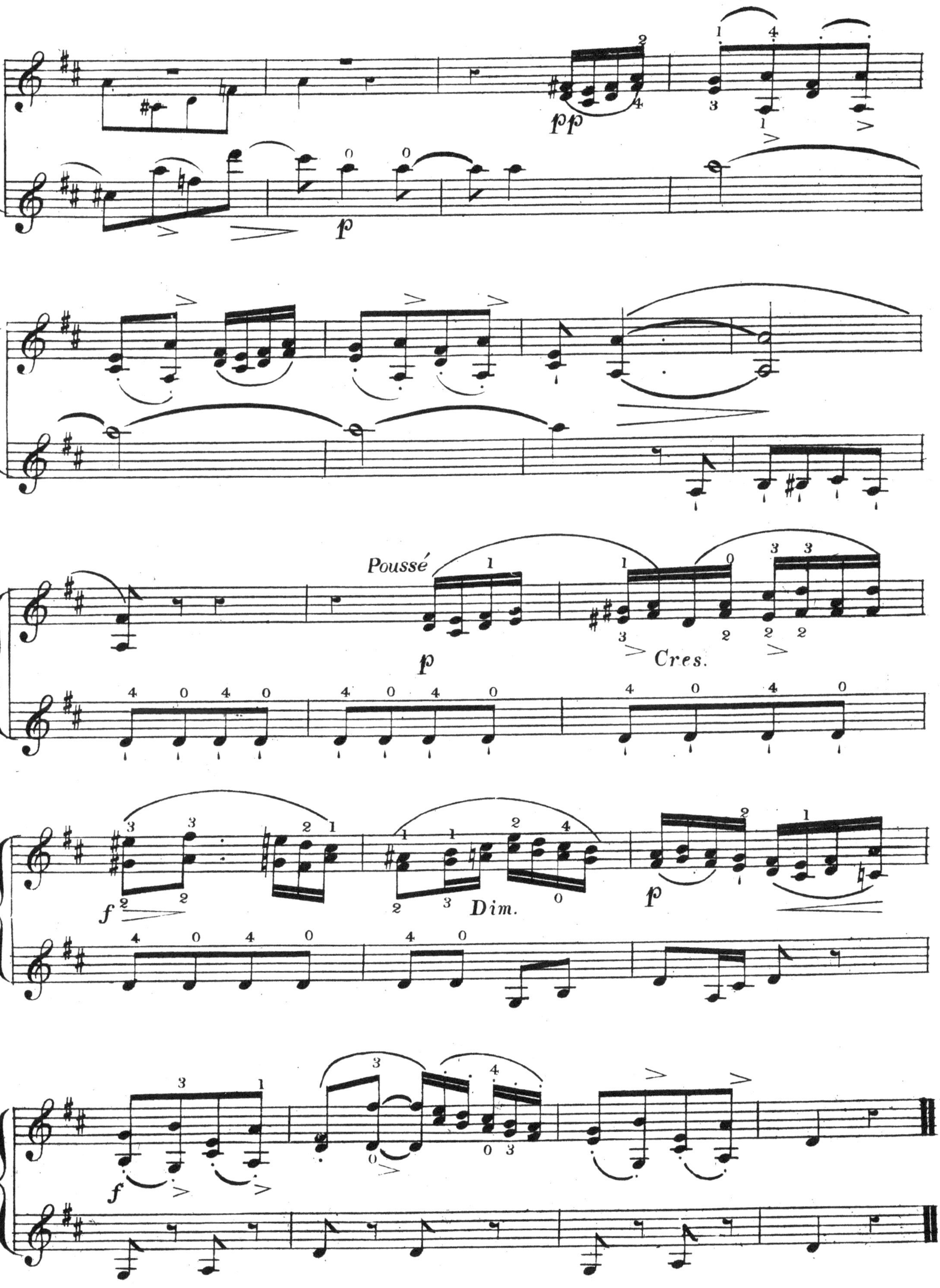
Poussé
Cres.
Dim.

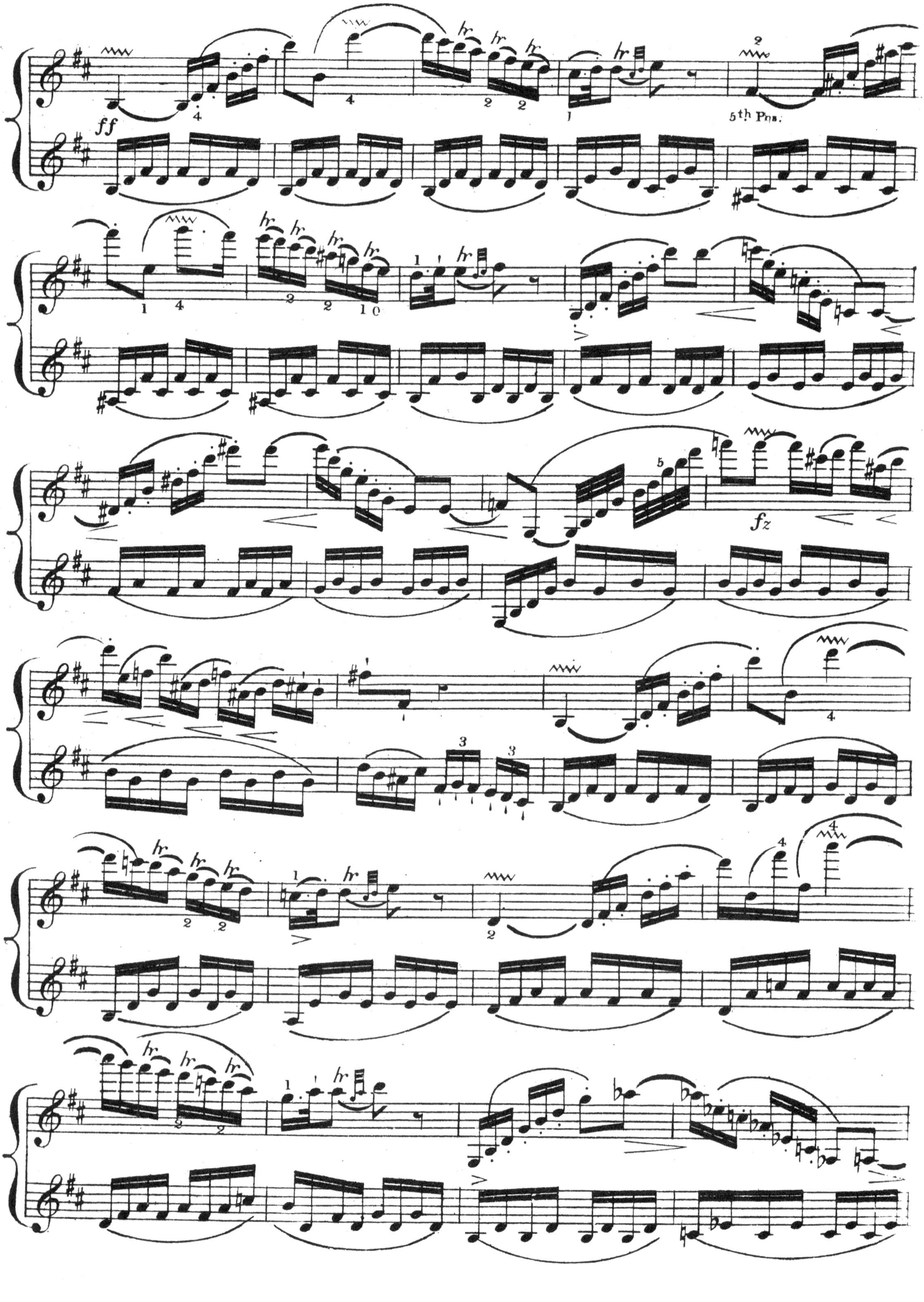
ff
5th Pos.
fz

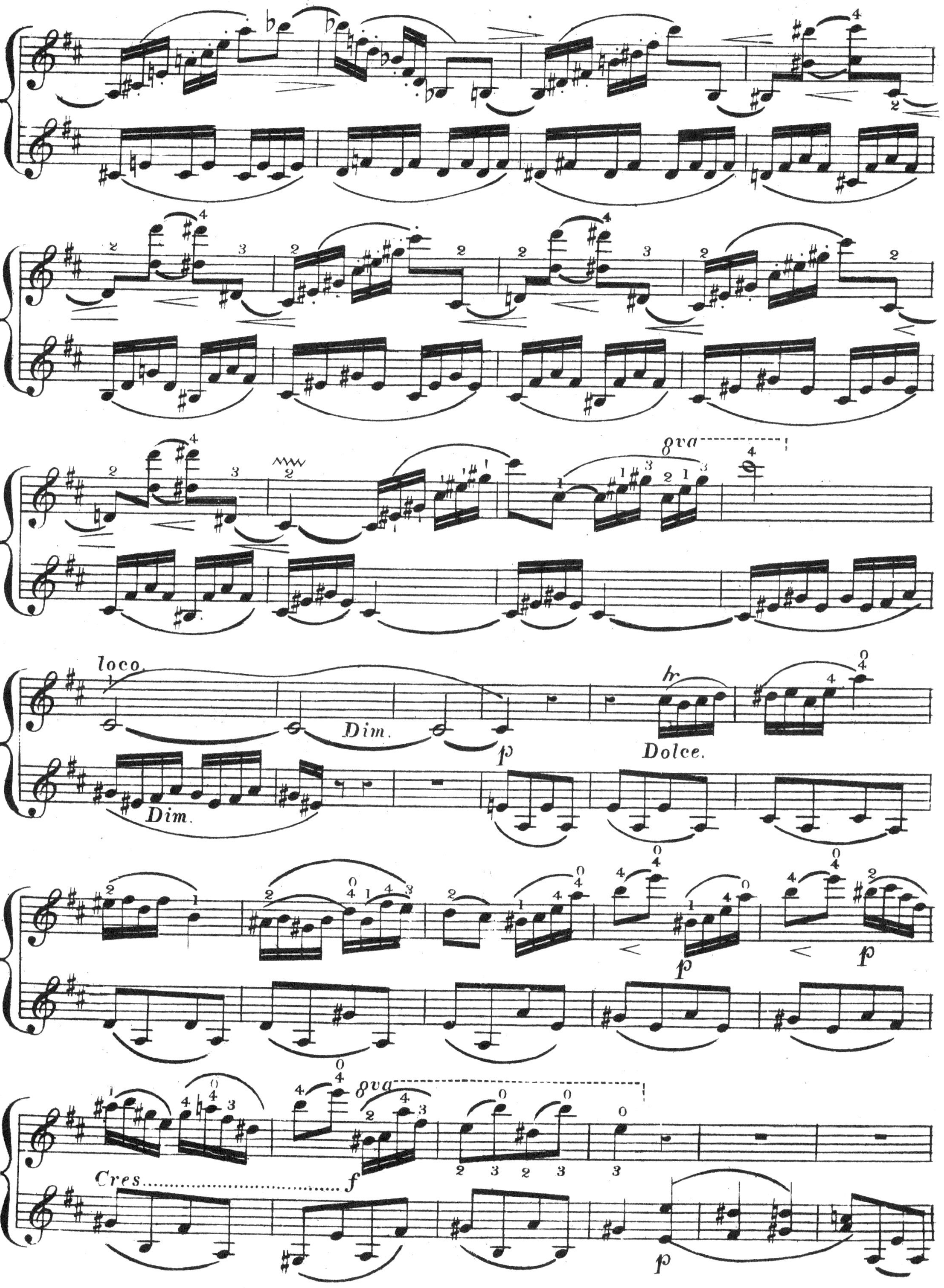
8va
loco.
Dim.
p
Dolce.
Dim.
p
p
Cres.
f
8va
p

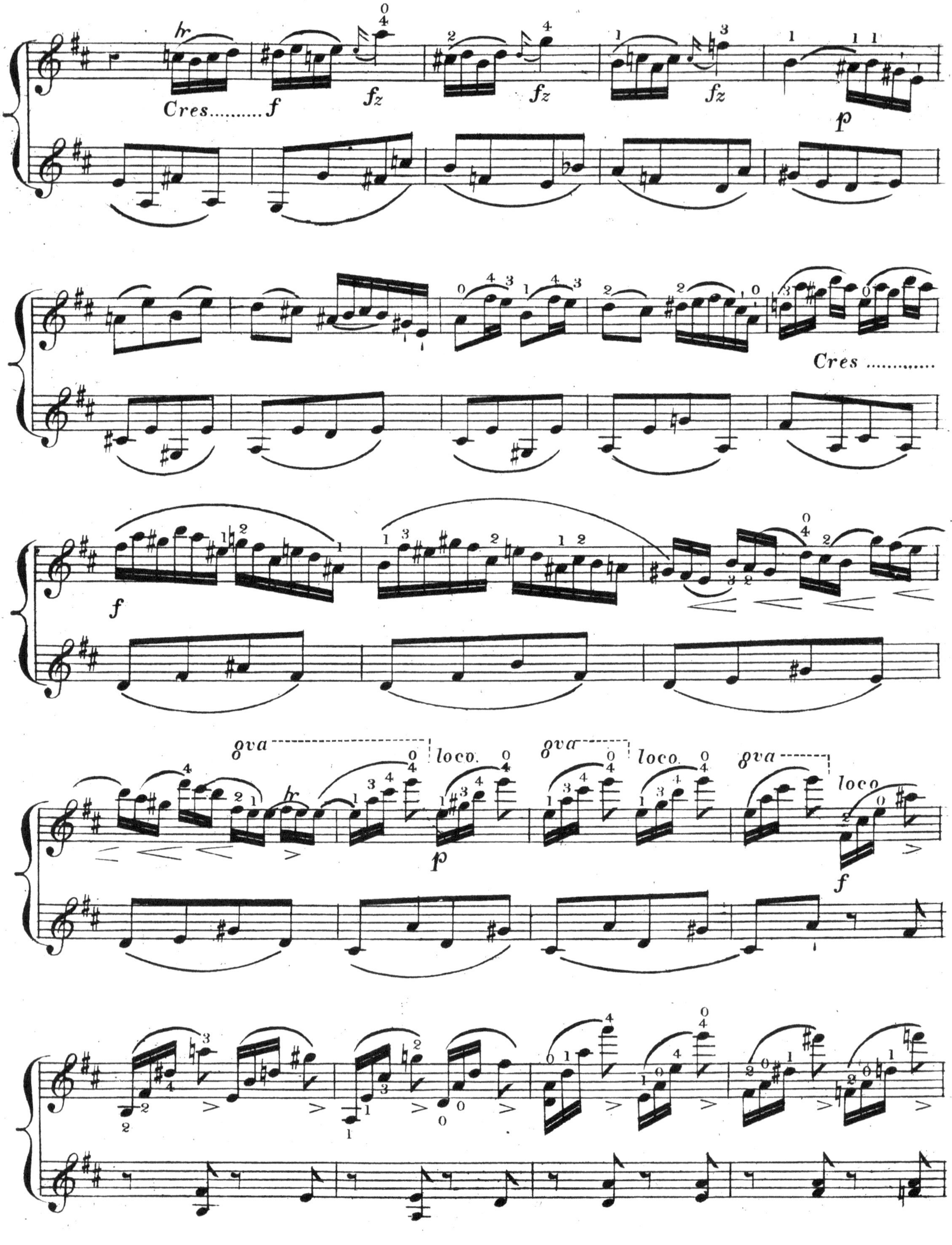
Cres..........f
fz
fz
fz
p
Cres ....
f
8va
loco.
8va
loco.
8va
loco
p
f

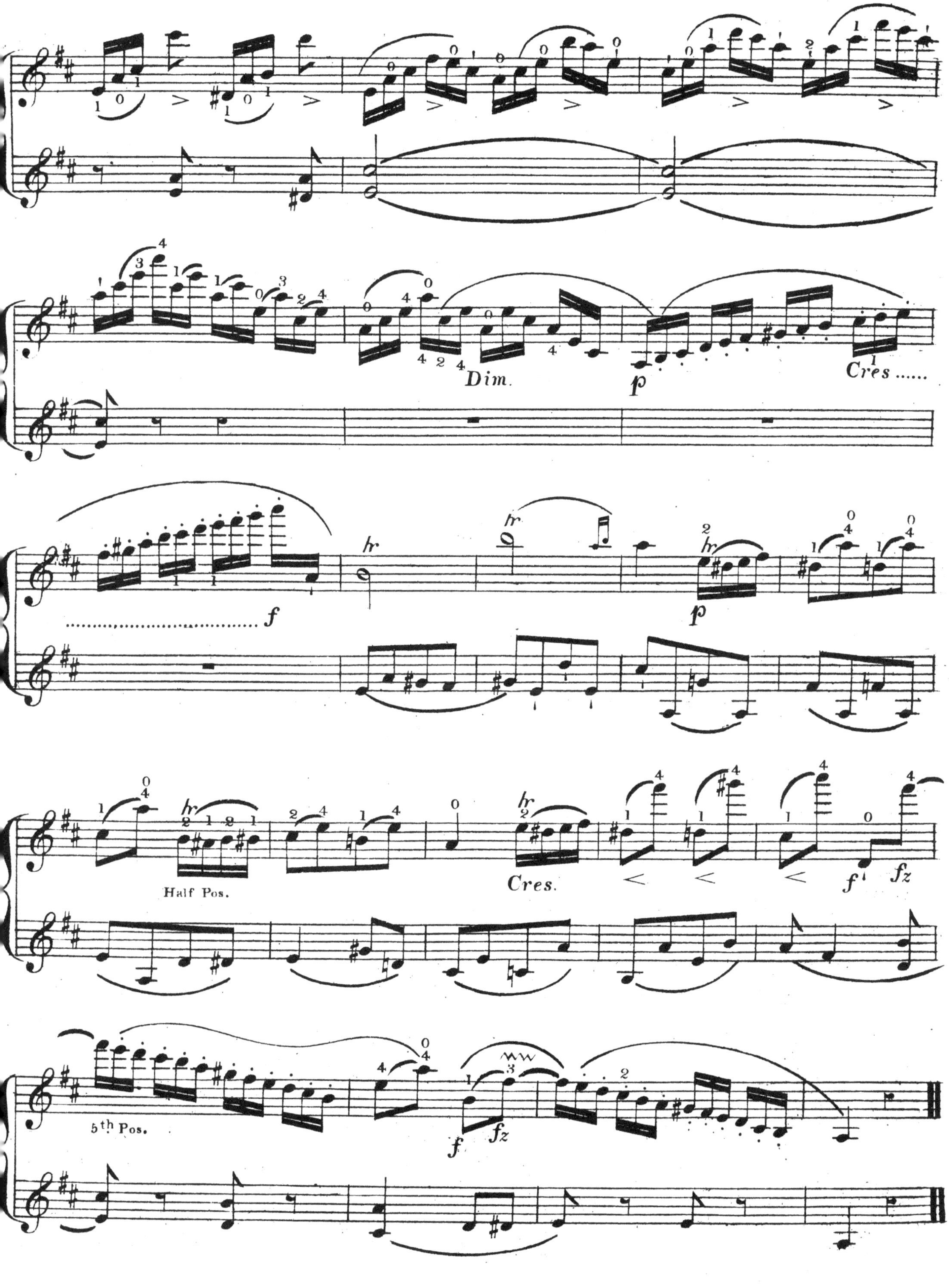
Dim.
Cres
f
p
Half Pos.
Cres.
fz
5th Pos.

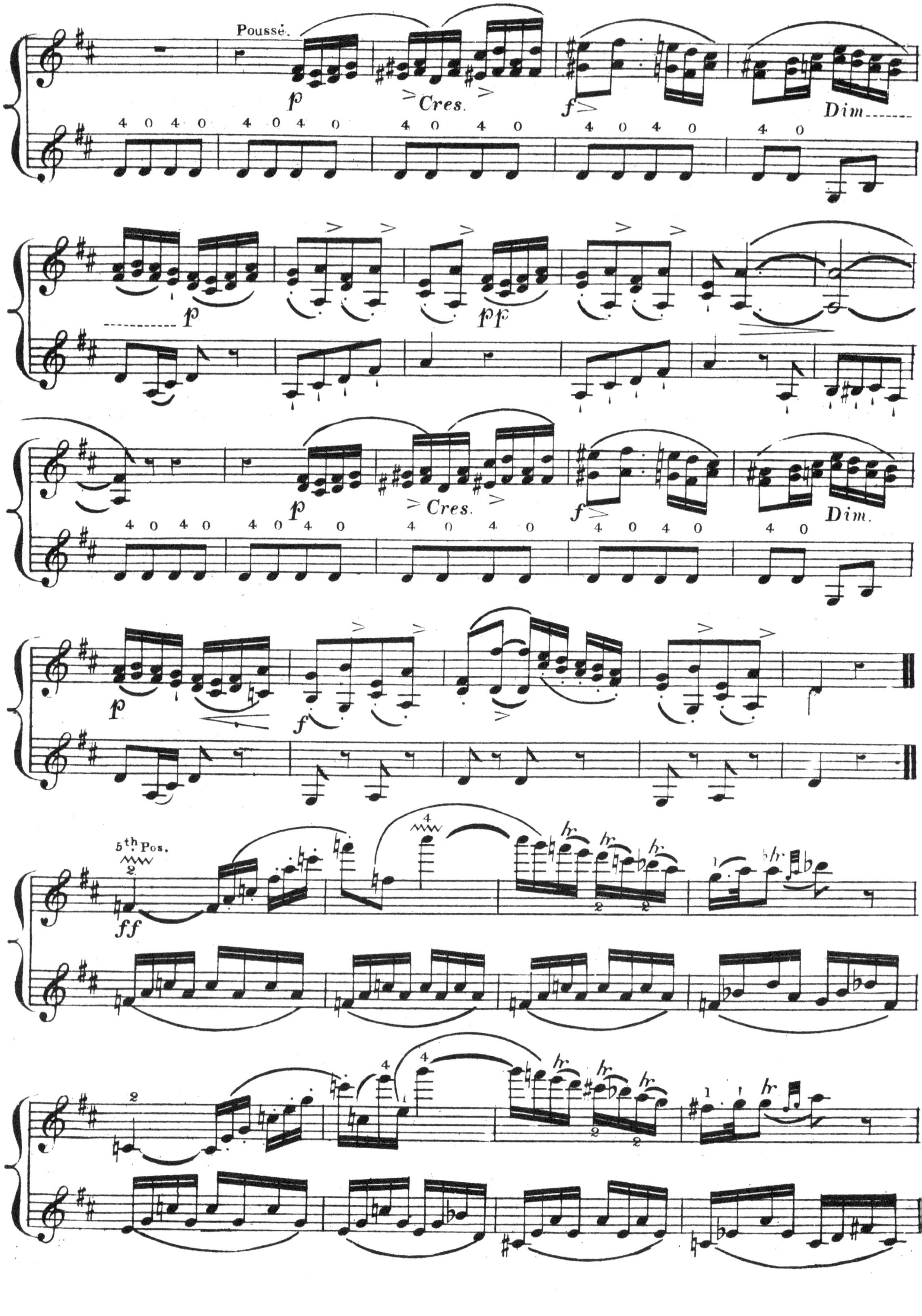

Poussé
p
Cres.
f
Dim
p
pp
p
Cres.
f
Dim.
p
f
5th Pos.
ff

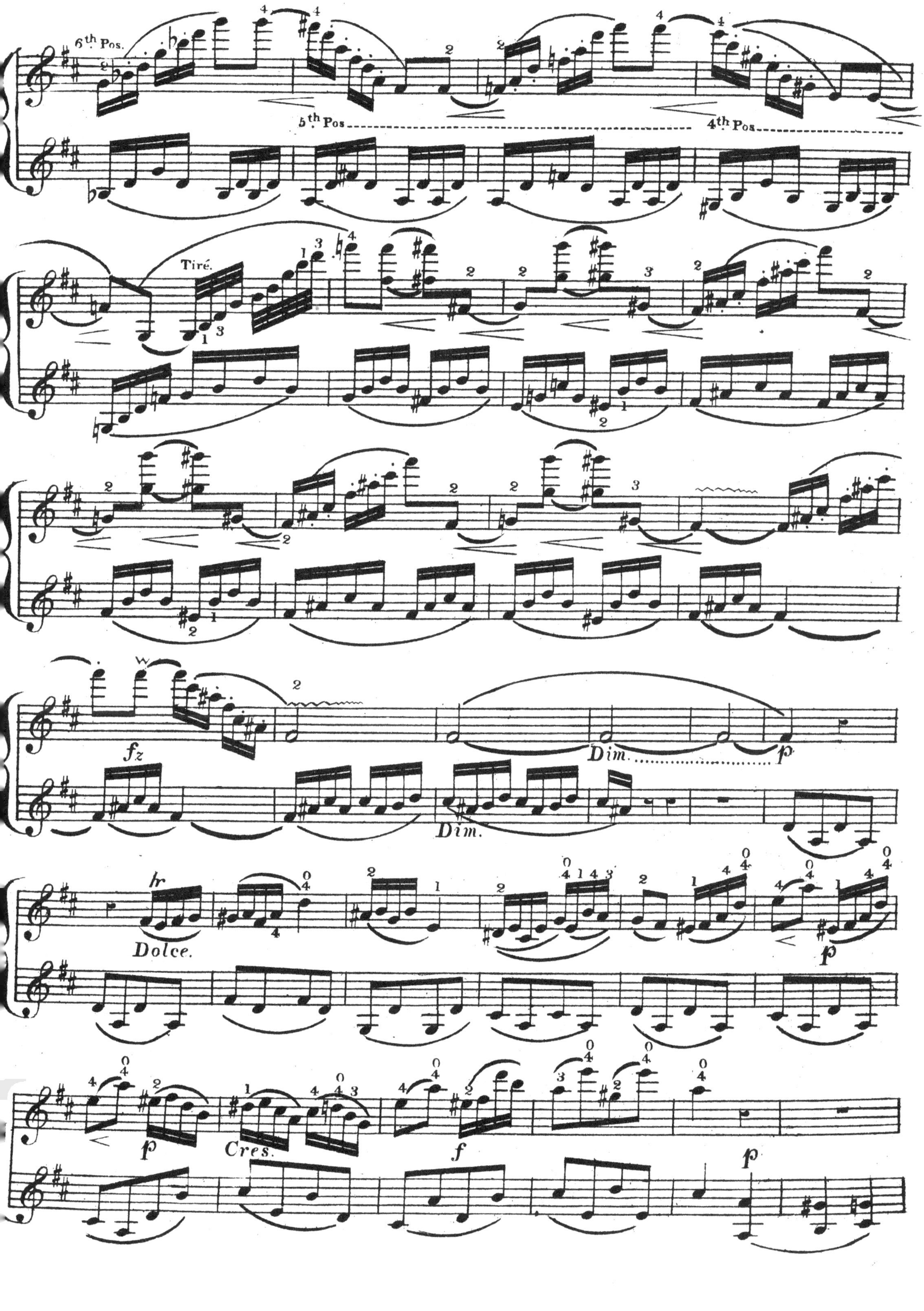
6th Pos.
5th Pos
4th Pos
Tiré.
fz
Dim
p
Dim.
Dolce.
p
p
Cres.
f
p

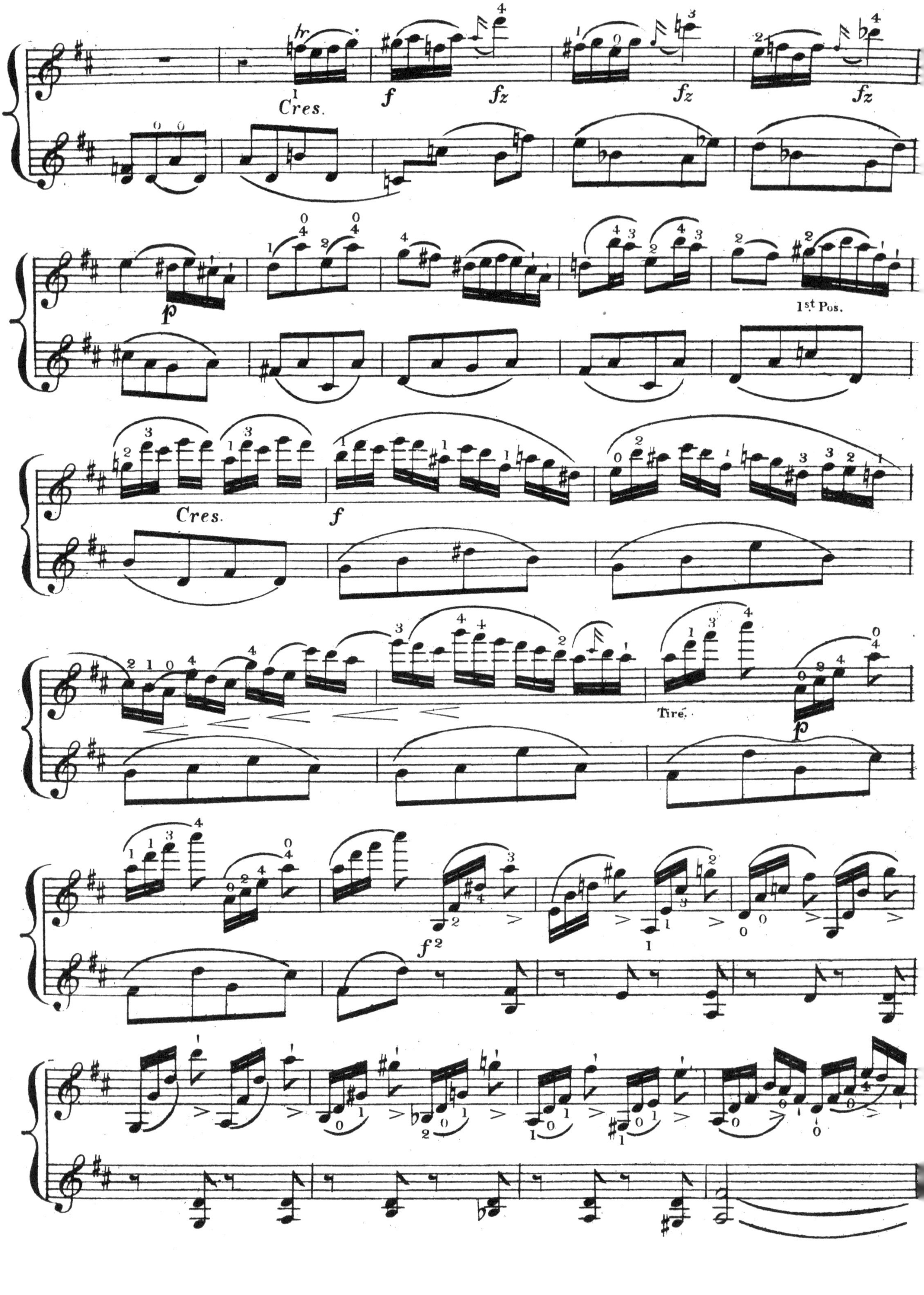
Cres.
f
fz
fz
fz
p
1st Pos.
Cres.
f
Tire.
p
f

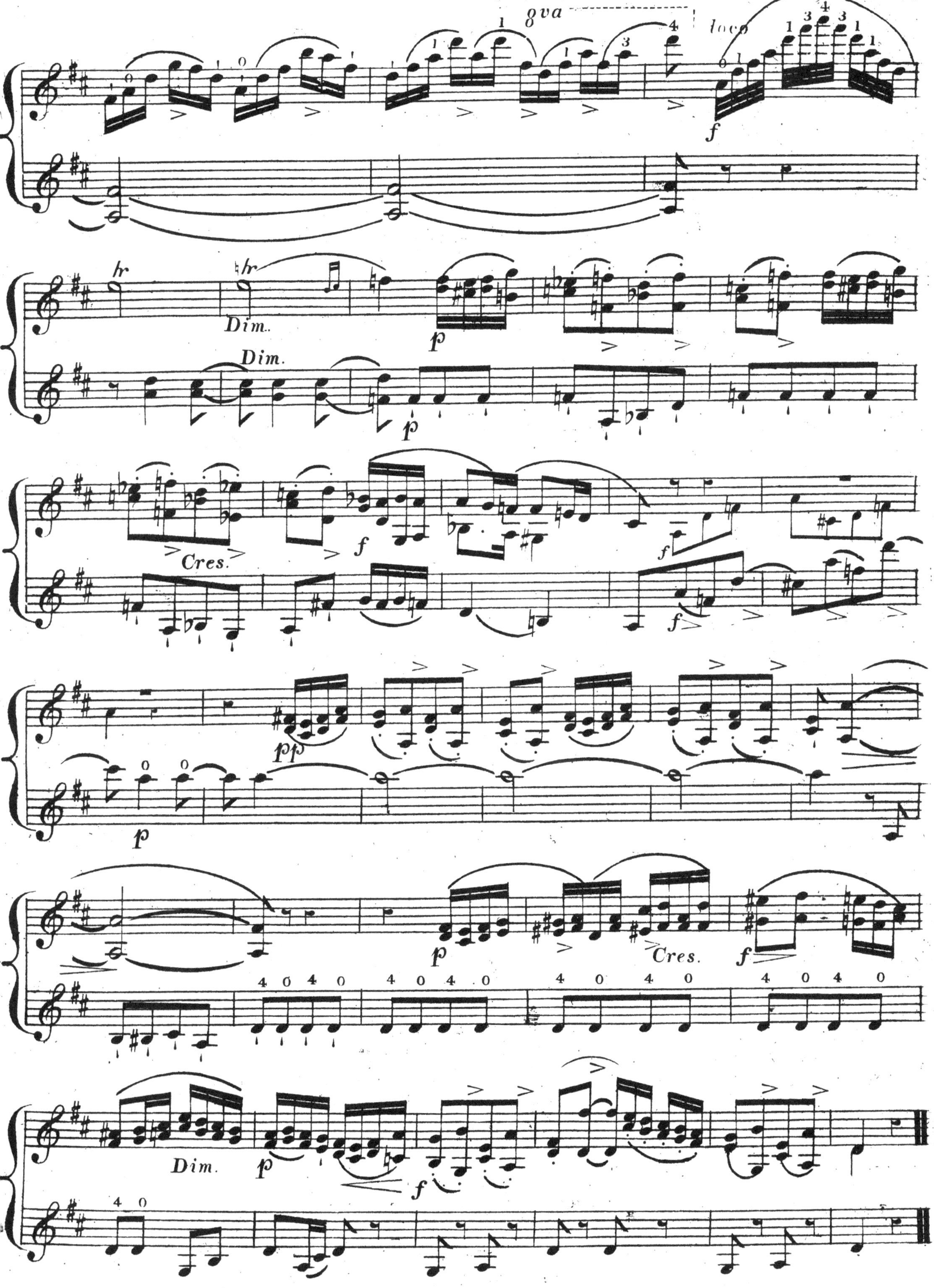
8va
loco
Dim.
Dim.
Cres.
Cres.
Dim.

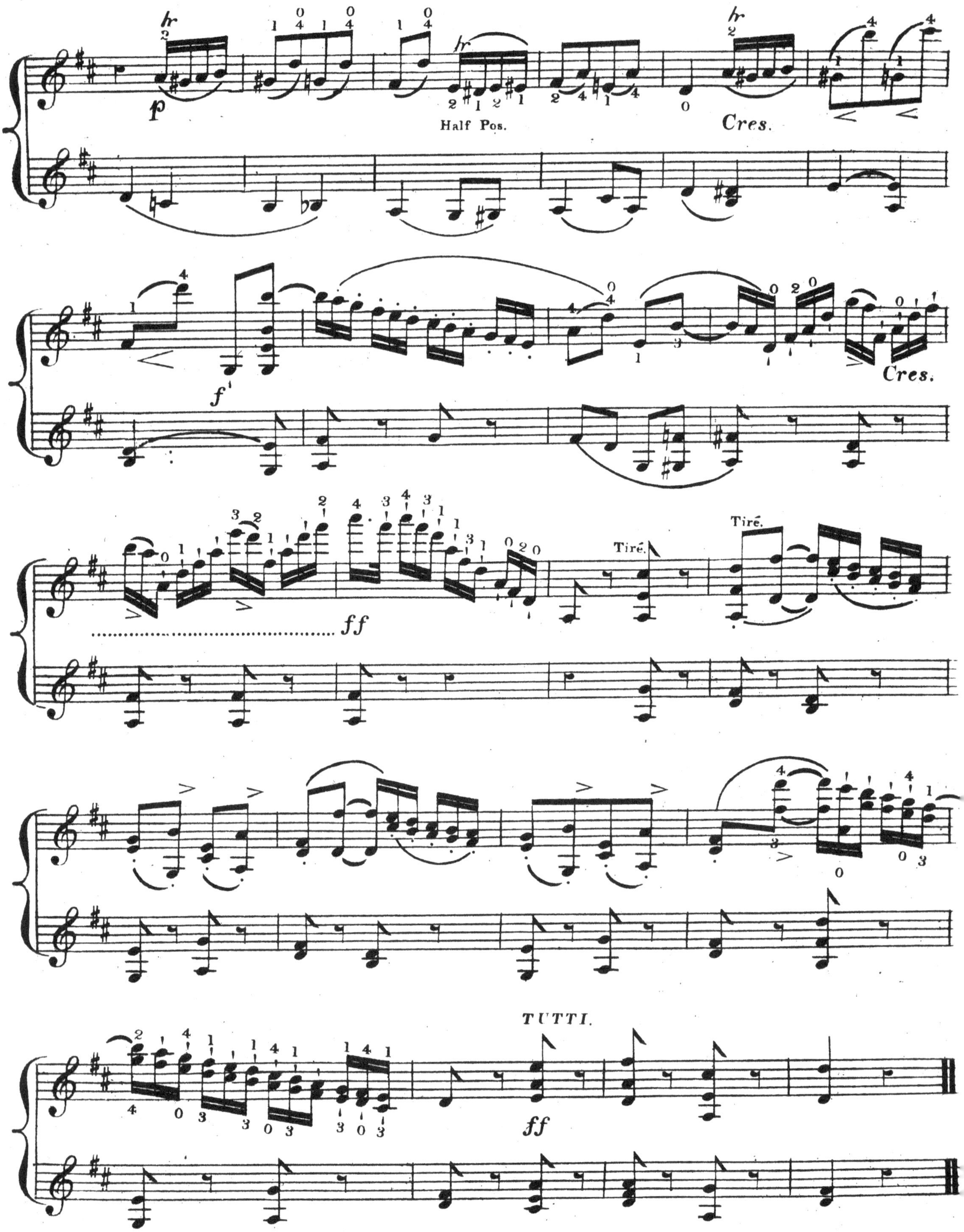
p
Half Pos.
Cres.
f
Cres.
ff
Tiré.
Tiré.
TUTTI.
ff

CHAPTER XXIII.

ON THE METHOD OF STUDYING NEW CONCERTO COMPOSITIONS.

Violin Compositions, although much improved of late are still very incomplete. If all Solo parts were as exactly marked as the preceding Concertos, it would be an easy mat_ ter to ascertain their style or delivery without explanation.

When a new Concerto piece is commenced, the Student will generally have to complete the signs of expression required throughout the composition; the following remarks therefore are worthy of attention.

At first, the notes must be studied; the Student should then seek for the most favourable positions, calculated to overcome the difficulties of the left hand and note them down; also to find out the best divisions of the bow for the Melody; and the most effective kinds of bowing for quick passages. The Pupil should next ascertain, how the style of delivery can be improved by introducing artificial shifting, (change of finger on one tone, sliding from one tone to another.) tremolo's, and finer degrees of light and shade, than those, the composer has marked, so as to heighten the general expression. Until all this has been accomplished, the composition should be perseveringly practised, both has regards the me_ chanical treatment and particular expression, thereby enabling the performer to give it that sentiment, which it is calculated to inspire.

Good divisions of the bow are most requisite for a fine performance, and although a great variety of Musical phrases exist, yet no special directions can be given.

General observations. $1^{\underline{o}}$ In the *forte* a more frequent change in the bowing takes place than in the *piano* $2^{\underline{o}}$ Single tones and all phrases which are to end very delicately obtain the *downbow* and for all tones scales and other passages to be increased in power, the *upbow* is preferable. The upbow is also taken for all concluding notes of broken chords and scales, if intended to be strongly accented or marked. Where the above observations are not applicable then, according to the old rule, the upbow must be used in the unaccented and the downbow in the accented parts of a bar. Commence as often as possible every bar with a down_ bow and finish with an upbow.

From the scantiness of these directions, the Student having paid strict attention to the signs of expression in the preceding compositions, will be able at first to rely much on his routine of playing.

The study of these, and a comparison with similar works already practised, will teach him to find out the best divisions of the bow and the right moment for applying other means requisite for a finished performance, untill such time, as he shall be guided solely by feeling, sentiment, and taste.

The Student will greatly facilitate his task by comparing the preceding Solo parts with the two printed Concertos, as originally published.

CHAPTER XXIV.

ON DELIVERY, OR STYLE OF QUARTETT PLAYING.

A new kind of Quartetts have been lately introduced, in which the first Violin has the Solo parts and the other instruments merely an accompaniment. To distinguish them from the regular Quartett, they are called Solo Quartetts. (*Quatuors brillans*) They are intended to give the Solo player an opportunity to display his Musical talent in small circles.

Their style of delivery may be classed with Concerto pieces. All remarks on the manner of playing the Concerto, are applicable to these and similar Solo pieces with accompaniment of 3 or 4 instruments, (as Variations, potpourris &c) with only this restriction that in a smaller space and with a weaker accompaniment. the tone of the instrument is not to be extract_ed with the greatest force. All roughness when the performance is close to the audience, should be carefully avoided.

The delivery of the regular Quartett demands a very different treatment. In such a composition it is not intended that one instrument should exclusively predominate, but that each should enter into the spirit of the Composer and delineate it accordingly.

The power of tone on the first Violin and the manner of playing must be in keeping with the rest, and where it is not the principal it should remain subordinate. As the style of deli_very should always proceed from the idea and spirit of the composition, it is required of the Solo player, in the Quartett to lay aside his peculiar manner of Solo playing, and accomodate himself to the character of the Music. Until he be capable of this, he cannot discern the cha racter of the separate parts of the Quartett and give proper effect to the variety of style displayed in classical compositions.

This will convince the student, how much is required for perfect Quartett playing and tho' perhaps less mechanical skill is called for than in a Concerto, yet it demands more of refined sentiment, taste and knowledge *

The combination of these qualifications will perfect the Quartett player; and nothing is more calculated to obtain it, than diligently playing those compositions. No opportunity ought therefore to be lost of joining a good quartett party.

The student should commence with the second Violin and learn the difficult art of accompani_ment. This consists in the facility of agreeing with the first Violin as closely as possible, such as, the power of tone, the trifling changes of tone, (sometimes caused by the first Violin.)

---

* The Pupil should now study the Theory of composition if he has not done so already.

strictly adhering to the prescribed bowings, slurs, light and shade, without however the f becoming shrill, or conspicuous, unless expressly marked.

The style of a good performer is to be attentively observed, and if the Student is then inclined to venture on the first Violin of a Quartett, he must mark the part previously, and practise it exactly as a Concerto piece.

Our principal Violin Quartett Composers were no performers, at least they were unacquainted with the mechanism of the Violin. The markings of their bowings in their quartetts is therefore more faulty than in their Concertos. The performer in supplying this deficiency, must use the greatest caution and reserve, and remember, that the intention of the regular Quartett is to display the idea of the author rather than the talent of the Violinist.

When a peculiar character of a musical idea is interwoven with other parts, the bowings necessary to pourtray it cannot voluntarily be changed, even supposing the performer knew how to change them for more convenient, or more striking modes of expression. The applications of other modes used in the Solo, require in the Quartett great caution, to prevent an interruption in the *ensemble* and destroy the meaning of the composer. In passages, *decidedly Solo*, the usual embellishments may be allowed.

The Quartett ought to be in Score, to mark it correctly, otherwise a perfect knowledge of it can only be obtained by frequently hearing it performed.

From the above we perceive the necessity for well considered marking of bowings, shifts &c. before the performance of any Quartett, until the Student can, by merely reading the notes, find out the best divisions of the bow, and other modes of expression, calculated to give the best effect to the composition.

C HAPTER XXV.

ON ORCHESTRA PLAYING AND ON ACCOMPANIMENT.

The Orchestra playing of the Violinist differs from the Concerto and Quartett playing principally because the same parts are performed by several others at the same time. Each performer ought to agree as much as possible with the other, in intonation, time, accentuation, light, and shade and lastly, in the division of the bowings.

The division of each portion of a bar, according to the value of its time, must in Orchestra playing be strictly observed. The *tempo rubato* (a slight delay on single or more notes) in the Solo of great effect cannot here be tolerated. The same applies to accents used in the Solo.

No deviation from the p's and f's is permitted, nor, as in Solo playing, add new shades of expression.

The greatest difficulty consists in the strict accordance in the bowing of the Violinists of an Orchestra. Even in the best practised Orchestra it is much neglected.

One principal cause of the difficulty may be traced to the negligent and faulty marking of the bowings of Orchestra pieces (more so than in Concerto and Quartett music) and also that the Violinists of an Orchestra never originate from the same School.*

---

* The Conservatoirs of Paris, Prague and Naples make an exception; their Orchestras have produced astonishing effects by the unity of the Violinists.

Thus every one has a different Method of bowing. The unity of the Violinists in the up and down-bows, while pleasing to the eye, is nevertheless absolutely necessary for giving proper accentuation, light and shade, in the *tout ensemble* of the performance.

Under this impression, I beg to remind the Orchestra player of the old rule, which prescribes the accented parts of a bar to be taken with a down-bow, and finish with an upbow.

The leader has, the responsibility of correcting and filling up, erroneous or omitted markings of the bowing (particularly when several rehearsals take place, as in Operas, Oratorios, Symphonies) and of endeavouring to effect the greatest possible unity.

Further rules for Orchestra playing are: to avoid every addition of turns, doubleturns, shakes &c. likewise all artificial shiftings, the sliding from one tone to another, the changing of the fingers on one tone, in short, every embellishment properly belonging to the Solo.

Appogiaturas or doubleturns found in an Orchestra part, require the leader strictly to determine, the length of the former and the manner of executing the latter, that they may be uniformly played by all Violinists. The time given by the leader or conductor is to be strictly followed, and an occa-sional glance at him will ensure the better observance.

The Orchestra player when accompanying a Solo performer, must be perfectly subordinate and never overpower. The f or fz of the accompaniment is therefore never so strongly marked as in the *Tutti*. The power of the tone should be regulated by the style of the music, as well as the size of the locality.

The Solo performer must neither be hurried nor retarded by the accompaniment; he should be instantly followed wherever he deviates a little from the time. This latter deviation, however, does not apply to the *Tempo rubato* of the solo performer; the accompaniment continuing its quiet, regular movement.

The preceding rules apply also to accompanying the voice. Generally the time is beaten by the Director, and therefore must be attended to and followed. The *Recitativo* having no uniform motion of time is with difficulty accompanied; as a guide the Vocal part is usually added in a separate line above the accompaniment. Both this and the director's beats are at the same time to be noticed, which will guide the performer when to commence with the accompaniment. There are different ways of giving the time. An attentive Orchestra player will, however, soon understand and follow his leader, provided it is firm, commanding, and unchangeable.

The tuning in the Orchestra should be as quiet as possible. The Leader should get the **A** from the Oboi, or better from all the wind instruments at once, and then, after his **A**, let the separate Violins &c be tuned. If one has done with it, he should not by useless preluding dis-turb the tuning of the others.

The general effect of the Music will be much heightened if, after the tuning, silence reigns for a few moments.

In recapitulating the above rules prescribed for Orchestra playing the Student will find, that the principal merit of a good Orchestra player consists in being subordinate, and willing to increase by that subordination the perfection of the whole.

These rules then are recommended to the Student, while assisting in the Orchestra.

CONCLUSION.

When the various instructions contained in this Work have been carefully studied, the greatest difficulties will then be surmounted.

Its Study must be vigorously persevered in, and daily practise is essential to retain the knowledge previously acquired, for in Music as in other arts, he who does not advance retrogrades.

If the Student be destined for the Profession, let him always pursue an honorable path and study to execute Music according to its strictest laws, and never permit correct taste to be sacrificed for the gratification of the multitude.

If he be ambitious of distinguished rank in the profession, let him choose for performance the best of classical music, and obtain a thorough knowledge of Harmony and theory of composition; an acquirement indispensable for a Leader or Director of an Orchestra.

The student should ascertain by frequent trials in composition if he be gifted by nature with talents for a composer.

Should he not possess these rare qualifications, he will however be amply compensated by a facility acquired in conquering difficulties, and moreover by that delightful intellectual enjoyment, which is inseparable from a correct knowledge of music and an accomplished performance.

When the Student has arrived at eminence in his art, he will then appreciate the endeavours of him, who has attempted to facilitate his career as a Violinist.

END.

LOWE & BRYDONE PRINTERS LTD. LONDON, N.W. 10.

NEW AND POPULAR VIOLIN MUSIC.

www.ingramcontent.com/pod-product-compliance
Lightning Source LLC
Chambersburg PA
CBHW081136090426
42742CB00015BA/2858